D0881128

"On April 15, the President issued a call for 75,000 men to defend the direct attempt at the destruction of the Union, and there came a spontaneous and patriotic response from many time 75,000 men who were eager to meet the foe and avenge the insult to the flag and startling was the response to the call and intense the enthusiasm that animated every man, women and child in the land.

The streets were filled with excited crowds hurrahing for Lincoln and the Union, the stars and strips were flutterin from numberless staffs, and the drum and fife resounded everyone."

Off to war Pierre went for 3 years of service. This is his Journey.

MOUNTAIN ARBOR
PRESS
Alpharetta, GA

ISBN: 978-1-63183-399-1

Library of Congress Control Number: 2018951458

Printed in the United States of America   0 9 0 6 1 8

∞This paper meets the requirements of ANSI/NISO Z39.48-1992 (Permanence of Paper)

Disclaimer: Much of the material in this book falls into the public domain, otherwise, rights and permissions have been secured. All photos, unless otherwise noted, were taken by the authors.

Pierre Starr wrote the Journal for his Grandchildren Sally and Bobby. This book is now a rededication to Sally-Bobby and all of Pierre's & Louisa's Children, Grandchildren, Great Grandchildren, and Great-Great-Grandchildren.

Thank you, Robert Starr the 3rd for allowing us to bring this story to the public and Civil War community.

If there are any spelling or grammatical errors in Pierre's writings it is my fault and error.

Brad Quinlin

Introduction

When a good friend Don McGilvary was on a visit to his cousin in Connecticut he meets Robert Starr the 3rd. Don and Robert started talking and Robert talked about his Great Grandfather and his Civil War letters and journal. Robert said he had tried for many years to get the journal published. Don mentioned me and my work on other manuscripts about the Civil War. We worked out the details of getting this unique manuscript published. When Robert first sent me the reminiscence part of the project, I read through it and was amazed at the written remembrance of Pierre. But my hesitation on proceeding with the project was that Pierre wrote it in 1912. He wrote it for his grandchildren, knowing that many would blast the reminiscence as being written late in life and that it had little value.

Then we got Pierre's Civil War letters! These brought enough information and facts to the project to validate the journal. In fact, when you read the reminiscence and then go to the letter section of the book you will find he not only directly referenced the letters but incorporated them word-for-word into some of the reminiscences.

With the added letters of George Cadman, and other members of the 39th Ohio, their regimental books and muster rolls I knew we had a gem of a Civil War manuscript, which will make a great Civil war journey. This is the story from the Regimental Surgeon of the 39th Ohio Infantry. All are incorporated into the story as the journal is left intact and the reader can draw on Pierre's Stories. Then there are Pierre's letters, with George Cadman's letters and some other 39th Ohio soldier letters.

Pierre was born November 18, 1839 in New London Connecticut, the son of Johnathan and Catherine Starr. Attended Williston Seminary, Easthampton, Ma. After his completions of studies at Williston Pierre attended Yale and graduated 1860. He then attended New York Medical University and received his degree as a M.D. in 1862. Pierre enlisted in the service of the United States in 1862.

After the war Pierre practiced medicine in Chicago from 1866 to 1871. He married Louise Green Tudor May 27, 1868 in South Windsor, Connecticut. They had three children, Mary born 1870, Louis, born 1872, Robert born 1873. In 1871, the family moved to Hartford Connecticut, where he practiced medicine until he retired in 1910. Pierre was a loyal member of the Trinity Church in Hartford. Pierre Died March 11, 1920 at the Hartford Hospital from the effects of a broken Hip. Pierre is buried in Cedar Grove Cemetery New London Connecticut. His wife Louise died April 10th,1921

The Story begins in a classic New England town, South Windsor Connecticut. Historic homesteads line "Old Main Street, some dating back to the 1700's. It was within one of these classic homes, at an after-church gathering., that the Starr's proudly brought out a few classic artifacts that they had saved over the years. My cousin Vicky was there, and she immediately thought of me when they brought out the written account of the civil war authored by their ancestor. They were gracious to share the treasures with me when I visited Connecticut later that year.

Being an amateur C.W. Historian (and Civil War Reenactor) myself. I was very excited and thought the manuscript to be very interesting. I passed a copy of it along to my friend Brad Quinlin who is an avid C.W. researcher and author. One thing led to another and this is the finished product.

I'm very glad to have been a part of this process and I hope you enjoy it.

Don McGilvary

Louisa Green Tudor Starr

Pierre in Uniform

Pierre Starr died March 11, 1920 at the Hartford Hospital from the effects of a broken hip. He is buried in Cedar Grove Cemetery, New London Connecticut.

At the time that Pierre was looking to enlist there were no regiments being raised in Connecticut so Pierre, worked to get an appointment in the navy. Gideon Welles the Secretary of the Navy, on June 21, 1862 gave Pierre the appointment to a Hospital in New York. Turning down the appointment with the Navy, Pierre moved to an enlistment in the Army as a surgeon. He was first assigned to the 11th Ohio Battery. Disappointed with that assignment he requested a transfer and was ordered to report to the 39th Ohio Infantry. The following are the orders for Pierre, during his Medical Service.

$$\star\star\star\star$$

Navy Department
June 21st, 1862
Sir,

You will receive an appointment as an Acting Assistant Surgeon in the U.S. Navy on temporary service, provided you are approved by a Medical Board of Naval Surgeon appointed to examine you in regard to your professional attainments the, on your reporting yourself to Surgeon B.F. Bache at the Naval Hospital New York. You will notify the Department whether you accept the above condition.

> **I am Respectfully**
> **Your obt. Servant**
> **Gideon Welles**

Hd. Qtr. Army of the Ohio
Medical Directors Office
July 20, 1862

Actg. Assist Surg. P.S. Starr will without delay report for duty to Colonel Gilbert comdg. 39th Ohio Regt.

W.R. Troll   **Med. Director,**
                          Army of the Miss.

Headquarters Army of the Mississippi
Medical Director Office
Iuka Miss. Sept. 8, 1862

Act. Asst. Surgeon Pierre S. Starr is relived from duty at the Genl.
Hospital at Iuka, and will without delay report to the Commanding
office of the 26th Ill. Vols. For duty.

> A.B. Campbell
> Med. Dir.

Army of the Miss.
Headquarters Second Division, Army of the Miss.
Div. Surg. Office Camp at Rienzi Miss. Sept. 30, 1862

Act. Asst. Surg. P.S. Starr is here by transferred from the 26th   Illinois
Regt. Vol. to the 39th Regt. Ohio Vol. and will immediately report
himself to Col. Gilbert Commanding 39th Ohio Vol.

By order of Medical Director of the   Army of the Miss.
> I.J. Crane Surgeon

2nd Div. Army Miss.
Head Quarters Stanley's Div.
District of Corinth Nov. 1st, 1862

Dr. Starr
39th Reg. O.V.I.

Sir,

You will remain at Corinth and assist Dr. Babb of the 47th Ill.   In
taking charge of the Div. Hospital situated at   the "Pink House" ¼
mile north west of these headquarters.

By order of
Brig. Genl. Stanley
G.M. Rowe 40th Ohio
Med. Div. Stanley's Div.

Jan 25, 1863 - Special Duty Corinth Mississippi at Seminary Building
Medical Directors Office

Corinth Miss. Feby. 16th 1863

Asst. Surgeon P.S. Starr of the 39th Ohio Vol. Infantry is hereby
ordered to resume the duties of Post Surgeon at Corinth Miss. And
relieve Asst. Surgeon J.H. Gilmore ordered to his regiment.

By order of
Brig. Genl. G.M. Dodge
W.R. Marsh
Acting Medical Director
Dist. Of Corinth

Medical Directors Office
Corinth Miss. Feby. 19th 1863

Asst. Surgeon S.J. Smith of the 3th Ohio Vol. Infantry will relieve
Asst. Surgeon P.S. Starr in charge of Post & small pox Hospital &
report to the commander of the Post immediately for duty.   Asst.
Surgeon Starr will turn over all medical & Hospital Property in his
possession to him & report to his regiment for duty.

W.R. Marsh
Act. Med. Director
Dist. Of Corinth

P. S. Starr

Asst. Surg. 39th Ohio Infry.

Head Quarters District of Corinth
Department of the Tennessee
Corinth Miss.
Feby. 24th 1863

Capt. Ferrand   {{{{Mustering Officer}}}

You will muster in Surgeon P.S. Starr to date from the 1st of January
1863.
By Order Genl. G. M. Dodge   Geo. E. Spenser
A.A.G.

Head Quarters District of Corinth
Corinth Miss. Janay. 25th 1863,

Special Order Order 36

Assistant Surgeon Pierre Starr   of the 39th Ohio Infantry Volunteers is
hereby detailed for special duty, and will report to W.R. Marsh,
Division Surgeon and Act. Medical Director at the Seminary Building
immediately.
                              By order of,
                              Brig. Genl. G.M. Dodge
                              Capt. J.R.R. Gone

Head-Quarters 16th Army Corps
Medical Director's Office
Memphis, Tenn. Aug. 22nd ,1864

Pierre S. Starr   asst. Surg. 39th Ohio Vols. Is relieved from duty with
the U.S. 3rd Cavy. And will resume his duties in the 39th Ohio, as actg.
asst. Surgeon White has reported himself recovered.

By order of Maj. Gen. Hurlbut
A.B. Campbell Surg. U.S.A.

August 27, 1863 - Ordered back to the 3rd United States Calvary
October 1863 - relieved from the 3rd United States Calvary returned to
the 39th Ohio infantry

Head-Quarters 16th Army Corps
Medical Directors Office,

Memphis, Tenn., August 27 1864

Special order No.-

Pierre S. Starr asst. Surgeon 39th Ohio, is relieved from duty with the
39th Ohio, and will report in person without delay to Capt. Geo. W.
Howland Commanding U.S. 3rd Cavalry for duty with that Regt.

By order of Major Genl. I.A. Hurlbut
Surg. U.S.V.
Medical Director

Headquarters 16th Army Corps,
Medical Director's Office
Memphis Tenn., October 7, 1863

Pierre S. Starr asst. Surgeon 39th Regt. Ohio Vols., is relieved from duty
with the U.S. 3rd Cavalry, and will report in person without delay to
the command   of my office 39th Ohio for duty .

By order of Maj. Genl. Hurlbut
Surg. U. S.V.
Medical Director

April 12, 1864 to June 7, 1864 – Appointed to 3rd Alabama Colored
Infantry

13

Headquarters Left Wing 16th Army Corps
Army In Miss. Off. Athens Alabama April 12, 1864

Asst. Surg. P.S. Starr, 39th Regt. O.V.I. Inft. Is hereby relieved from
duty with his regiment and will report without delay to Col.
Commanding 3rd Ala. Regt. Of U.S.C.   Troops at Sulphus Branch
Trestle Ala.

                         By order of Brig.
                         Brig. Gen. G. M. Dodge
                    Norman Gay U.S.V.
                    Army in Miss.

                         Approved
                         by command of
                         Maj. Gen. Rousseau

Headquarters Department and Army   of the Tennessee
Acworth Ga. June 7, 1864

Special Field Orders, No. 32

Asst. Surg. P.S. Starr 39th Regiment Ohio Infty. Vols. Is relieved from
duty with the 3rd Alabama Colored Troops and will forthwith rejoin
his regiment in the field for duty.

                    By order of Maj. Gen Jas. B. McPherson
                         Wm. I Clark
                         Assistant Adjutant General

June 7, 1864 - June 14, 1865 - Surgeon to 39th Ohio Infantry

Headquarters Left Wing 16th A.C.
Near Atlanta Ga. August 18, 1864
Special Field Orders No. 65

Asst. Surgeon P.S. Starr, 39th Ohio Infantry Vols., is hereby detailed from special duty in Hospital and will report to Surgeon J. A. Follett 39th Ohio, in charge of 16th A.C. Hospitals at Marietta Ga.

By order of Major Genl. G. H. Dodge
J.W. Barnes
A.A. Genl.

July 9, 1865 - Mustered out of Regiment

Brief history of the 39ᵗʰ Ohio Infantry

- Mustered in at Athens, Ohio on August 16, 1861.

- Organized and trained at Camp Colerain and at Camp Dennison Ohio.

- The 39th was sent to Mississippi where they fought in the Battles of Iuka, Corinth 1862.

- Stationed in the Mid-Mississippi area until January 1863.

- Moved to Memphis and Middle Tennessee in 1863 to April 1864.

- Attached to General Sherman's Army for the 1864 Atlanta Campaign. Fought at the Battles of Resaca, Dallas.

- Moved to Acworth and Big Shanty.

- Stationed at the North East side of Kennesaw Mountain and saw action on the line June 27, 1864.

- Charged the Rebel works at Nickajack Creek and action near Atlanta on July 22, 1864.

- Journeyed with Sherman's Army thought the March to Sea, up to the Carolinas and fought at Bentonville North Carolina.

- After the fight at Bentonville and the following surrender of General Johnston Confederate Army the 39th Ohio marched to Washington D.C. for the Grand Review on May 25 and 26.

- Taken by train to Louisville Kentucky and Mustered out from service July 9, 1865.

The Narrative 1912

A Reminiscence:
By Pierre Starr

"As strained relations of the northern and southern states during the several preceding years, and the more recent threatening attitude of the southern representatives culminated on April 12th, 1861, when the first guns were fired on Fort Sumpter from Charleston Harbor, South Carolina. Until then hope had remained of saving the Republic without blood-shed, but now Civil War was undoubted. The first cannon ball had shattered the peace of the country for the seceding five years.

On April 15th, the President issued a call for 75,000 men to defend the direct attempt at the destruction of the Union, and there came a spontaneous and patriotic response from many times 75,000 men who were eager to meet the foe and avenge the insult to the flag. Startling was the response to the call and intense the enthusiasm that animated every man, women and child in the land.

The streets were filled with the excited crowds hurrahing for Lincoln and the Union, the stars and stripes were fluttering from numberless staffs, and the drum and fife resounded everywhere. Railroad stations were crowded with zealous throngs, bulletins and extras were frequently issued to assuage the clamor for news, and young men were hurrying to the nearest enlistment points, lest no place left for them in the regiments hastily forming.

The bloody assault of the Sixth Massachusetts Regiment as it was passing through Baltimore to the protection of Washington, when four men were killed and thirty-six wounded, caused the first blood-shed of the dreadful conflict and produced an electric effect on the popular mind in the north. A patriotic exaltation surged over the country, and everybody was ardent to do and to serve. Flag raisings were held in every town and hamlet, and the pent up emotions of the assembled enthusiasts were given full vent as the stars and stripes of the beloved flag was hauled to the peak of the lofty pole amid the cheers of the crowd, the beating of the drums and shrill notes of Yankee Doodle" or the "Star-Spangled Banner"; and many a one had a bit of a catch in his throat and frisky thrills running up and down his spinal column as the national emblem fluttered in the breeze and "Rally Round the flag" was sung with reverence never before put into the spirited strains.

Then popular speakers or would-be orators would mount a convenient table, and with furious gesticulations, passionately voice the fervent sentiments of the applauding crowd. School boys thrusted aside their books and hurried away to enlist; college students hastened to join the ranks; lawyers, clerks, ministers, mechanics, and doctors all joined in the rally for the Union. Peaceful pursuits were speedily exchanged for "grim visage war", plough shares were turned into swords and pruning hook into spears.

Returning to Hartford from New York in the spring of 1862 with a medical diploma from the New York university Medical College in my pocket and confronted with conditions such as I have alluded to, it naturally followed that I desired to be a participant in such occurrences. Connecticut had already filled her quota of regiments called for by the government, and the opinion prevailed, in which I concurred, that the contest would last but a few months and that our erring sisters would come back to the fold. None realized the persistency or fierceness of the conflict.

So, despairing of joining a Connecticut regiment and disposed towards the sea, I wrote to the Navy Department at Washington my application for appointment as Acting Assistant Surgeon. To this I received a reply form Gideon Wells, Secretary of the Navy, directing e to proceed to New York for examination by the medical board of Navy Surgeons. To New York I at once went but calling on my former medical quiz teacher there I was diverted by his representations of more life and actions in the field, to go to go before the Board of Army

Surgeons, and there I obtained my appointment as acting Assistant Surgeon in the Army and was directed to the Medical Purveyor's office for orders. I then took the night boat for New London, arriving about one o'clock in the morning, aroused and informed my mother that I had enlisted in the service. She was somewhat dazed at the unexpected announcement, but soon rallied and concurred with me that it was all right, but I fear she slept no more that night.

The next day with "good-bye" and "god Speed" I left for Hartford bid adieu to friends, donned a suit of Army clothes, (in which, while feeling quite conspicuous, I did not seem to attract the particular attention I was entitled to) and on to New York and Army Headquarters, where I received an order, dated July 5th 1862 from R.S. Slaterly, Surg. U.S.A. "to report, without delay, to Pittsburg Landing Tennessee, to Gen. Hallock's headquarters and report to Surgeon Chas. McDougall, Medical Director for Duty." That afternoon, having received my transportation papers from the quartermaster, I started for Cincinnati, Ohio. Reaching that city early on Tuesday and interviewing the quarter master, I learned that no boat left for Pittsburg Landing, to which place I was ordered to report, until Wednesday evening. The intervening time was spent as far as the weather would permit for it was intensely hot, in looking about then "Queen City of the West".

On Wednesday evening, on the steamer, Nashville, I started down river. On the boat were some seventy-five soldiers and a dozen Officers, with whom I made pleasant acquaintance, among whom were two or three medical Officers all returning to their several commands from furlough or sick leave. Among other stoppages for freight or wood the next day was one at a place called Union Town, on the Kentucky side of the river.

Here I encountered the first blood-shed of my career in the army. As the steamer drew up to the landing many of the soldiers jumped onto the wharf boat. As I was leaning over the upper rail looking down upon the scene, I noticed a long-haired chap with a sombrero head covering slouching down the embankment. As he approached a group of the men he quickly pulled his pistol and fired into the bunch. Then he ran up the bank, jumped on a horse held by a confederate, and was off. The men's guns were all stacked on deck, out of immediate use, and there was no chance of successful pursuit. The ball pierced a soldier's face, breaking his jaw and knocking out several teeth. We left him at the Army Hospital at Paducah Ky. Farther down the Ohio, and there our boat turned into the Tennessee River, following which we reached Pittsburg Landing Sunday morning, July 13th.

The medical doctor to whom I was ordered to report, and the hospital had removed to Corinth, Miss. So, we-that is an acquaintance of the steamboat and one of the surgeons-procured an ambulance, a pair of mules and driver, and late in the afternoon started for Corinth. We passed over the battle field of Pittsburg landing or Shiloh as it was called, fought by General Grant a few weeks before, where our troops came near being defeated and shoved into the Tenn. River, but were on the second day victorious. The splintered trees, the cannon balls remaining in some of them still- the majority having been taken away by curiosity seekers- the graves of the dead, the ovens for baking, the remains of the tents and camp fires, and the fields for several miles completely cleared of grass and shrubbery, all attested to the presence of a large army and severe fighting.

The distance from the landing to Corinth is twenty-eight miles, we were seven hours making it, for the road was extremely bad and much of it corduroyed. We reached Corinth about midnight, tired and hungry, but our endeavors to relieve either condition were in affectual, as we could find no place to sleep and nothing to eat. Accordingly, we had the ambulance hauled up among a lot of government wagons and soon went to sleep to be awaked at daylight by fife and drum of patrolling soldiers, braying of mules, and the hubbub of a thousand men who had been asleep on the ground around us.

In its peaceful past, Corinth, with its few thousand inhabitants, its shaded streets, neat homes and well-kept lawns, was doubtless an attractive little town, ninety-three miles east of Memphis and Ohio

R.R.s. It was strategically important to the confederates, who after their defeat at Pittsburg Landing, made strenuous but ineffectual efforts to hold it. Thus, marred and mutilated by contending armies, it was now a most furlong place.

Tishimingo House Corinth Mississippi (1)

After a very unsatisfactory breakfast at the "Tishimingo House"a hostelry with which I was destined to become well acquainted during my frequent sojourns in Corinth and then over crowded with all sorts of hangers-on of the army, dirty and disreputable-I reported, as ordered "to Surgeon Chas. McDougall, Medical Director of the Army of the Mississippi", with a surgeon whose acquaintance I made on the boat to Cincinnati and who came to Corinth with me in the ambulance. I went to the headquarters of the army of the Mississippi, about fifteen miles south of Corinth, where there were some forty thousand troops under General Rosecrans, and finally, by Dr. Thrall, medical Director of the Fourth Division, I was ordered to the Eleventh Ohio Battery, third Division of the Army of the Mississippi, and there I arrived on the evening of July 14th; this being my first detail of service.

Here I was introduced in a measure to camp life, the first night of which was a unique one for me. It was extremely hot and the Sibley Tent, in which the Officers-of whom I was now one, slept, raised a couple of feet from the ground, on which I slept, not being provided with a cot as were the others. About midnight I was awakened from a fitful sleep by thunder pearls and lighting flashes, quickly followed by a downpour of rain. Soon the water was trickling under my blanket and wetting my clothes, but as my comrades did not seem disturbed and it was intensely dark, I lay quietly until the storm was over, dolefully wondering on the very probable results- none of which happily materialized.

Assignment to this battery was not to my liking for various reasons, I was too isolated and devoid of experience, distrustful of my own resources and had no medical Officers congenial and the mess table was very poor. After a week with the battery, to effect a change if possible, I have recourse to Dr. Thrall, who proved a good friend and assigned me to the thirty-ninth Ohio Infantry, with which I remained the succeeding three years-until the close of the war.

It was one of four regiments of first brigade, being made up the Eighteenth Missouri, Twenty-seventh Ohio, thirty ninth Ohio, and Sixty fourth Illinois, it was one of the crack Regiments of the west and comprised about seven-hundred and fifty-men with a full complement of Officers, all recruited from, and near Cincinnati. Col. Gilbert, Civil Engineer from Cincinnati, was there in command. He was wounded a few months afterwards and went home.

The command then devolved upon Col. Edw. F. Noyes, who was promoted to the Colonelcy. Noyles was a young lawyer, graduate of Bowdoin College and a very bright man. After the war he was governor of Ohio and Subsequently was U.S. Minister to France during President Hayes administration. He had a remarkable memory and his copious poetical quotations ad literary reminiscences were much enjoyed. Henry McDowell was Lt.Col. a recent law school graduate of about my age, a handsome fellow, a dexterous boxer and a
22

fine vocalist. McDowell and I were comrades. We always tented together, when there was a tent, and when there was none we pooled blankets and slept on the ground. After the war he related to an Atlanta Newspaper as editorial writer. The major was Lathrop, a young Cincinnati Lawyer. During the war he went home and was married. Shortly after he was made Colonel of a colored regiment and was killed in battle with most of his command. John Follette was surgeon, he too was a Bowdoin, Chidlaw was Chaplain, but was with the regiment only a month or so after I joined it. Chaplains did not seem to be regarded as necessary to the force. These with the adjutant and myself compromised the Colonel and his staff.

My short enrollment in the eleventh Ohio Battery is punctuated in my memory by my first attempt as an equestrian. One day following my advent, the battery was ordered out and a spare artillery horse was assigned to me for a mount. The horse was a large robust raw-boned animal about eighteen hands high. Ill fitted it seemed for me for a novice in horsemanship. However, as I had sworn to enlist in the U.S. Service for the sake of the imperiled Union, I mounted, though fearing a tragic beginning and a premature ending of my valuable services. Seemingly at a dizzyingly height and apprehending an ignominious fall I had but time to clutch with my legs the horse's broad sides when the bugle sounded, and we were off. The gun carriages' loud rumbling, the horses galloping and the sabers clashing made a tumult very disconcerting for a tyro in the saddle. As we rushed down a hill of stones and wagon ruts, the clatter was redoubled, and frantically clinging to the saddle bow, I had a realistic sense of being grounded to bits under iron-shod hoofs as they pounded down the rock-strewed road and the resounding wheels of the fast-following battery. However, I got back to camp still on the animal and glad to return to teera-firma.

The camp of the thirty-ninth was on the side of a gentle declivity, along the base of which ran a babbling brook which gave to the spot the name of "Clear-creek camp". The surrounding scenery of hills and woods and snowy tents presented a very pretty picture. The tent assigned to me about eight feet square was on the side of the hill in a beautiful grove, the surgeon was on the one side, the Colonel and the

23

rest of the stall on the other. The company Officers and the privates' tents higher up the declivity.

After sleeping for a few nights on the ground, I procured a cot and this, with a box for a seat and some meal sacks for carpet, furnishing my temporary house. The regimental band was locked on a hillock on the opposite side of the creek. Sick call was sounded at eight thirty A.M. when thirty or more complaining ones would appear. These attended to, I would go through the hospital then where there were as many more. This occupied me till noon and the remainder of the day I passed as I chose. My pay was $125.00 per month and a horse. The headquarters mess was very good indeed for camp, and by sending out foraging parties we managed to procure from the secesh there about, many luxuries. The weather was hot, over 100 degrees in the shade, while the nights were comfortably cool, a blanket usually necessary. There was always had dress parade of the regiment at 6. P.M. supper at 8 O'clock and a serenade from the band for an hour afterwards. We were well supplied with contrabands, each one of us having a servant

There seemed to be about that country no neat farm houses or cultivated fields, such as we have in New England. Riding from camp to Corinth, seven or eight miles, one passed not a single house. Rebel fortifications were stretched along the road, which had been strengthened and improved for future use if necessary. While Columbiads and rifle pits were at every turn, government trains and droves of horses and beeves were passed. Riding back in the evening when camp fires were lighted on the hills for miles around, and the numerous bands were playing. The effect was very fine. Retrenchment of the government expense was soon a order however, and all our music, save one band at brigade headquarters, was mustered out and the fife and drum made our only music.

Our Surgeon Follette, having returned from a sick leave of a couple of weeks, was detailed to go to Iuka, Miss. About 20 miles distant and assist there in the General Hospital. This hospital had been a large summer hotel and now contained some six hundred patients. Contrabands were coming into our lines daily. There were several

24

hundred of them at Iuka, -a motley crowd of Uncles and Aunts and picklnninies. The men were kept busy mending roads, driving, and when we fortified, doing the digging, and all appeared happy in their ignorance of the future. It became necessary, a couple of weeks later, to evacuate the place because of the approach of the Rebel General Price.

BATTLE OF IUKA, MISS., Sept. 19th, 1862.
11th Ohio Battery in the Foreground.   Ohio Brigade Coming Up Double Quick
This Battery lost more men in two hours than any Battery in any Battle of the War.

We had considerable difficulty in getting away undisturbed, the next train being fired into and several of our men shot. Having removed all the sick to Corinth, the train, with two hundred and fifty soldiers and another surgeon and myself attempted to return to Iuka to get some remaining stores. We were intercepted however at Burnsville, about six miles from our destination, the Rebels having gained possession of the road beyond. Here during the day, there had been considerable skirmishing and several houses were in flames. The battalion was now disembarked and after remaining there a couple of hours.

We with a couple of prisoners and a few soldiers to guard them, started to return to Corinth. As we pulled away, some Rebel cavalry attempted to capture our train by riding along parallel road for a couple of miles with the intention of taking a cross road which would intercept us. We could see them dashing ahead of us and there was an

25

exciting race as to which would first reach the crossing road. All steam was put on and we just succeeded in escaping; the baffled Rebs. having but the satisfaction of firing a few harmless shots after our retreating train.

I remained in Corinth with a lot of the sick for a week, and learned that my regiment had, the night previous, in a pelting rain been ordered to march, leaving behind all tents and baggage except blankets. Everyone now knew that a fight was expected and under the circumstances, I did not wish to remain in Corinth. Desiring to get to my regiment I was relieved from hospital duty by the division surgeon, -the same whom I accompanied to Burnsville the week before.

He and I then- with a chaplain who was on horseback, - procured an ambulance and driver, and started out to find our second (Stanley) division, though quite uncertain of its location. Late in the afternoon we heard cannonading and learned that there had been a severe fight and hastened on. It became quite dark and we hurried along meeting, much to our surprise, no pickets. Finally- about midnight we were brought to a halt and challenged.

"Who goes there?"

"Friends"

"Give the countersign."

We did not have any.

BANG! went a musket and a bullet whizzed over our heads. Others followed as our ambulance was quickly turned and our horses lashed into a gallop, tired as they were The Chaplain who had been riding ahead, was captured. We had run straight into the enemies videttes, having slipped through a defective part of our picket line and in the darkness traveled about two miles beyond. Probably we were mistaken for the advance of a large force. At any rate the Rebs were thoroughly alarmed by two unarmed doctors and a harmless Chaplain for as the horses were being urged into a run and the bullets were flying over us, the pickets along their lines took up firing, the long roll was sounding and probably the whole force was called under arms. In about half an hour we were halted again, this time by our own guards, whose lines we had reached. Thoroughly tired, we halted up by the roadside and slept.

In the morning we continued the pursuit of our division and came to the house used as a hospital during the battle of the previous day. The ground about was strewn with the wounded and those who died of their wounds since brought there. The sheds adjoining were filled and in all there were between two and three hundred disabled. Many were shot through the head and their shattered skulls and scattered brains presented a horrible appearance. There were many lying about for whom a small red spot in the breast told the tale. There were shots in almost every part of the body. One poor fellow I saw who had received a ball in the back of his head, it made its exit at the eye and the organ, completely torn out was hanging by a shred and bleeding over the cheek.

There were many such instances but there is no use of recounting them, I was to remain there and assist in getting the wounded into ambulances and taking them to Iuka where there was a large hospital. The fight took place five miles from Iuka, - General Rosecrans commanding. I worked all day with nothing to eat but a few hard crackers for thirty-six hours and then tough beef and cold potatoes seemed the best.

I slept in the field that night, found my regiment about noon the next day and in the afternoon, rode over both battle fields, -- hard fighting everywhere, dead battery horses, in one bunch I counted twenty and those were of the Eleventh Ohio with which I was connected for a short time. Its dead cannoneers laying with the rammers and lanyards still in their hands. Trees were splintered by cannon balls and marks of musket balls everywhere. Splendid Enfield Rifles of the finest English manufacture which belonged to the Confederates, blankets,

27

knapsacks, butternut coats, often bloody, were scattered about in great confusion. It was then about twenty-four hours after the fight, and long mounds of freshly thrown up earth told of the burials of many. Over six-hundred wounded secesh were brought into Iuka. Among the killed found on the field was the body of General Little. It was supposed that General Price would renew the fight the following day, but apparently, he had had enough and withdrew.

The next day the regiment marched until nine P.M. when we turned into a cornfield, and as all tents and baggage had been left behind. We just laid down in the soft furrow and slept. The "Battle of Iuka" was fought on the nineteenth of Sept. and the following ten days, pursuing and skirmishing with General Price, the regiment had no rest. Having no tents, we, of course, slept on the ground, which is no hardship when it does not rain, precluded a change of clothes, removal of boots and attention to various details which from habit, had become to be regarded essential to a civilized being. When It rained we were encased in mud and when it did not we were stifled with dust. Food was monotonous, hardtack, salt pork, and onions being the invariable menu. By October first we had reached Rheenzi (Rienzi, Mississippi) and that night the regiment encamped within four miles of Corinth.

The next afternoon I rode into the town to see about some our wounded who had been sent there, intending to return the following day. I found that the command had been ordered away in the night and I knew not where it had gone.

I had plenty to do however. The combined forces of General Price and Van Dorn, constituting their whole army of that district, were on their way to make a grand effort to retake Corinth. This attempt had been anticipated by General Grant, who, on the departure of Halleck to Washington to assume the position of which included the district of Mississippi. A chain of redoubts had been thrown up covering the whole front of the town and protecting the flanks, in front of which was a strong abatis of fallen trees, then a deep wide ditch and then the forts filled with cannons. Learning of the approach of the confederate forces General Oglesby, with a large command was sent out to meet them.

On Friday, October third, the Rebel force was largely increased and the fighting, about four miles outside of Corinth became quite severe. The wounded then began to arrive, and by evening we had a large depot and the two hotels, the "Tishimingo House" and another one on the other side of town, - filled with them.

Among these were two of our Generals, Hackelman of Indiana and Oglesby of Illinois. I was in the room with Hackelman where he was lying in full uniform on a couch, breathing his last. His robust frame and strongly developed muscles indicated a man in the acme of efficiency in marked contrast with his pallid face and labored breathing. His adjutant was kneeling by his side with ear close to the dying Generals lips to receive the last faltering words for the family at home. General Oglesby was in an adjoining room, shot through the lungs and not expected to survive the night. He, however recovered, returned to the army, and was afterwards Governor of Illinois.

Late in the afternoon the fighting had got quite close and the cannonading and musketry was rather disquieting, particularly since it was apparent that we were getting the worst of massed columns rushing forward to meet them with flags flying and drum beating. The cheers of our men and those of the enemy were distinctly heard as one or the other made a successful charge. Night brought an end to the contest for the present. We had nothing over which to be jubilant.

All seemed depressed as gathered in crowds about the hospitals and other places, the incidents of the day were narrated, and anticipations of the morrow discussed. All were serious, on the morrow would be the decisive battle, and if no more successful, we would be badly whipped and prisoners or worse by the next night.

I had been working to the limit all that afternoon attending the wounded of whom there were many hundred and felt used up. So, about midnight with a couple of friends, I went to a private house, for there were a few families still remaining in the town, roused the inmates and announced our intention of spending the remainder of the night.—we were not welcomed but that made no difference—

During the night of the third, the Confederates were heard planting a battery a few hundred yards from our redoubts and about four O'clock of the morning of the fourth we were aroused by the heavy booming of artillery. The enemy was furiously shelling the town, and I got a reluctant acquaintance with their formidable missiles. After watching the fusillade for a few minutes, we started for the hospital. Now if there is any time when one feels less valorous than another it is about four o'clock of the chilly morning when one is empty of stomach, tired in body, and depressed in spirits and screaming shell are bursting over one's head.

It seemed to me that I was doomed as, one another, they came with their blood curdling hisses, as if they were huge steam locomotives hurtling through the air, and then bursting, with terrific clamor into a thousand jugged instruments of death. One crouched involuntarily, as if from the loudest thunder clap. Then before one could straighten up and realize that he was not torn to bits, another shrieking demon of destruction would explode with a deafening roar.

To state it mildly, I was just then uneasy about my temporal, welfare, and someplace, - any place, -far from the seat of war would have been aggregable. Yet if one could eliminate the personal equation he might admire the graceful curves of these engines of destruction and delight in the fiery trails their burning fuses left behind in their furious flights through the darkened sky.

But we hurried on to the hotel, which was filled with our wounded the night before, to find that because of its proximity to our line of defense nearly all had been removed farther to the rear. A few minutes before we reached the hotel it had been struck by a shell, the victim of which lay mangled and dead at the foot of the stairs and over whose body we had to step. Welcome daylight had now come and the four guns of the Rebel battery which had been shelling us were silenced by the parrot guns of "Fort William" and two of them taken by our infantry, skirmishing then opened at various points in our front, constantly increasing to the magnitude of a battle.

Outside of our breastworks were forty thousand men of the combined forces of General's Price and Van Dorn, the grand army of the west. Inside were twenty --five thousand men under Rosecrans to defend the town. While greatly outnumbered we had the advantage of artillery, of which the enemy had but little, and we were on the defensive, behind breastworks.

About nine-thirty, threatening masses of confederate troops were suddenly discovered, assuming a wedge like form and impetuously advancing. Now our batteries opened and made hideous gaps in their lines. As the Rebels assaulted, a whirlwind of bullets, grape shot and canister poured into their faces; but, as if insensible to fear, they pressed on.
Again, and again with the greatest bravery and recklessness they assaulted and our cannon on the right and left were blazing with an almost continuous roar, while the crack of the enemies' muskets could be heard very close when the noise of the heavy guns would permit.

Hundreds of the Confederates crossed the ditch in front of our works, climbed into the forts and clubbed the men at the guns only to be shot down. The head of the enemy's main column reached within a few feet of Fort Robinette, and Colonel Rogers with a Rebel Flag in one hand and a revolver in the other led his men straight up to its crest. He was shot down by one of our drummer boys who had crept to the firing line, seized the musket of a disabled soldier and made good use of it. Colonel Rogers was said to have been the fifth standard bearer who had lost his life at that point.

One of our divisions wavered, fell back in consideration disorder, and a panic was barely averted by strenuous work on the part of the Officers. All around, the enemy made a most desperate charge in solid columns, through whole companies seemed to go down as the shells ploughed through them. The firing was closer, the enemy was in the town. Rosecrans headquarters was reached and hand to hand combats were waged in the streets. Commissary wagons were seeking a place of safety, ammunition trains were on the run and intense excitement prevailed.

Musketry firing on the part of the Rebels seemed redoubled and bullets whizzed about most flagrantly, and our cannons were belching out deafening roar Ordeilles on their horses were galloping and it looked like a panic, though, in truth, there was none, since the seeming confusion was but the hurried execution of orders, and the double-quick movement of troops from point to point as eminency demanded quick movement of troops from point to point as exigency demanded. Now we had orders to remove the hospitals further from town, we began to comply, when the pleasing assurance came that the wounded were safe in their present quarters and the enemy was repulsed.

We had lost much ground when the defection of General Davis' division began, and Fort Richardson seemed about to be taken as the Rebels rushed in with a yell, but the fifty-Sixth Illinois made a charge and held them, when our whole line advanced and the Confederate columns were broken, and they fled to the woods. The battle was over by eleven-thirty. I was not aware until then, having been busily engaged by order of the division surgeon, in attending to the wounded as they fell, with the position of my own regiment, the thirty-ninth was few; it, most of the time, having been held in reserve behind Fort Robinette. Our Colonel Gilbert was badly injured and sent home, and Lt. Col. Noyes was promoted to the Colonelcy. As soon as the enemy was known to have retired, another Surgeon and I took an ambulance for the battlefield after the wounded.

There were awful sights, the dead and wounded, friends and enemies, mangled and torn in the unseemliness manner. Many were without heads, others armless or with legs torn off. , some literally cut in two; such were the secesh who had been killed by our artillery, while our men had been killed or wounded, early in the day by musket balls. Colonel Rogers-whom I have mentioned-was found dead, lying against a tree in his stocking feet, some vandal having pulled off and appropriated his boots. I saw some dead negroes who had apparently been fighting on the Rebel side. Dead and wounded were scattered all about the field for a couple of miles.

I was glad to get orders that night to join my regiment and at three o'clock the next Sunday Morning. The whole army started by different roads in pursuit of the retreating foe. We left everything behind in the shape of baggage, the men had neither tents or blankets. My baggage consisted of an overcoat and blanket strapped behind the saddle. We were victorious and after a flying enemy and cared little for inconvenience.

For the first two miles of our march we were going over the battlefield of the previous two days. A young surgeon and myself would at times ride into the woods and, at every few steps, our horses would snort at the dead body of a secesh soldier. Splintered trees, fragments of shells, torn and bloody clothing were evidence of a hard-fought battle.

We kept on and in a few hours had proof of Price's hasty flight, Tents, blankets, cartridge boxes, ammunition wagons, cooking utensils, etc. were strewn along the road in direct confusion. Hospitals filled with wounded, Rebel surgeons having been left in charge, were passed at intervals. The surgeons were very friendly and communicative; with one of whom I divided a batch of papers I had recently received from home.

In one of the houses were three Colonels, two of whom had had a leg amputated. All acknowledged a severe defeat. In a little while we met a body of three hundred men, under a Colonel with a white flag of truce sent back to bury their dead. For nearly a week we continued the pursuit and at Ripley we were ordered back by general Grant.

We had captured one thousand prisoners, eleven guns, and ammunition and baggage trains, but failed to catch up with the main army as we had hoped.

For many a twenty-four hour, I as the rest of the staff, for we all fared alike, had nothing to eat but hardtack. There had been no rain for weeks, thousands of wagons and men had just travelled over that road and the dust stifling. Hot, hungry, and tired I was nearly played out and at times could hardly stay on my horse. Though the weeks trip none of us took off our boots, while in addition to having little sleep, (for we were always on the march again by midnight.) had nothing to eat but crackers and pork, and as we rarely halted long enough during the day to fry pork and were too tired at it's close to attempt cooking, we subsisted mostly on crackers.

On Friday, on our way back, my regiment was rear-guard. The rain then poured in torrents and we were soaked to the skin, the wagons stuck in the mud (the mules were soaked to the skin, the wagons stuck in the mud (the mules too tired to pull them Out) and drenched and shivering, we would stand for an hour or more, until, of logs or neighboring fence rails, a corduroy road was made. With men at the wheels and a concerted pull of the mules we would start again to repeat the performance at no great distance on. I never supposed I could become so dirty as on that trip which the soldiers declared was the toughest they had ever taken. Sunday, we reached camp at Corinth, passed in review before Rosecrans and began to recruit.

Sherman writes "the effect of the battle was very great and changed the whole aspect of affairs in that quarter" Our loss had been three-hundred and fifteen killed, one thousand three hundred and twelve wounded, two hundred and thirty-two prisoners and two parrot guns. Of the Confederate, were one thousand two hundred and sixty-eight killed and buried, two thousand two hundred and sixty-eight prisoners.

We had been in camp near Corinth about three weeks when, assuming that we would stay some time longer, we had our headquarter tents floored over, brick chimneys built, drains dug, and everything was comfortable and stylish for our camp life. We had however hardly got settled when orders came to march.

At the same time, I received orders to remain in town and with a brother surgeon take charge of the Division Hospital. It was lonely to be without the regiment and I was glad soon to be ordered to rejoin it at Grand Junction, Tennessee. With two or three companions I took the train to Jackson, a place of considerable size and quite pretty, the headquarters of General Grant, who was then commanding the district. I stayed there overnight and in the morning, took cars for

Grand Junction, ordered an ambulance and rejoined the regiment in the evening.

It was then the middle of November - delightfully warm - rose bushes were in full bloom and other flowers in great abundance, overcoats were quite unnecessary, and we laid out of doors as in summer. We remained in Grand Junction a few days and then, on the seventeenth, moved to Lagrange, a place of seven or eight thousand inhabitants and the seat of a large university. While there I had a sharp attack of chills and fever. My first, but by no means my last while I was in service. The Rebel army, numbering some thirty thousand as told by a deserter who came into camp, was about fifteen miles in our front and our brigade was in the advance of the army in that direction. We remained in that part of Tennessee skirmishing with the enemy, who was burning bridges and interfering with the railroad, for some time.

In the meantime, I had become somewhat dissatisfied with anomalous rank as acting Assistant Surgeon in the contract service of the United States. I had no defined rank in the army and did not feel identified with any regiment, though with the thirty nines the greater part of the time, I was liable to be transferred not only to some other command in the Army of the Mississippi, but to some other part of the country, or my contract might be annulled whenever the Medical Director saw fit, or an assistant surgeon appointed from Ohio to secede me. Accordingly, having been in the service five months, I resigned, with the intention of seeking a commission as Assistant Surgeon. When I entered I cared not where I was sent, but my few months association with the Thirty ninth had endeared the regiment to me and I was loath to sunder my connection with it.

So, on December first, I severed my relations with the army and started for Ohio for examination by the Medical Board for obtaining a commission. I left the command few miles south of Holly Springs, our brigade having the previous day made a reconnaissance to the river, briskly skirmishing with the enemy. With a couple of Officers who were going north on furlough I took the train from Jackson Tennessee.

There were no "Pullmans" on that line so we climbed into the next best offered which happened to be a rather dirty box car that had brought down commissary stores. We made ourselves as comfortable as its flooring would permit. We reached our destination about twelve 0'clock of a miserably, cold and cheerless night.

Jackson was shroud in darkness and we knew not where to go but were quite sure we had a surfeit of such conveniences as that box car afforded. Groping about the town in search of a hotel or some place of entertainment, for we were both sleepy and hungry, we met no one. As we were passing the dim outline of a house on a venture, I tried the door. It opened. Attached by loud snoring farther on, we cautiously advanced through an interminably long and densely dark passage to the room from which emitted those unmistakable sounds. Pushing in the door three darkies were disclosed noisily slumbering before the dying embers of a wood fire. With the toes of our boots they were finally awakened and told to seek repose elsewhere. We added more wood and before the blazing fire, filled the vacated places of the departed negroes.

But alas scarcely had we entered dreamland when measured steps were heard coming through the hall. The door opened and in tramped a corporal and four men. Bang went as one, four musket butts upon the floor and we were ordered to report forthwith to the Provost Marshall of the town. Such an order was not to be questioned, - the town of course being under military rule, - So, grumblingly, we put on our overcoats and, "Forward March" we went to Head Quarters. There our papers were sufficient identification for the Marshall and we were escorted back. It was then about two A.M., when we resumed our places by the fire and slept undisturbed until daylight.

The following day I resumed my journey and reached Cincinnati Thursday night, stopped at the "Burnet House" and the next day went on to Columbus, the Capital, and reported to the Medical of examiners. The examinations, written and oral were held in the Hall of Representatives on the State Capital. Having passed all right, I two days afterwards, received from Governor Tod, my commission as

Assistant Surgeon with the rank of Captain. I had brought with me complimentary letters from Colonel Noyes requesting that I might be ordered to the Thirty ninth, also, from the Medical Director and the Division Surgeon. Colonel Noyes had asked that then Assistant Surgeon, who was a German, might be transferred to a German Regiment; thus, opening a vacancy that I might retain my connection in the Thirty Ninth.

I returned to Cincinnati on the eleventh stopping at "The Burnet" found some Yale class mates in the city and remained until the twentieth, by which time the $175.00 with which I had left the regiment had become so reduced that my departure seemed discreet. I left Cincinnati Saturday on a steam Packet down the Ohio river from Columbus, Kentucky. My transportation from and back to the regiment being allowed me by the government, the only expense would be I thought, the rations during the short trip. Before leaving Cincinnati, I had heard rumors of the burning of bridges and the destructive raids by guerillas between Columbus and Jackson, - my destination, yet I thought I could get through somehow, at any rate, it was expedient that I should start.

On Christmas day the packet stopped for freight at Paducah Ky. And with an acquaintance made on the boat, I went to see the town; staid a little too long and returning to the river, to my dismay, found that the boat had gone. We could see her cheerily steaming away around a distant point. It was impossible to overtake her. There being no railroad, and there was no knowing when another steamer would come along, and the probability was that she would go on to Memphis. Her destination, and we would not see her again. The outlook was pretty discouraging since my commission, my appointment for which I had gone to Columbus and my clothes were all in a disordered state in an unlocked state-room which I had occupied with the fellow who was with me.

Hoping to catch the Captain at Cairo, -a government depot at the junction of the Ohio and Mississippi Rivers, I telegraphed him to put my luggage on the wharf there, and that I would be along on the first available boat. We spent the remainder of the day and nearly all the night at the river's edge, watching for a possible steamer, for there was no regularity in their trips. Not until the following day did one come. Reaching Cairo, sixty miles, I was immensely relieved to find among the number of other crafts, the one in which had left us behind. The Captain had been unexpectedly delayed by business; had received my telegram and I found my belongings in a pile on the wharf. I surely had not had a pleasant Christmas!

On Friday I reached Columbus on the Mississippi river with but $5.00 at my disposal; however, as I expected to go on without delay, it made little difference. On interviewing the quartermaster in the morning however I found the worst rumors I had heard verified. The guerillas had burnt bridges and torn up railroad for some fifty miles and were even then within a few miles of the town in some force and expectations of an attack were rifle. Government stores had been moved to the river bank for immediate shipment to Cairo and general confusion was in command.

The previous night I passed at what was called the best hotel in town and half a dozen soldiers shared the room with me; their sonorous slumbers and creepy denizens of the bed were fatal to sleep. All though that part of the county a room for the night, always divided with others cost fifty cents. The bed was a narrow mush used canvas cot; the bedding consisted of one soiled army blanket. Whenever obliged to stay overnight at the "Tishimingo House" in Corinth the only smaller place at which had ever stopped. I always had my own blanket and slept on the piazza. Breakfast fifty cents, lodging and meals always paid in advance. Therefore, in the morning on my visit to the quartermaster I had but four dollars on which to subsist for the one or two weeks before the road would be open. Uncle Sam owed me four hundred dollars, but my official papers were with the regiment.

I proposed to the quartermaster to reach Jackson by the way of Memphis, but he assured me that the chance of getting through was not as good as remaining in Columbus, and that he had received orders to notify all seeking transportation to that effect. There was no one with whom I was acquainted, though I wandered a long time seeking in vain to find someone with money to lend to an impecunious M.D. Then I went to the Medical Director, introduced myself, and told him I was on my last cent, and, not being able to reach my regiment, desired to be detailed to the hospital and to make myself useful for my bed and board. He said that the hospital had been cleared out in expectation of an attack. He was very pleasant about it, but could not suggest anything, really; would be very glad to help me etc.

A disconsolate looking man who was near and had overheard what I had said then introduced himself and remarked that he was in about as deplorable fix as myself. He had a little, a very little money. However, he owned a mess-chest supplied with cooking materials, was corralled in this detestable town by the Rebel raids, which he eloquently cursed, and was getting anxious as to his future food supply. He proposed if I could get a tent or a room somewhere, that we form a syndicate, pool our wealth and eke out a living until times were more auspicious. He had two dollars and I had four, my extra investment in the business of the concern off-setting his contribution of the mess chest.

I very willingly acceded to the proposal, since at the usual cost of living at fifty cents a meal and fifty cents for lodging-cash payment in advance, -my funds would be exhausted in just two days. The Medical Director suggested where he thought we might be accommodated-viz, -in a certain house which was used only in part as a regimental Hospital for the one hundred and eleven Illinois; so, there I went and told the Surgeon of my needs. There were about thirty patients, and the room not occupied by them was one in which the nurses and steward slept. However, all I asked was a place on the floor to sleep and the privilege of cooking our simple meals on the outside, and this they willingly granted.

On the twenty seventh then, our furniture, the mess chest, having been transported, the stranger and I began housekeeping. He was an odd, uncouth, good natured chap from away out west, long in expletives and short in table manners, had no connection with the army and for what he was lugging that huge mess chest around I never understood. We slept on the floor, no blankets and lived, -just lived- on two poor meals daily, -only two because more would have been extravagance, and also, because there were troubles a plenty without adding to the number of times it was necessary to chop wood, peel potatoes, fry pork, and wash tin plates. My undeveloped abilities were soon revealed, I found I could live on two shillings a day, and that I had the attainments of an Irish Scullion.

A couple of days later there was quite an excitement about an unexpected attack of guerillas. Women, the sick and government stores were removed to an adjoining hill and our small force of combatants placed in position to do their best. The anticipated attack resulted only in a further destruction of the railroad near the town. About ten days later I determined to dissolve our partnership and get away if possible. My patience and money were exhausted, and the Christmas holidays had not been hilarious. The road had not been completely repaired, some miles being still at the mercy of the guerrillas, and the quartermaster would not give transportation through to Jackson.

However, with three others who were ready to take the chance, I started. The train ran all right for some thirty miles, then burnt bridges and trestle work destroyed for some miles ahead, stopped further progress. We disembarked from the box cars into the woods at the edge of a swamp. My baggage consisted of a small carpet bag containing a very limited amount of wearing apparel, which I could carry, and a good-sized valise replete with various alluring articles, some of which were breakable, with which I proposed, in company with the rest at regimental headquarters, to celebrate my return with a commission. These I could not carry. Providentially, there happened to be at the place at which we stopped two or three contrabands.

Now, a darky in that region was bound to obey the order of a white man, especially if he was in Officer's clothes, so I impressed the bulkiest one of them into my service by putting my valise on his back

41

to tote. The portion which we had to travel was through low swampy tracts over which the cars had gone for the most part of trestle work and which abounded in bridges over numerous creeks and little streams. All this woodwork the Rebels had burnt and in consequence I had to walk through mud and water, sinking nearly knee deep at every step. Creeks, in many places quite deep, had to be crossed on treacherously rolling log usually ended in a miss-step and a slide into the water. Eight long miles I tramped and somewhat after dark reached the completed portion of the road, awfully tired, thoroughly wet and desperately hungry, having had, since an early breakfast, nothing to eat but some dry bread, and the prospect for supper was not good. I deplored my inability to give that weary darky a few dollars for his invaluable services, but what could I do with only fifteen cents in my pocket?

We had stopped by the side of the railroad in a wood. A fire was built, someone supplied hard tack, and bacon was fried and a bottle of whiskey from which we all gladly drunk (and) was passed around. My companions prepared to roll themselves on their blankets and to go to sleep before the fire. While I was in Columbus the weather had been delightfully warm but now it had become cold and the prospect of sleeping out without a blanket was not enticing, so with the view of mitigating the condition, I scraped acquaintance with some track men who had been repairing the road and got the privilege of sleeping on the floor of their box car. The next day about noon a train arrived, and we could get to Jackson, Tennessee, about fifty miles distant.

As I stepped from the train, to my immense relief, (as I did not know where my regiment was), I met Lt. Col. McDowell and my first inquiry was

"Have you any money?"

He confessed to a very limited amount, yet sufficient to supply something to eat and a place to sleep. The next morning the Colonel was obliged to leave town on some duty, expecting to return in the afternoon and left me one dollar, - nearly half of all he had, - for the paymaster had not been seen for some months. I paid fifty cents for a

42

dinner and when supper time came, the Colonel had not arrived. Now, with my remaining half dollar, should I omit that meal and make sure of a place to sleep? I decided as it was cold and rainy, to adopt the latter alternative and went to bed super less. About two A.M.I. was aroused by the loud calling of my name in the hall and was glad to have McDowell enter.

My difficulties were now at an end and on the morning of January eleventh, we got back to the regiment at Corinth, having been gone six weeks and glad enough to be with old friends again. In the evening at the Colonel's tent the valise, containing various tasty viands, was opened and corks popped.

During my absence the regiment had been off for two weeks, had a fight with some cavalry, captured four hundred prisoners and many horses, (one of which, a fine animal, was turned over to me), and having no tents had slept out in the rain, and, altogether had met with a pretty tough time; all of which I had lucky escaped,--- although I had had my own troubles--, A couple of days after, the regiment was ordered out as guard with a forage train into the country, One doctor remained with the sick in camp and I accompanied the command.

We started at day- break with blankets and three days rations. It was snowing had and right cold. The people thereabouts declared there had been no such weather for years. It was too cold to ride, and I walked nearly all day. After dark we halted in an open field to bivouac and soldiers soon built for their comfort huge fires of the nearby fence rails. Close by was a neat house owned by a secesh, and occupied by himself and his two daughters. We, that is the Colonel and staff, preferring a house to the field for sleeping quarters, called upon the occupants and informed them of our intention to make their house our headquarters. Our reception was as frosty as the weather. It was doubtless a bitter pill to give a Union Officers a good supper and comfortable beds while our soldiers were burning their fence rails and our horses and mules eating their corn, but it had to be taken and they did it with frigid politeness.

The next morning, we started again early and, from the full corn cribs of the secessionist thereabouts, got nearly two thousand bushels of corn, all we could carry. We then returned to camp. That afternoon we marched as far back as our quarters of the preceding night and our very kind southern friends once more provided us with a hot supper and comfortable quarters, while our men burned more fence fails and our animals ate more corn. It was most comfortable to get before that roaring fire on those cold nights, and we thanked our entertainers heartily, - they did not ask us to come again.

About a week later we received orders to be ready to start for Memphis, Tenn. But after the rest of the division, consisting of three brigades, (a brigade being made up of four regiments,) had gone, the order, as far as our brigade was concerned, was countermanded.

Camp life is a very lazy one. The regiment has certain duties on the way of drilling and the company routine of pickets, etc. is kept up, but the staff has little to do but to read, smoke, play cards, race horses, - for which impromptu course was laid out, - and write letters. A foraging party into the country occasionally relieved the monotony. This brought chickens, eggs, hams, etc. in quantities, and for a time we would live quite luxuriously. Our headquarters cook, Watson an ex attaché of a Cincinnati restaurant detailed from Company B. could construct some quite nice dishes, if he had the materials, with his Dutch oven and wood fire. Sutlers' prices were steep, -potatoes $4.50 per bushel; butter $.75 to a $1.00 per pound, rancid at that and everything else in proportion; but sutlers charged whatever they choose. When the commissary had such articles as we wanted prices were quite reasonable.

Corinth had been strongly fortified since the Battle of October third and fourth, and a few thousand troops were considered capable of holding it against a large force, and our brigade was left as a garrison for the places. The regiment had been but two or three weeks in Corinth before the idea became prevalent that we would remain for a long time. Accordingly, the Lt. Col. And I (we were tenting together) concluded to have a house built. We were actuated by the fact that our

44

tent was leaky, and the rain had pattered down upon us many times of late. So, a detail of men with a wagon and mules were ordered out to a saw-mill some miles distant, and the owner, with a natural reluctance, compiled with the enforced request to furnish logs and lumber for our projected abode.

Carpenters were plenty in the regiment, indeed every trade and occupation had representations in the command, and these artisans were always pleased to be detailed for special work. Soon we had a beautiful log house erected; floors were laid, tables and bunks constructed, and even a portico extending six or eight feet in front. Not content with all these luxurious equipment's, we sent into the country and got turf and trees for further adornment. After occupying these quarters for a short time, I was ordered to take charge of a small pox hospital.

The disease had caused quite a commotion and all the troops were vaccinated. The hospital was a large building, a mile outside of the breast -works, and here I had a dozen patients. I had quarters in the adjoining "Corona female Seminary" which, for obvious reasons, had not been devoted to classical education of females for some time. I remained a month and then returned to my regiment.

On the morning of April Fourteenth our usual peaceful avocations were interrupted by the receipt of an order to have teams harnessed and the men ready to march. All was bustle; blankets were hurriedly rolled and strapped on saddles, a few rations put in haversacks and shortly we were off. Artillery, cavalry and infantry were all on the move, ---an exciting and interesting scene, quite different from a holiday parade, - as the cavalry, one thousand strong or more galloped by us, the infantry cheering and they responding and the field pieces rumbling along with their sixty horses to each gun and caissons clattering after. After all, the result was nothing. There had been a few casualties, but it was not the object to, then, follow up the enemy.

On April seventeenth there was a celebration of the battle of Shiloh. The whole command, which had been lately re-enforced by infantry, cavalry and artillery, was called out and presented a fine lot of war torn veterans, an oration was delivered by Colonel Bain, who lost his right arm in the battle, and, a fine band playing, we passed in review before General Dodge, Commander of the Post.

On the next day, a force of six thousand men started for Florence Alabama, on the Tennessee river sixty miles east of Corinth, to destroy bridges across the river, thus cutting off communications between Vicksburg and Chattanooga and the transfer of Rebel troops. General Dodge, the commander, met the enemy thirty miles from Corinth; had a loss of one hundred killed and wounded and two companies taken prisoners, and then sent for the Ohio Brigade to reinforce him. So, the Thirty Ninth with the rest started at once. To my regret, I was left behind in charge of the hospital with the line Officer and a very few men. All pickets and outposts having been removed, a few guerrillas could easily capture our whole concerned.

(13)

DEFENSE OF BATTERY ROBINETT BY THE OHIO BRIGADE. BATTLE OF CORINTH, MISS., OCTOBER 4TH, 1862.
Sketched by D. Auld, 43d O. V. I.

43d O. V. I.
Changing front forward on 1st Co., crushing the right flank of the Confederate columns.

63d O. V. I.
Being cut to pieces but holding their line.

27th O. V. I.
Capturing flag of 9th Texas.

39th O. V. I. In reserve.

In a few days the expedition returned from their raid into North Alabama. It had been very destructive to the enemy's possessions. Hundreds of heads of stock were brought back, and property of all kinds destroyed. Among the buildings burnt was the Alabama Military Institute and residences of militant secsh. Thousands of darkies of both sexes came straggling along with our forces, eager to be free and thinking that within our lines flow milk and honey, and that every happiness awaited them. There were also many refugees with pitiful stories of hardship and want, following affluence and comfort.

At last, May twelfth, 1862 came an order to leave Corinth, for which we had been waiting so long. We were glad to leave this locality which had been the camping ground of thousands of Rebel and Union forces in the past twelve months; of a sanguinary battle and he is burying places of thousands of soldiers, horses and mules. We had become heartily tired of camp life there. The weather was getting very warm and the dust plenty, and all the trees had been cut down for fire-wood, still we had been occupying our stylish houses and had made up our minds to while away the summer the best we could.

Sunday evening four companies of the regiment started for Memphis ninety miles northeast. With these went Lt. Col. McDowell and I, leaving the other field and staff Officers to go with the rest of the regiment. The train carried, beside the four companies, a battery of six guns with horses, wagons etc. A freight car was the best accommodations offered the Colonel and me, upon the floor of which, rolled in our blankets, we slept comfortably, well used to hard beds.

Reaching Memphis about six the next morning, after disembarking, a staff Officer of General Veitch conducted us to a temporary camping ground. Adjacent to our camp was a large handsome house with extensive and well cultivated grounds. The house was occupied by an old gentleman, its owner, and his young attractive rather dashing wife. To these, the staff Officer, who had conducted us hither, introduced us, and the Colonel and I were cordially invited to make their house our headquarters until the regiment arrived. As we were without tents, the invitation was very acceptable. The old gentleman and his youthful spouse were very hospitable and everything in the wine cellar, which apparently was well stocked was at our disposal...

All this seeming friendliness was of course on their own account, for in those times, a federal Officer, was a safe guard in a private house and quite welcome as an inmate. Without exception all residents of that city were naturally Southern Sympathizers, their sons, brothers, and nearly all their relations being in the confederate army. The lady at whose house we were staying, for instance had, she told us, three brothers in the secesh army and though, for prudential reasons, avowing neutrality, would undoubtedly have viewed our butchery with great complacency. All of which was evident on conversing with her; for it required but a few inappropriate ad loyal remarks by one of us to provoke a display of the real and ardent sentiments she wished to, but was unable, under provocation, to conceal.

This somewhat intemperate display of devotion to the Southern Cause was entertaining to us, and she knew very well that, through us, it would not react to her. The old gentleman was prudently mum. We certainly enjoyed, for the first time in many months, sleeping on a luxurious bed in a handsomely furnished apartment, and eating at a well-appointed table abundantly supplied with dainty food, prepared, I am sure, by a darky cook of extraordinary culinary abilities.

With all this comparative sumptuousness we, in our heavy riding boots with trousers, well worn, stuck in the tops, our flannel shirts without collars and our bronzed faces and hands, did not well accord. All the same we did not feel abashed. But, alas! This oasis was not for long our abode, for in three days the remainder of our regiment arrived, and our camp was moved. As our former location was too contracted for our eight hundred men, we went to a point half a mile from the city in a beautiful wood called by the dozens of the town "Picnic Grove". Here we were supplied with new tents for the whole command and their snowy whiteness under the thick overhanging trees made an encampment that was very delightful.

The surrounding country was naturally rich and well cultivated., the land diversified with hill and dale; and handsome residences of Southern merchants were scattered numerously about. The rides were delightful; quite different from those about Corinth, where I rode only for exercise. The city was attractive, of some forty thousand inhabitants and had been, as one of the cotton marts of the Mississippi river, of great commercial importance, King Cotton, however, was then defunct, through business of various kinds connected with the army was carried on and the streets had a lively appearance. The great river, too, was always an interesting point, and we frequently rode down to the levee to see the heavily freighted flat-bottom steamboats come in, blowing their musical calliope from away above the city until they hauled up at the wharf boat. The markets, too, were a great luxury as we could buy many things that for a long time we had been without.

Many months before, when we were in Mississippi on a march, we bought a fine cow for a confederate twenty-dollar bill which one of our boys picked up on the Corinth Battlefield. This bill I purchased from a soldier for a dollar and fifty cents, desiring a souvenir. But, as the owner of the cow thought it worth more than an equal amount of United States money, he got it. For this cow, which cost me one dollar and fifty cents, we were offered one hundred and twenty-five dollars in gold, -- we did not sell. Milk in Memphis cost one dollar per gallon.

The weather was very warm. We usually laid about the camp during the day, playing cards etc. About five P.M. our horses were saddled and two or three of us rode down town with an orderly to look after the animals; travelled about the city until dark; played a few games of billiards and then returned. We had been ordered to Memphis to relieve a Division sent down to Vicksburg, one hundred miles further south. General Grant had for some time invested that place with General Pemberton in command; and it was a fore-gone conclusion that it would soon be ours. Grant was having hard fighting and hundreds of his wounded were coming up the river to be taken care of in Memphis.

In June, a large number of prisoners were sent up from Vicksburg to be taken north, stopping at Memphis on the way. I was ordered to accompany a steamer carrying about a thousand of them, many of whom were sick and all of them ragged, dirty, and emaciated. On boarding the boat, I found most of the men on deck with their clothes off, busily engaged in striving to get free of the vermin which had infested them. The steamer went up to Cairo, Ill. Where the prisoners were transferred to cars for Philadelphia, and, from there, taken to Fort Delaware, a few miles down the river where they were to be confined, and where I turned the sick over to the Surgeon in Charge.

I had been to Fort Delaware just previous to the war, where General Newton (4) with his family was then stationed, and there I had hoped to meet my sister Anna, but was disappointed, as she had left the island a while before as she left the Island a while before. Being near home, I took the opportunity to run up to Connecticut to see my mother in New London and my friends in Hartford, who took the occasion at that time to present me with a sword, for which I had no more use for than a base drum.

My visit to the nutmeg state was short, reaching New London at two A.M. Friday and leaving Hartford the following Sunday night. My stay was hurried because I had no leave of absence and I had stolen the time from duty. I therefore hurried on to Columbus, Ohio, there meeting one of our regimental captains. I was informed that the detachment that had accompanied the prisoners from Memphis had received a furlough with orders to meet in Cincinnati the following Saturday, -- which was vexatious after hurrying home.

So, I went to Cincinnati and put up at the "Burnet" for the remainder of the week. Fortunately, I met there a former classmate from San Francisco and some Officers. Sunday morning, our men having got together, we started down the Ohio, - our voyage was greatly delayed by low depth of the water and consequent stoppages on numerous sandbars, and Monday evening found us but three miles below Louisville. It being likely that the boat would remain there all night, three of us got a carriage and rode back to the city.

There were plenty of amusements, Louisville being a particularly lively city during the war. We reached the boat by daylight and continued our journey. It took eight days to get to Memphis. In the Mississippi the amount of water is very variable. At times it is almost confined to a narrow and circuitous channel, and again it spread over miles of adjacent country.

At one of the stoppages on a sandbar, a number of men went swimming, among them was one of the accompanying negro servants. He was having a fine time when he saw a chance to slip into the channel and, being unable to swim, underwater he went. The current was swift.   Up to the surface he came as he was swept along, screaming with fright only to again disappear. His struggles once more brought him to light and then, with feebly waving arms and inarticulate cries for help that could not be rendered, he sank and was seen no more... There were all sorts of stories regarding guerrillas; in fact, nearly all the boats we passed reported having been fired into, but we escaped the sight of, so many blue-coats perhaps contributed to our being left unmolested.

After a month's absence I was glad to get back to the regiment arriving Sunday evening. Vicksburg had now been captured by Grant. Port Hudson had fallen into the hands of Banks, and the river was open to its mouth. Riding to the levee, I saw a canopy sign hung our "For New Orleans" the first time the passage could be made since the war began.

In the preceding two months there had been taken by the "Army of the Tennessee" over forty thousand prisoners, and an immense number of arms. We at Memphis, had no direct connection with the capture of Vicksburg, but still were contributory there to and were elated and proud to belong to the "Army of the Tennessee" Therefore it seemed quite appropriate to celebrate. Accordingly, the big guns boomed; the small arms crackled; the bands played their loudest, and the numerous drums and fifes added to the clamor. Later, there was a grand review by Major General S.A. Hurlburt of all the troops in the vicinity, consisting of many thousands to which I added the effluence of a new hundred-dollar military suit and my newly acquired resplendent sword. After all of which we went down town and drank Champaign for the glorious cause and the star-spangled banner, -- long may she wave!

August twelfth I received an order detailing me for duty to the United States Cavalry. There I remained about a month during which time I had a well-remembered attack of chills and fever and nearly shook my teeth out with cold while I was rolled up in blankets and the mercury was over one hundred in the shade.

Many times, we went out after guerrilla bands, always returning after a little skirmishing with a number of prisoners. It was exhilarating to start out at daylight of a bright summer day with four or five hundred cavalry men. At the bugle sound the whole troop would spring into gallop as the horses felt the pricking spur. And their many hoofbeats, the clashing of sabers and the shouts of the men would make the scene as one of a holiday, while a little later a few whizzing bullets added to the fine excitements of the raid.

On returning to the regiment my horse having become lame, I brought another one, and very soon lost him. There were a lot of vagabonds in Memphis who made a business, apparently of stealing horses. If one had no orderly with him when going down town from camp, his animal was quite likely, if left in the street, to be taken, put in some cellar, branded, mane and tail cut, and, thus disguised, sold to whomever will buy.

Well this horse of mine had been gone two weeks, eluding every effort to find him and I was about to appropriate another, - for I did not propose to buy again, - when as McDowell was going down the street one day, he thought he recognized my horse with a secesh on her back. The Colonel jumped from the ambulance in which he was riding, sprinted down the middle of the street, like a marathon racer, seized the animal by the bridle and ordered the rider, excitedly protesting, to the Provost Marshall's Office; and, after turning the fellow over to the guard, proceeded in triumph to camp with the mare. The next day I went to the office, made charges and the examination was to be the following morning but that day the regiment was ordered to move, and as far as I was concerned, the case ended.

While in Memphis we had a pleasant and rather lazy time. I had had one or two desirable details, had made a trip north and had formed many good acquaintances. However, I, as well as other Officers and the men, was glad to have a change. In those stirring times we did not like to remain long in camp. Campaigning, with all its discomforts and hardships, so-called, was more to our taste. Since the fall of Vicksburg, furloughs had been generously granted by the General to Officers and men alike. A few of the former in a regiment were away all the time and five percent of the whole command on a twenty-five days absence.

For a while our headquarters mess was destitute of the Colonel who had gone to Cincinnati on duty for getting drafted men to fill the regiment to the maximum number. The Lt. Col. Was away on sick leave and the surgeon was in New England, being a New Hampshire man. We had yet the largest regiment in the department, having seven hundred men in camp, and enough of detached service to foot up over eight hundred, which number for a regiment that had been so long in the field was regarded as remarkable.

By the first of October, all had returned and on the seventeenth, the regiment with the rest of the division started on it peregrinations. After a six day march we reached Corinth about ninety miles away. It looked as familiar and uninviting as ever. We remained but twenty-four hours and then took cars for Burnsville, fifteen miles distance. This was a miserable little village, boasting of having sent out two full companies of guerrillas, though it could never have had more than three hundred in habitants in its most flourishing era. There we remained three days, and then again eastward we went to Iuka, our old summering and fighting ground. After a short march of ten miles we struck the Tennessee River and Eastport, Tenn. Arriving there we expected to cross the river at once but in this were disappointed, there being about fifteen thousand men already waiting; accordingly, we were marched down to the bank of the river and encamped in the mud for a couple of days.

We had experienced all sorts of camping grounds during the past two years, but never had there been allotted to us one as detestable as this: Nothing but soft black mud around and beneath and surrounded by reeds nearly as high as one's head. Finally, the other commands, - those Generals Blair and Osterhaus, (6) -having crossed, we gained possession of the transport and, in a few hours, our brigade, consisting of four regiments and two batteries with their horses, numbering two thousand five hundred men, were in Alabama. We then marched a couple of miles and went into camp and waited for the remainder of the division, -about eight thousand men. Taking up the march later, we soon reached Pulaski, a good-sized town with three or four churches, a large court house and many fine residences.

We were now cut off from all connection with the north; our railroad in our rear to Corinth broken up. Since getting in to Alabama we had been living off the country which was abundantly able to supply us with all we desired as food for ourselves and forage for the animals. We found turkeys, chickens and all kinds of game abundance and wild hogs were rooting in the woods by the hundreds. Of one thing, however, the country was destitute, viz. - young and able-bodied men. The young fellows were guerrillas hovering about in the woods, very shy of any considerable force but certain to shoot or gobble up any straggler from the command.

At night we would usually receive orders from headquarters to march the following morning at daylight. Consequently, reveille would sound an hour before, tents were then struck. The time that intervened between four thirty and reaching camp late in the afternoon, together with riding all day with but two or three crackers to munch on the way, gave us a most glorious appetite. We had an excellent cook who, with a Dutch oven and a battered frying pan could serve, for hungry fellows in the open, from the chickens, wild turkeys, sugar cured hams, the most delectable dishes, it seemed to us, that were ever concocted.

We reached Pulaski about dusk after a tiresome day's march, company roll was called, head-quarters tents were pitched, and preparations made by our cook, Watson, for supper, our first meal since an early breakfast - the intervening hunger being appeased by a few hard-tacks munched as we rode. Our faithful cow was stripped of what milk she had laid up during her long march, tied behind the hospital wagon; and the cloth was laid upon the grass. Our cook had succeeded in capturing a few chickens during the day and had fried them over a wood fire. These with some beans and corn bread with molasses, furnished for us an admirable supper. After smoking our pipes around the camp fire and recounting the doings of the day and the probabilities of the morrow the bugles of our and the surrounding regiments musically sounded the" Tattoo" for the men to go to quarters, and "Lights out" and all was quiet, and the men, rolled in their blankets on the ground went to sleep.

By this time our servants had started a smudge before the respective tents to drive out the mosquitoes and leaves in abundance had been gathered for each one of us to have a good bed. The headquarters tents had been set up on a slightly knoll; The Colonel's on the right of the line; the Lieutenant Colonel's and I next, and Major Lathrop nest to us, and others on the left of the Major. Major Lathrop was a young lawyer from Cincinnati before entering the service; a very gentlemanly clever fellow and a good Officer, but somewhat reserved and formal, and inclined to be restrained in the frivolities that might be indulged in about the camp fires. For some trivial affair, he seemed to have incurred the disfavor of McDowell, - the Lieutenant Colonel, - who, though realizing his worth as an Officer and treating him worth the utmost consideration yet withheld intimate companionship. Lathrop was afterwards Colonel of the Colored Regiment, to which I was detailed for a while, and he was killed.

In due time, we all turned in to our leafy beds. There was never any elaborate preparations for that ceremony. It was a simple affair of taking off boots and outer clothing, while a thick pile of leaves covered with a rubber blanket furnished a sufficiently good bed for any one was living out of doors, and a day in the saddle was invariably rounded out with a sound sleep.

But for some unaccountable reason McDowell on this occasion broke the rule. He couldn't inveigle the God of Sleep and the demon of restlessness got into his legs. After long and futile efforts to woo the one and banish the other, he was in despair at the unwanted condition, and to relieve the stress got up. Then, afterwards told me, when he heard the still distant thunder rolls, it occurred to him that no trench had been dug around the tent, -as was usual, when rain was indicated or a longer detention in camp was expected, -and the novel idea came to him to undertake the task and so allay his restlessness.

Accordingly, he jumped into his boots, donned an overcoat, and started out, passed a word with the surprised sentinel, pacing to and fro his nightly beat in front of headquarters, found a spade and went to work. Now the Colonel was never suspected of doing any unnecessary labor; anything not in the line of his official duties, and that could as well be done by someone else, was delegated to that somebody to do. It is no slight undertaking to encircle a tent with a working trench, but it was finally completed by the Colonel after an hour's hard work, enlivened by frequent lighting flashed; and finished in the pouring rain.

Hot and tired he returned to the tent, somewhat boastfully told of his worthy action, received my commendation for such a startling exhibition of energy of his part, and went to a well-earned sleep, undisturbed by thunder claps and the torrents of rain.

By morning the storm had about cleared away; the sun was striving to edge its way between the rolling clouds; and bits of blue peeped out near the western horizon. But our tent was nearly flooded, and rivulets, large and small, were winding over the grassy floor; our boots were in a puddle, our clothes, carelessly thrown down, exhaled an unpleasant moisture and our beds were soggy. The colonel was amazed and wondered, if such was the condition despite his labors, what would it have been if he hadn't dug his ditch.

Opening the flaps, he looked out, then walked all around the tent with a "well, I'll be _____!" and stopped. Words were inadequate to express his chagrin and disgusted when he realized that in the darkness he had digged a trench around the Major's tent and Lathrop was the only man in the regiment that he would not have gone out of his way to serve; but he wouldn't for anyone, have dug a trench.

We are in General Sherman's department, General Dodge being the commander of the division of which our brigade was a part. The duty apportioned to us was to open the railroad which the enemy had destroyed from Pulaski to Athens, a distance of about twenty miles; to repair the bridges; restore the torn-up rails and ruined culverts; and, from there to Decatur on the Tennessee river. This would open connection with Chattanooga by transports and obviate the necessity of guarding the whole railroad from Nashville. While in this vicinity the original enlistment of the regiment for three years expired, and one month's furlough was offered to such as would re-enlist for three years or for the war. Nearly the whole regiment reenlisted and took their month's leave.

At the same time, I had a leave of absence and went north; passing the time in New London, New York and Hartford, to which latter place Colonel McDowell came and a week with me. I went to Poughkeepsie with him for a few days to visit his sweetheart, and then returned to Hartford. Our orders were to report with the regiment at Cincinnati February tenth. We did not leave Hartford however until the night of the ninth, thirteenth at three A.M.

Looking at the papers in the morning, we learned that the command had left the day before for the seat of war. We had expected that it would remain some days in Cincinnati, but a dispatch from General Dodge had hurried the departure and we were left behind. However, as the regiment was to go to Nashville, on the Cumberland river by boat, we knew we could overtake them by cars. So, the next day, Sunday, we took a packet to Louisville; remained there Monday, and Tuesday morning started by cars, for Nashville, reaching there in the evening. We stopped at the St. Cloud, one of the fashionable and abominable hotels of the town, for the next three days, when the regiment arrived.

We all then took the cars for Pulaski and marched and marched to Athens, Alabama. Athens was a pretty town of one thousand five hundred inhabitants and seemed to be a place of considerable wealth. There were many handsome residences and a large female seminary still in operation and to which we were often invited for afternoon teas. The people of the town treated us very kindly and we expected their favors whenever agreeable to us without inquiring whether they were offered out of love for us or themselves, probably they were more concerned for their property than our happiness. The teachers were much afraid we would take their building for the education of the community; just as the churches were taken to store commissary goods in. There was quite a union sentiment there when the war broke out and the stars and stripes were nailed to the flag staff of the courthouse and kept floating for some time after the secession of the state.

On my return, I found that my contraband servant, a bright fellow of eighteen years, had died. It seemed that on return to camp with my horse from our point of departure on the cars he froze both his feet. Darky like, he preferred, under any circumstances, riding to walking, though he had been warned of the danger, for those negroes were very susceptible to cold, and they rarely encountered it to such a degree as we experienced on that march.

At first, we occupied for headquarters a pretty gothic school house which answered our purpose very well, but soon took possession of a fine brick house which was even better. The Rebs were in considerable force on the other side of the river and their pickets and ours were skirmishing every day except when they made an agreement not to shoot one another, and instead to swop papers or other articles.

58

We frequently sent foraging parties into the country which returned with supplies of chickens, eggs, etc. We now had two cows, a good cook and a new mess-kit bought on our furlough. The result of the combination is self-evident.

On one of these foraging trips Colonel McDowell and I succeeded in gaining possession of a buggy and a double harness. With this unique camp equipage, which we had so much. We had many pleasant rides over good roads, though we could not go far from town without being stopped by a sentinel; and, if without escort, as we sometimes were, we crossed the picket line on a "pass" we were in some danger of being captured by some one of the guerrilla bands that swarmed the country round.

My very agreeable camp life at Athens was unexpectedly cut short, - though nothing really is unexpected in the army, - by an order, April Twelfth, eighteen sixty-four, from headquarters relieving me from duty with the thirty ninth and sending me to take charge of the Third Alabama Colored Troops stationed at Sulphur Trestle, Alabama; the medical Officer in charge being sick. This regiment of negroes, about eight hundred strong, - had been recruited not long before, and was on duty at that point to guard a very long and high trestle on the Nashville R.R. which the enemy would have been glad to destroy and thus block our communication with Nashville.

On reaching the command I found as black a looking set of men as could be conceived - not a mulatto among them - and they all looked to me exactly alike. When the Rebels evacuated this part of the country they probably took with them their house servants, usually most of mixed blood, so that the residue was very black. The Colonel I knew well, of course, having been major of the thirty ninth and very recently promoted to the Colonelcy of the third Alabama. The company line Officers were white, as of course, were the staff. About seventy-five cases of measles greeted me, and subsequently, there were nine or ten cases of small pox, and I vaccinated the whole command.

There was but one tent on the ground and that was allotted to me. The privates were sheltered on log cabins; they sleeping in bunks ranging one above the other around the enclosure and holding twenty or twenty-five men in each cabin. One cabin was reserved for the sick, which accommodated, in a way, about twenty men; the remainder remaining in their accustomed bunks; making an exceedingly smelly mess. By constant drilling the men because quite efficient in the manual of arms, and the parade made a fairly good appearance.

As an additional protection for the trestle there was a block house with a couple of cannon. The men were panicky, easily alarmed and nightly disturbances were common, for they were in mortal terror of Rebel Raiders who had sworn to show no quarter to negro soldiers. The grunting of a wild pig in the woods or the rustling of a rabbit among the leaves at night would startle the wary sentinel, ever ready to be alarmed. Bang! would go his gun; the adjoining picket line would add to the din; the whole command would be called out to man the breastworks. Then, an inspection would prove the futility and needlessness of the alarm. Such disturbances were nearly nightly occurrence.

While on this detail, I really removed my clothes at night, since these disquieting occasions were so frequent. But one night, having had a severe chill and fever that day and feeling particularly wretched I ventured early to undress and go to bed. During a fitful sleep I was suddenly aroused, not by a musket or two, but, as it seemed to me, by a whole battery of heavy artillery, or the blowing up of a powder magazine, as the thunder loudly pealed, and the lighting flashed, while a terrific wind snapped my tent ropes and before I was fairly awake the rain was drenching me. Up to that time I had not thought I could sprint, but when by the lighting's flash I saw my tent speeding through the camp, I jumped from my cot and in bare feet made quick time to my hospital steward's cabin, fifty yards distant; and had no sooner scrambled into his bunk, when--- rip! Went half of the slab roof! There being no other refuge, I had a tarpaulin thrown over me, and remained until morning.

At day light search disclosed my clothes in all sorts of places to the very limit of the cam. The next day, my tent being badly torn, I had a team and men sent out, who took down a small unoccupied house belonging to a neighboring Rebel. This replaced my former frail tenement and, while I remained, I occupied quite stable quarters. On June seventeenth I was ordered back to my own regiment, - this had been an unpleasant detail and I was glad to return.

About ten days later Forrest's cavalry, which had long been a terror to colored soldiers, and known to be near Sulphur Branch, swooped down upon this isolated command, which really had no ability for fighting properly, and massacred nearly the whole force; of the Officers it was said but three escaped... among the killed was the Colonel Lathrop, - Our Former Major and the Assistant Surgeon who relieved.

I left Sulphur Branch on the nineteenth for Nashville, spent the night at St. Cloud, and went on was ordered to the regiment, at the front with general Sherman. The journey from Nashville to Big Shanty, which was the terminus of the union end of the railroad a few miles from the camp of the Thirty Ninth and about thirty miles from Atlanta, Georgia, was made in dirty box cars, and much exposed to guerrillas. I was detained for two days at Ringgold, Ga. The Rebels having burned some bridges in advance of us.
For thirty miles of the way, a friend and myself rode on the head of the cow-catcher, as a diversion from the hot and stuffy box car and found it very enlivening. But a wild pig appeared on the track and showed no intention of leaving it on our approach, so we nimbly retreated to the engine cab, not wishing to be a buffer for quadrupeds.

We were continually passing the charred remains of bridges or cars pitched off the tracks and shattered to pieces by torpedoes, or remains of long trains but lately destroyed by guerrillas. We passed, also, those places but lately made historic by Grant, Sherman, Rosecrans and others in advance toward Atlanta against Johnson, --- Chickamauga, Chattanooga, Dalton, Tunnel Hill, Look Out Mountain, Buzzards Roost, and about midnight, stopped at Big Shanty, the then terminus of the Tennessee and Georgia R.R.; glad to reach our destination, for it was a rather perilous road to travel. Until daylight, I slept in the car with other Officers on some sacks of corn, and in the morning, procured a horse and started for my regiment.

On May fifth, eighteen sixty-four, the great campaign in Georgia under Sherman was begun. Ringgold, Tunnel Hill, Dalton, Resaca, Altoona, - positions in the mountain range most eligible to defend, were strongly fortified by General Johnston's troops. However, they all had successively fallen under the masterful strategy of Sherman and the splendid valor of his army, and now our forces had reached Big Shanty under the Kennesaw Mountain. Johnston of course had destroyed the railway as much as possible in his retreat from point to point, burning bridges, blowing up tunnels and obstructing passes.

But Colonel Wright, a railroad engineer with two thousand men had skillfully and swiftly repaired damages so that by the middle of June a loaded train ran up to Big Shanty, and the engineer detaching his locomotive, ran it forward to a water tank within range of the enemy's guns on Kennesaw Mountain., which were opened on him. The engineer pluckily got his water, answering the guns with shrieks of his locomotive whistle heightened by cheers of our men.

I found the regiment on the extreme front, at the base of Kennesaw Mountain within a few hundred yards of the enemy and unpleasantly exposed to the musket balls and shell which were continually flying over. Our headquarters was in a hole in the ground eight or ten feet square and a couple of feet deep with an embankment of the same height on each side and the front, over this was simply a tent fly, - there was no tents in the army, as men bivouacked, over the fly was a covering of green boughs and leaves. This was so that the white of the canvas might not afford a mark for the enemy's sharp shooters, who took every opportunity to plant a musket ball where it would do the most good for themselves and the most harm for us, -- and they could shoot very accurately. Bullets were continually zipping about the camp, wounding men and peppering everything in sight; while every now and then the enemy's big guns would open with shells or shrapnel from the summit of the mountain.

During the eighteen days we were under Kennesaw not a candle was lighted after dark, and to light one's pipe, it was expedient to get in some place of concealment. One night after coming in from picket duty with the regiment, I thoughtlessly dropped at the base of a tree, fronting the mountain, struck a match and before my pipe was fairly lighted, a musket ball struck a foot or two above me, and I hastily retreated to the other side of that tree. When a bullet comes as close as that, one does not hear a wiz that is so noticeable when the ball is passing at a little distance, very frequently men were wounded at night - the only Officer killed in camp was shot when he was asleep.

I had just begun a letter one day when a soldier brought to me wounded in the leg and such casualties were happening continually. What little cooking was attempted was done in a hole in the ground or behind some protecting embankment. Of course, we slept on the ground and made no pretense of undressing.

There was a battery of eight guns, commanded by a young West Pointer, Named Murray. Which had been with the brigade a long time. This battery was stationed on an elevation about one hundred and fifty feet to the rear of our headquarters and would throw shells over our heads in a quick succession for an hour or two at a time and would afford to us much diversion as we watched the effects of the shot; the Rebs jumping and dirt flying whenever the parapets were struck, which was very often. Many times, at night this battery would have a duel with the enemy's guns, thought all of which would sleep undisturbed, so accustomed had we become to the roar of artillery.

Ordinarily a picket line is made up of a detail from the companies, which is relieved at intervals. Before Kennesaw the whole regiment was turned out at once for twenty-four hours, relieving the regiment which had held the position the previous night and day. This change of pickets was necessarily made after dark since the enemy's lines and ours were so close that any exposure during the daylight was exceedingly hazardous.

To protect themselves the men made, as best they could, simple defensive works in the form of a lunette, or horse shoe of dirt, or logs, if procurable. They covered the outside with dirt sometime a log across the top with sufficient aperture beneath to admit of a rifle barrel. Thus, they were fairly well protected if they remained still, but this they were not content to do; and so, a continuous duel would by going on through the twenty-four hours, and numbers were killed or wounded daily. When a soldier on the picket line was wounded, perhaps early in the day, there he had to remain until relieved at night, since an attempt to retire during the day would be death from the opposing line not more than a hundred yards away.

One evening, when our companies were relieved, several men were brought in wounded, but one corporal was missing and was afterwards found, dead at post, fly blown and putrid, having laid in the broiling sun all day, probably shot early in the morning. And so, it would be nearly every day and yet, our men would go out to take the place of dead and wounded with as much alacrity as if were on some pleasant diversion. The grit with which these soldiers endured suffering and encountered danger and death was really wonderful. Through commanding Officers received most recognition and reward, the glory of the war belonged to the private soldier, who is the least regarded; yet one finds in him truest bravery, heroic devotion and a splendid exhibition of coolness and courage.

The enemy's forts lined the mountain crest and their pickets were almost down to its rocky base, within talking distance of our lines, of which latter condition the men sometime took amicable advantage. The "Yanks" and "Johnny Rebs" as they were called, by mutual consent, suspended firing at each other and substituted talking and exchanging of commodities, such as tobacco and coffee, of which latter the "Johnny Rebs" were destitute.

One night our men came in from duty complaining that the Rebs were exceedingly surly, would hold no conversation; and returned every advance with a musket ball. Such contumaciousness, it seemed, resulted from the fact that on the previous afternoon, while a truce was in progress and the Rebs had come to our lines to exchange papers, two of their men had been persuaded to desert, and when the others returned to their lines one of our men followed them in and gained considerable information.

A group of men on the mountain top could plainly discerned from our lines, and any such cluster was generally annoying and dispersed by a shot from one of our batteries. One such group we noticed observing us with glasses. It seems this group consisted of three major Generals, Johnston, who commanded the army, and Hardee and Polk and about them was a number of soldiers belonging to the battery close by. General Johnston, after the war, said that he noticed preparations of our battery to fire; cautioned those about him to scatter, and he likewise hurried behind the parapet, but general Polk not wishing to appear to hurried in the presence of the men, and was struck in the breast by a shell and was instantly killed. Polk was a West Point Graduate, who afterward entered the ministry, and at the breaking out of the war was the Bishop of Louisiana The Church Militant being less compelling than the army Militant, he resigned his episcopacy to become general in the Confederate Army.

Earthworks of the 5th Indiana Battery where General Sherman personally gave the order to fire on the beloved Southern General.

Kennesaw, one thousand eight hundred feet high, and Lost and Pine Mountains is the same range, all steep rugged and heavily fortified, were impregnable to any assault from the front. Such an attempt was unsuccessfully made one by Sherman and met with heavy loss of Officers and men and was not repeated. Other tactics were necessary to dislodge the enemy from his strong position. Accordingly, all dispositions were made by the army, now consisting of one hundred thousand men. These dispositions were made for a flanking movement to gain the rear of Johnston's Army, thus gaining possession of his Railroad and cutting off his supplies, compelling a retreat or a fight in the open.

With this in view, certain movements had been going on for two or three days and on the night of July Second our division of the Sixteenth Corps, was ordered to be in readiness to march. It was essential to the success of the movement that Johnston should be unaware of our departures from his front. So, about dark, to convince the enemy that we were still in position, all our artillery opened fire and a most terrific shower of missiles was poured upon the Mountain.

When darkness came the sight of almost countless shells with their fiery trails bursting as they neared their destination was a grand spectacle. Such a bombardment, with its deafening roar was kept up for a couple of hours. Then the artillery wheels were muffled, and precautions taken that our movements of our trains might not be perceived. We had been ordered to start out at midnight, but the massing of our foes on our right being supposed to indicate an attack, the order was countermanded. So, the regiment laid on its arms, and we tried to get a little sleep. We were not disturbed during the night.

At sunrise, I was up with the others, and, looking towards Kennesaw's rugged heights, the welcome and glorious sight of the Stars and Stripes proudly floated in the morning breeze from the frowning betterments that had so long been pelting us with deadly missiles, and our soldiers in blue lining the crest of the mountain greeted our eyes.

The enemy, for seeing our intention, had evacuated their impregnable position during the night, and before the sun rose on July third our pickets had discovered that the Johnny Rebs had ingloriously decamped.

After a hasty breakfast of hard-tack and beans, (we should have had the same menu if we had not been in a hurry, and ditto for dinner and supper), we ordered our horses and the Colonel, and I started for the summit. As far as the animals could travel we rode up the steep and rugged mountain side, then leaving our horses with an orderly, we clambered the reaming seven or eight hundred feet.

Bodies of dead soldiers marked the ascent. At first blue and then gray, - those who gave their lives for the Union preservation, - those who had laid for days in the blistering sun and pouring rains, --- a sight on which one would not care to linger, -others who, musket in hand, had lost their lives only the night before in the last volley at the retreating foe. Trees splintered and broken down by our shells obstructed the way but at last, we reached the summit.

The view from the top was splendid. The little town of Marietta seemed right under us, and through it the rear guard of the enemy was winding its way skirmishing as it went, with our cavalry sent out to reconnoiter. And it was interesting to see the arrangements the enemy had made for our reception in case we assaulted. A few hours after their departure our army started in pursuit and marched about ten miles.

The next morning was the fourth of July. That historic day was celebrated with enough noise and excitement to satisfy the most patriotic youngster in the Country.

After advancing some three miles from our camp of the previous night, our brigade being on the right of the line, the command was halted and a company of the Thirty ninth sent out as skirmishes. They soon ran upon the pickets of the enemy and the regiment was ordered to advance. Bullets whistled numerously and spitefully about, though

67

few were wounded, and none killed, and the Rebel skirmishes were quickly driven back to their rifle pits. It seemed that we had bumped up against the strong rear guard of their army intrenched at Smyrna Camp ground, six miles below Marietta.

Our brigade was now halted, and, about three hundred yards from the Rebel rifle pits, breastworks were thrown up; shots were being continually exchanged and we lost a few men. In the early afternoon my regiment and the twenty-seventh Ohio got orders to be ready to charge the enemy's works. Immediately in our front was an open field, on the opposite side of which were rifle pits filled with bristling muskets which the two regiments were to assault We waited a couple of hours before the final order came. When confronted by actual danger to be met at once men have less fear than after long delay affords time for contemplation. Lt. Col. McDowell was engaged to a girl in Poughkeepsie, a very attractive young lady, whom I met in that city when I went with him there while on our furlough. Their letters helped to weigh down every mail that came to and from our camp.

During the delay referred to the Colonel had abundant time to muse on what might happen. His pocket was crammed with letters from his dear Julia. They might prevent a bullet from going through the doting heart over which they laid, and again they might not. In the latter case, which seemed the more probable the longer he mused, irreverent eyes might gloat over endearing words from Julia, so the Colonel took the precious missives from his inside coat pocket, and, hurriedly glancing over them, tore them into bits and cast them on the ground.

Then, the bugle sounded Forward; on the double quick, CHARGE! And altogether the two regiments with a cheer started off for their appointed work. The excitement was great, the cheer was taken up by the rest of the troops and as our men rushed across the field the Rebs opened with a musketry fire that was startling, like a pack of fourth of July fire-crackers under a barrel magnified a thousand times. Our troops did not fire a gun but went at them with the bayonet and in a few minutes from the time the bugle sounded the regimental colors of the thirty ninth were floating over the Rebel's rifle pits and the enemy was retreating at full speed.

Now came the sad part of the affair for all who went out did not come back. The first one brought in was Colonel Noyes, his leg badly shattered by a musket ball. In the evening the limb was amputated. We were extremely sorry for the Colonel's ill luck. He was a fine Officer and very popular. Of course, he went home. He had married a few months before when on a furlough; was breveted Brigadier General and did not return to the army.

McDowell, who was in the thick of the affair, was not wounded and might have retained his letters. He was now in command of the regiment. The thirty-ninth lost in killed and wounded, thirty-six privates and three Officers; twenty-seventh lost forty-one. The enemy had fallen back about two miles to the second line of works. Our troops remained on the field the night of the fourth expecting another encounter in the morning, but it was then ascertained that the confederates had retreated again, leaving strong works without a struggle.

On the morning of the fifth I walked over the abandoned rifle pits and found there a southern newspaper. It was a small affair printed on dingy coarse paper, the usual publication during the war. In it I was interested to find an article clipped from our "Hartford Courant" giving a somewhat lengthy description of an elaborate and costly brick barn just erected by henry C. Beckwith on Concord Street for the stabling of his fast horses. Appended to this article were comments by the Southern Editor on the silly extravagance of Northern mudsills in General and Beckwith, bombastic laudation of the Southern Army and prophetic annihilation for the Northern invaders and vituperation in abundance. As a serious paper it was very amusing. I sent the paper to my brother Jared.

I also found a crumbled piece of note paper the following touching bit of poetry. It was presumably written by some very best girl to her soldier swain who, during his often its words of sweet sympathy and coy confession, had been startled by our sudden assault and had dropped in his hasty flight.

"It's hard for you-uns to fight the Yanks

Its Hard for you-uns to live in camp

It's hard for you-unstand we-uns to part

Cause you-un got we-uns heart."

At noon we were again on the march but did not meet our enemy and stopped about three miles from the Chattahoochee river across which their army was making the best of its way harassed by our troops. It was so fearfully hot down in that country it would seem to have been impossible to march or fight, yet our troops did both, though many fell by the way under the burning rays of the Southern Sun.

We were living at those times in very rough style. For headquarters we had one tent-fly, the men bivouacked at night, and we were in such close quarters with the enemy that the regiment had at all times to be in the alert, never for weeks taking off our clothes. Beans, Bacon and hard tack our unvarying food day after day.

No green vegetables did we see after entering Georgia, and a potato, even a sweet-one, -which I detest, - would have been a luxury. Since entering on the campaign, we had lost seventy-five men and several Officers. Two weeks previous I lost my mare. She got away once before, when we were in Memphis butt now I gave her up. Colonel McDowell procured another for me, however, young and promising.

Now, about three miles from the river, cannonading could be quite plainly heard; the Rebels having strong fortifications and considerable heavy artillery. On the morning of July seventeenth, the army received marching orders and we were early on the road to Atlanta. During the day we were continually skirmishing with the Rebel cavalry and on the eighteenth, crossed the then much talked about peach-tree creek, where General Newton, -my brother-in-law, - had just had a severe fight.

On the evening of the same day we were in the vicinity of Decatur on the line of the railroad from Atlanta to Augusta and about five miles from Atlanta. The twenty third corps halted about a mile from the town while our corps, the Sixteenth, was ordered to advance and occupy this place.

The thirty ninth was on the right of the line and with flags flying, drums beating and fifes shrilling, lines dressed, we entered the town and had just reached its center by the court house when, most unexpectedly, a Rebel battery opened, the shells crashing through the trees and bursting about us in the most careless manner, wounding many, among others, our division Surgeon. A piece of shell fractured his thigh. Very quickly Murray's battery came up on a run, and, soon unlimbering, got a line on the disturbing guns and stopped further interruption. Few besides women remained in town, and they were not cordial.

A couple of days before this, one of Sherman's spies brought to him an Atlanta paper containing the relinquishment of the command of the confederate forces about Atlanta by General Johnston, and Hood's order assuming command thereof> Johnston was regarded as one of the best Generals in the Confederate Army, but for some reason, was not in the good graces of President Davis, who, dissatisfied with the Georgia Campaign, took this opportunity to relieve him.

Though Johnston had held positions impregnable by direct attack from Chattanooga down to Atlanta, he had been forced by Sherman's tactics, to relinquish them one after the other, in order to retain connection with his base of supplies, and it was no lack of judgement on his part that the frequent retreats were made. General Hood was a West Pointer known by Sherman to be bold, even to rashness, and courageous in the extreme, but by no means the equal of Johnston's in Military ability, the change of commanders was a welcome one to

Sherman, who foresaw that now would come the opportunity which he desired, viz. a fight on anything like equal terms instead of running up against prepared intrenchments. SO, now, every division commander was cautioned to be always on the alert for battle in any shape.

On the twenty first we were within two miles of Atlanta, and from various parts of our line we could see the houses inside the city. Our army was in line of battle and the enemy similarly disposed; the skirmishers keeping up a continual rattle of musketry, and every few minutes the artillery would roll out. The night was very noisy while the morning of the twenty second presented a marked contrast, soon explained by learning that the enemy had left our front.

Library of Congress

During that morning my regiment was resting at ease, having no marching orders. At headquarters we were lolling about under the trees in the shade, anticipating, in our blooming ignorance, a speedy and easy entrance to the city for which we had been maneuvering and fighting so long. As very likely any company of young fellows with keen appetites, who had been living for weeks on salt pork and hard tack would, we were detailing at pleasurable length all the daily things to eat and drink we would order at the best hotel in the city.

Just then General McPherson commanding the army of Tennessee, of which we were a part, passed with his staff and orderlies. McPherson was then in his prime, thirty-four years old over six feet in height, a very handsome military figure, He was riding a finely caparisoned horse boots outside his trousers, gauntlets on his hands, in full Major General's Uniform and sword belt. We rarely saw at that time a General Officer so elegantly dressed. After reconnoitering for then or fifteen minutes, he and his staff returned, leisurely riding.

Very shortly, sharp musketry firing was heard about a mile in our rear, and an orderly came dashing down the road, on the double quick. We at once jumped on our already saddled horses, bugles sounded and the regiment with the rest of the division was no the run. After about a mile and a half we reached a large open space in which the teams, about two thousand in number, were parked. The enemy was in sight rushing down in great force to capture them. Immediately the line of battle was formed, and the fight was on. Our artillery belched out shells and canister and the bullets, whistling through the leaves and tearing up the ground about us, made things very lively.

I had been under fire of shells and musketry many times before, but surely never felt that I was so near the terminus of earthy interests as in the succeeding few hours. Bullets came too threateningly for calm sightseeing. I was by no means calm; indeed, I was badly scared. When the wounded had not come in to keep one busy, and cannon balls are shrieking overhead and bullets spitefully hissing close, it is the easiest thing in the world to picture one's head knocked off or a bullet going through one's body, and continued contemplation does not make one placid. Still, with engrossing eyes, I had a splendid view of a big battle, though I would hardly care to take the risk again even for such a gladly exciting scene.

THE BATTLE OF NICKOJACK, GA., JULY 4th, 1864.
The 27th and 39th Ohio going over the Confederate Works

13

The two lines were at times touching one another as charges followed charge with flags flying and men cheering. We could see the enemy's men and Officers dropping, and, as standard bearers fell, others took their places, seized the drooping flag and hastened on to meet the same fate, and there was havoc too, on our side, for our soldiers went down by the score, as, undaunted, they rushed on the foe regardless of everything but gaining the victory. Of course, the troops in my vicinity were but a small part of those engaged, our brigade numbering about two thousand five hundred men; while the whole of McPherson's army of the Tennessee was in the battle, consisting of twenty-five thousand soldiers.

The total Federal loss in this battle, called the "Battle of Atlanta", was three thousand seven hundred and twenty-two. The enemy's dead in front of our lines was, by actual count, two thousand two hundred. Their total loss was three thousand, two hundred and forty killed, three thousand prisoners and many Officers of high rank. We had irreparable loss in the death of the brilliant General McPherson.

Between the sixteenth Corps, to which the Thirty-ninth belonged, and the Seventeenth Corps was a wooded space of about half a mile not occupied by any troops. A report that the enemy was moving around to the left of the Seventeenth Corps and was pushing in through the unoccupied space mentioned induced McPherson to hasten there. This was before the battle had really begun. The General sent a staff Officer for a brigade to fill this gap in the line; and himself, with an orderly, went through it on a cross road, which, unknown to him, had already been occupied but h enemy's skirmishers, and, when too late to retrace his steps he was within fifty feet of them, and was shot down.

I saw him pass up the road and distinctly heard the crack of muskets a few minutes afterwards. Then back came his horse, wounded, bleeding and rider less. The spot where he was killed was shortly taken by our troops and within an hour his body was brought to Sherman's headquarters. He was dressed as when he rode past us in Major Generals uniform with gauntlets and boots, but his pocketbook, money and watch were missing. His pocketbook contained papers from Sherman detailing important movements, very valuable to the enemy. Fortunately, the pocketbook was afterwards found in the haversack of a prisoner of war captured at this time.

McPherson's body escorted by his personal staff, was taken to his home in Clyde, Ohio, and received with great honor and buried in a small cemetery close to his mother's house, which cemetery was composed in part of the family orchard in which he used to play as a boy. Over his body is now erected, under the auspices of "the Society of the army of the Tennessee", an Equestrian Monument.

The battery of eight guns, which had been in our brigade so long, was lost. Murray, its commander, had just graduated from West Point when he came to us, a fine fellow to whom we were greatly attached. All the horses were killed and most of the Cannoneers. Murray was taken prisoner ad we afterwards heard he died in a Rebel Hospital.

Not very long after the battle began, wounded began to come in and the surgeons of the brigade had a busy time. Twice we had to move our location to get the wounded out of range of the enemy's shells which came bursting among us ending the suffering of many. By night we had we nearly had four hundred to take care of and with insufficient means at our command. It seemed hard that men badly wounded, or whose limbs were just amputated should lie all night on the ground and many without a blanket to cover them and nothing to eat. Yet such was the case. Knapsacks and Haversacks of most all having been lost in the fight, and our trains were in such confusion that they could not be reached that night.

Our trains had been in imminent danger of capture being within easy musket range. Many of the teamsters and mules were killed during efforts to get the wagons to a place of safety. The next day we made the wounded more comfortable under canvas and sent them north as soon as possible. My regiment during the preceding month had lost two hundred men and five Officers.

During the night Hood with his army retired inside of his fortifications about Atlanta, leaving us in possession of the field. Our commanding Officer having been killed, General O.O. Howard was appointed by general Sherman to command the "Army of the Tennessee". Howard was a graduate of West Point. Now thirty-two years old. He had high standing in the army of the Potomac and had lost an arm at Gettysburg.

The month of July had been hot in the extreme, and one of almost constant conflict, with casualty lists by the thousands. The official report of General Johnston for July Showed a loss of ten thousand eight hundred and forty-one, and the official report on our side, nine thousand seven hundred and nineteen.

The enormous strength of Atlanta gave promise of a long and perhaps successful defense; At the same time an active cavalry force operating on Sherman's flank might so seriously interrupt our communications with our base of supplies as to compel him to retrace his steps or even abandon the campaign. Our forces too had been subjected to daily depletion, as we advanced, by the necessity of garrisoning captured places and guarding lines of railroad. While Johnston, moving constantly nearer his supplies and re-enforcements, was relatively stronger then he reached Atlanta, than when he started from Dalton.

Well, here we were at last in front of the city not more than a few hundred yards from the enemy's main works. The artillery and skirmishers of each side continually firing at one another and neither side gaining anything, each being afraid to assault the other's works; for' of course, on investing the place, strong breastworks had been thrown up and heavy guns mounted by our forces. Every day, and perhaps several times each day, the big guns opposite our division would bombard us. Each heavy gun had its characteristic roar and was individualized by when it paid its complements to our camp. One day, when at our dinner of hard tack and bacon, a shell came ripping through our tent-fly. It hurt no one through such an intrusion somewhat ruffled a quit repast.

Here I lost my cow. I called her mine because it was my worthless confederate money that bought her, and, because, not drinking coffee, I was the largest beneficiary of her very small output. We had at one time two cows in the train, but the other one did not long survive the rigors of camp life. This one travelled with us, tied behind the hospital wagon, for hundreds of miles since she came into our possession in Mississippi. She was really an admirable animal, faithful to the Union Cause, devoting all she had to its maintenance, living on the barest necessities of cow life, trotting along mile after mile without a murmur.

She had a razor back, liked a wild hog, and the more attenuated she became the longer got her legs. Until she more resembled a lean horse then a buxom bovine once was. She was tough to the last, as we found out when in due time we came to eat her. While standing a short distance from headquarters her heart was pierced by the enemy's bullet. Such is the fate of warriors and there is no exception for cows.

After remaining at the front ten days I was ordered on August eighteenth to the General Hospital at Marietta, twenty miles to the rear. Though disliking to leave the regiment, it was not altogether an unsatisfactory detail, for I was thoroughly tired of the booming of Artillery, the side stepping of shells and the crackle of musketry.

I am now left our very contracted Camp Quarters and came to live in a great stylish brick house of some departed Rebel of the pretty little town of Marietta, though which I saw, from Kennesaw Heights some weeks before, the Rebel army hurrying. Here we lived on a deal of quiet and comfort. We had a hospital for the whole division and nearly nine hundred sick and wounded and more coming from the picket line every day. We occupied for their care three churches, eight or ten large number of tents. There were seven medical Officers to attend to them.

The ascent of Kennesaw Mountain from the south was much less difficult than from the north side against which we were so long bumping. The Rebels had made a road up which to haul their artillery and supplies, and up this a couple of Officer and I rode one afternoon. From the summit we had a magnificent view. Our works were plainly to be seen at the foot. To the west were Lost and Pine Mountains and surrounding territory, all of which had been fought over.

Fifteen miles to the north the Altoona Mountains loomed where the Rebels made a stand and confidently expected to stay our progress. On the summit of Kennesaw Mountain was a signal station, a conversation at the time being carried by flags with the signal Officer at Altoona. The works in which the enemy had their guns were badly battered. I had often been behind one of our own batteries when firing and seen the clouds of dust fly as our shells would explode in these same forts.

As we were going down the gorge between Kennesaw and Lost Mountains, - (little Kennesaw) we met a couple of soldiers, one carried on the point of his bayonet, the whitened skull of a soldier found in one of his rifle pits, the other, the rusty musket that was lying at its side. These, with the bones, were all that remained of some poor Reb.

While in Marietta there were daily rumors of cavalry raids into the place, but somehow, they did not trouble us much. About three months before, I lost my mare at Decatur and Colonel McDowell had given me another, -a fine horse of which I had great opinion. While at Marietta an orderly took a valuable horse bought from Cincinnati three years before by Colonel Noyes and left with us after the colonel lost his leg, and mine a little way from the town to graze, forage being scarce.

Through the carelessness of the orderly both animals got away and ran outside the picket line. They were both followed as far as the orderly was permitted, then he returned for a pass that he might go outside the lines and told him to go until he found the horses. Neither orderly or horses were ever heard from. He probably got into some Reb prison and I was out a horse and a new housing, saddle and bridle, which I had brought back with me when last north.

When I left the front, August eighteenth, the contending armies were facing each other, and neither gaining any advantage, so Sherman, after a little waiting, devised other tactics. He was too impatient a man for a siege and was unwilling to order a direct assault and perhaps unnecessary loss of life.

The capture of Atlanta with its vast stores and costly machinery would so cripple Rebel resources that the simple suggestion of such a counting effort, sent a thrill through the entire confederacy. In the opinion of many, its importance was not second to that of Richmond. There were established the machine shops of the principal R.R.s; the most extensive rolling mills in the south, pistol and tent factories; and numerous work under the direction of the Confederate Government for casting shot and shells and the manufacture of gun carriages, caps, shoes, clothing and other military supplies. Strenuous efforts were therefore put forth for its defense

Leaving but one corps, -the twentieth under General Slocum, - Sherman one night quietly started out with the remainder of the army and twenty days rations, and marched forty miles south of the city. In the meantime, finding our camps abandoned, Hood supposed that our army retreated, and there was consequently great rejoicing in Atlanta that the "Yanks" had gone. This news was telegraphed all over the south and trains of excursionist came up from Macon to celebrate the great victory.

After the larger part had got away to the south, Slocum, as was planned, started with his one corps from the north, and Hood, thinking it was the rear guard of our retreating army, naturally followed with all forces. Slocum, of course, before the whole Rebel army, continued to the north and decoyed hood to the Chattahoochee river, twelve miles from Atlanta.

Hood by this time had found out that he had been fooled and then he turned and made with all haste for Sherman, hoping to keep his communications on, which depended the sustenance of his army, intact. But he was too late. Sherman was a night and a day's march ahead of him and Hood's R. Rs, on which he depended, were now utterly destroyed by our troops. Slocum now, the ruse having worked, finding that Hood was retracing his steps as fast as he could, turned south again and cautiously reconnoitering, found that Atlanta was abandoned, and in he marched, and took possession of the City, September second, 1864. Our goal was won.

The glad tidings flew on the wings of electricity to all parts of their husbands, brothers, and sons fighting for them way down in "Dixie Lands", and congratulations came pouring in. From President Abraham Lincoln came the following "The national thanks are rendered by the President to Major Wm. T. Sherman and the gallant Officers and soldiers of his command before Atlanta for the distinguished ability and perseverance displayed in the campaign in Georgia, which under Divine favor has resulted in the capture of Atlanta.

The marches, battles, sieges and other operations that have signalized the campaign must render it famous in the annals of war and have entitled those who have participated there in to the applause and thanks of the nation". General Grant telegraphed, "In honor of the great victory a salute was to be fired with shotted guns for every battery bearing upon the enemy." These dispatches and others were communicated to the army in General Orders, all felt elated by the praise of those competent to bestow it. As the good news spread through the army, the shouts wild hollering and hilarious laughter were a full recompense for the dangers, labor, toils and hardships endured by all in the previous three months.

In Marietta, at General MacArthur's Headquarters, this placard was put up.
"Atlanta is ours, Glory to God, Bully for Sherman"

Everybody in the army felt that he personally contributed something to the glorious result, and rejoiced accordingly. There was a general jubilee.

I was indeed sorry not to have been with my regiment when it pulled out from before Atlanta with Sherman, through rather glad to get away for a while from the din of battle in which I had so long been. I soon, in the comparative quiet and monotony of Marietta, became impatient to return.

There is a fascination in being at the front amid all the excitement and life and vicinity of forward and unexpected movements, of skirmishers of bivouacking in the open, and even in all the chances that an energetic and fighting army entails, and such a magnificent army as was ours; Every place it had gone for had fallen, and, though to be sure, many of our men had fallen with it. One could not help feeling at times that one's self might perhaps be the next.

Marietta had now become a place of secondary importance. It previous to the capture of Atlanta, was one of the army depots and rather lively, but was now almost deserted except for the wounded and sick, and these were rapidly recovering and being sent to the front. After remaining in the town for six weeks, I at last on September thirty-first, received orders to return to the regiment.

After the capture of Atlanta. Instead of pursuing Hood in his flight southward (west), Sherman moved the army back to that city to enjoy a short period of rest, and our "Army of the Tennessee" was assigned to Eastpoint, five miles south of Atlanta and there I found the regiment encamped.

Sherman resolved to make the city a purely military garrison and had issued orders that all citizens and families should go away, either north or south as their feelings or interest dictated. He was well aware that the enforcement of such an order would be severely criticized. "If the people "said he, "raise a howl against my barbarity and cruelty I will answer that war is war and not popularity seeking. If they want peace they and their relatives must stop war. As a result of this order a very spicy and angry correspondence between Sherman and Hood ensued which is well worth reading as showing the feelings in the actors of the game of war at that particular crisis. *(see Excerpt: Correspondence Pertaining to Sherman's Forced Evacuation of Atlanta)*

So, in accordance with the order, a long train of cars and two wagon trains daily left the city, crowded with its former inhabitants and what few household goods they were allowed. Under a flag of truce, they were taken twenty miles south and delivered over to the Rebels. They were given one day's rations, and, that being consumed, they had to live off their own government, all sutlers and hangers-on to a great army were ordered at once to clear out and to go north of Chattanooga. The army was now resting in and abut Atlanta and being paid off, we not having seen a paymaster for eight months. Five present of the men were being furloughed and leaves of absence quite freely given to

Officers.

I made no application for leave. It was a long journey to the north and hitherto had proved a pretty costly one. The day after reaching the regiment I rode into Atlanta. It was surrounded with fortifications of the strongest description which Hood would have delighted to have us assault. Circle after circle of works., beginning at its edge and extending two or three miles out. Indeed, one might say they extended all the way to Chattanooga, one-hundred and fifty miles, as the Rebel army had this place to defend, and its preservation to the confederacy its great endeavor.

Atlanta's Whitehall Street Bernard Photo Library of Congress

As a city Atlanta did not amount to very much and had, before being depopulated, about twenty-five thousand population. Its most important features were its railroads to every quarter of the south, and manufactories of every description for army use. The arsenal and the works attached were all blown up when Hood evacuated the place, also the engines and railroad cars.

The city was pretty badly battered by our artillery. riding down the principal business street, - Whitehall, - I saw hardly a building that was not struck by our shells; great jagged holes were made in brick walls and, if a wooden house, nearly the whole side would be knocked out, and, of course, general havoc made of the inside. In one at which I stopped, - a pretty cottage with a handsome lawn and shade trees, - a large hole was made in the side and the missile had evidently burst just as it entered, there must have been forty or fifty holes in the side, ceiling and floors, making a prefect sieve of the place and not a whole window was left. A negro told me that half a dozen shells exploded within ten yards of the house, and nearly every other building had a similar experience. A shell exploded one night in a church where many women and children had taken refuge. Many were wounded and one or two killed.

That the inhabitants were in great terror was evident from the great number of "Gopher Holes" they dug in which to protect themselves. There was hardly one house unprovided with one. These "Gopher Holes", as they were called, were holes dug in the ground, or preferably in the side of an embankment, eight or ten feet square with a height of about six feet; logs were thrown across the top and covered four or five feet with earth. There was an opening at the side and steps leading to the bottom of the hole. In there the frightened ones took refuge whenever our guns shelled the city. I went into several of these. They were mostly floored over, with niches dug in the side for various articles, or a bed if a family had lived in them continually.

Probably not more than four of five hundred of the aborigines were remaining in town when I was there. Generals Sherman and Thomas were occupying fin residences in the town. One day I saw one hundred and fifty of our Officers just returned by exchange, or who had escaped from the Andersonville prison pen. They had been in the enemy's hands but two or three months yet showed the results of their harsh treatment.

All were pale and haggard, and many had to use canes to get along, among them many were bare footed. Their shoes having been taken from them, and all were dirty, wearing ragged clothes of variegated hue, their own having been appropriated by the Rebels. Here I learned that Murray of our brigade, to whom I have referred, had died in the prison. There were two fine bands in town belonging to the Massachusetts second and thirty third regiments, that gave much pleasure.

We had expected to remain restfully in camp for some time. Illustrating the uncertainties of war; on the third night after I reached the command, the whole "Army of the Tennessee" was ordered to move. The left wing, sixteenth army corps, consisting of two divisions, to one of which the thirty ninth Ohio was attached, had just been broken up. General Dodge, its Commander, having been wounded in the head, had gone home, and our division, - the first, -was transferred to the Seventeenth Army Corp commanded by General Frank P. Blair.

Our period of resting and recruiting was broken up on account of Hoods whole army getting in our rear and making strenuous efforts to destroy our communications with Chattanooga, thus cutting off the supplies which were vital to us. Forrest with cavalry had for some time been interfering with our railroad and had not accomplished much. But now Hood with his army of thirty or forty thousand men was seriously threatening us and it was necessary to keep him off our main route of supply.

Accordingly, on October third, we started out to overtake, and fight him if we could catch him. We crossed the Chattahoochee river twelve miles from Atlanta ad rendezvoused at Smyrna Camp Ground, our old battle field of July Fourth. The next day we reached Marietta and Kennesaw Mountain in the rain. From the summit of Kennesaw, we had a superb view, for it was beautifully clear after the rain of the preceding day. There could be seen the smoke of the enemy's camp fires for a long distance. The line of the railway from Big Shanty to Altoona was marked by the blaze of burning ties. At Altoona, fifteen miles distance, was one of our commissary depots and there were stored fifteen million rations of bread and it seemed now to be the projected point of attack.

From the signal station at Kennesaw, General Corse at Rome, some twenty-five miles distance, was ordered by Sherman to hurry to the relief of the small garrison in the block house at Altoona. General Corse hurried over and reached the little fortress just in time receive from General French, commanding the enemy's force of about four thousand men, the following note by flag of truce.

"I have placed the forces under my command in such position that you are surrounded, to avoid a need less effusion of blood, I call upon you to surrender your forces at once. And unconditionally. Five minutes will be allowed you to decide," ETC. To this General Corse Replied: "Your communication, demanding surrender of my command I acknowledge the receipt of, and respectfully reply that we are prepared for the "Needless effusion of blood" whenever it is agreeable to you" ETC.

Then the fight was on. For the defense there were, behind redoubts and in the block house, one thousand nine hundred men, while French had two brigades and two cannons. There was a hot fight and both sides lost heavily. Finally, French withdrew, unable to take the little fort. During the contest, in answer to a question from Sherman, Corse sent the following dispatch, "I am short a cheek bone and an ear but am able to whip all hell yet." And that was the spirit that made an invincible army.

My division reached Altoona just after the battle. The ground was strewed with dead and wounded Rebels. Among the prisoners taken was Brigadier General Young who said that French's loss was nearly two thousand. Corse's loss officially reported was seven hundred and seventeen, -nearly one half his entire force. After marching all night, in hot pursuit of Hood's army which was doing a lot of damage to the railroad, we reached Acworth at Four A.M. Four hours later at eight A.M. we started again, getting into camp in the evening.

The following morning, we went to Kingston and in the afternoon eight miles farther towards Rome, reaching camp at midnight. The next evening, we were again on the road marching all the night to Adairsville and laid in a barn yard a couple of hours until daybreak, and then took the cars to Resaca arriving there at noon. There had been a fight during the preceding day, and when we reached there the whole Rebel force was but a few miles off.

During the evening the thirty ninth and the twenty seventh Ohio were sent out in a reconnaissance to Snake Creek Gap in the mountain Range; had a skirmish and lost eight men. We returned ordered to march. We skirmished with the enemy all day and made about twelve miles.

On the Fourteenth we marched through Snake Gap Creek some ten or twelve miles long. The road was at the base of a range of high hills rising steeply on one side of the rad, while Snake Creek, of conservable size, bordered the other side. We were in close pursuit of Hood, but a few hours in advance of us, who gone through this same gap.

Now our headquarter were near Atlanta, had found, and appropriated for its own use, a light covered wagon and a pair of horses and harness to complete. All of which made quite a natty turnout, on which we prided ourselves greatly as being the most stylish equipment in the army as well as a great convenience in transporting our mess-chest, extra blankets, etc. Though conflicting with orders, it being unwarranted addition to the wagon train, we had sneaked it along thus far and trusted to escape detection. But the Gap proved its ruin.

Hood, in his march had left there a trail of felled trees and broken bridges to obstruct our pursuit and he had succeeded mighty well. At one point, where the command was completely stalled, Sherman unluckily came along, impatient to get at Hood and in an ugly mood at the annoying delay.

Spying our wagon, an unjustifiable impediment, - he apparently boiled over, and there was such a gush of perverted words and sulfurous condemnation as would blister the paint on the wagon and paralyze the horses. Then having told his orderly to unhitch the horses. Then having told his orderly to unhitch the horses he ordered a fire built under the wagon and the whole outfit went up in a lively blaze.

I was in the rear of the regiment where I usually rode, and viewed with dismay our mess-chest, (an unusually fine one with uncommonly elaborate contents for the army), blankets, and sundry other conveniences, such as we should not have thought of had we not been tempted by their easy conveyance, ruthlessly destroyed. But protest would have been useless. Indeed, no excuse could have been made for us. And no one, after hearing Sherman's fervid language, would have cared to claim the slightest connection with the concern. Fortunately, I had one blanket strapped to my saddle as usual. That night each one of us depended on the other headquarters for a meal, and it was sometime before we could beg or forage enough to partially make up our losses.

The chase after Hood was kept up to Galesville, Alabama, but we could not catch him, because we were delayed so much by obstructions, and Hood would not fight. He destroyed about thirty miles of railroad between Atlanta and Chattanooga and many bridges. Much to the surprise of the Rebels, it did not take very long to make repairs, for the Army Chief railroad engineer, Col. W. Wright, was a wonder and by distributing ten thousand men along a break it was soon restored. One of our spies heard the following: "Well! The yanks will have to git up and git, for General Wheeler has blown up the tunnel at Dalton and the Yanks will have to retreat because they can get no more rations." "Oh hell!", said a listener, "Don't you know old

Sherman carries a duplicate tunnel along with him?"

On October 21, we reached Galesville. It had not been a long campaign, but it was a very hard one. Many times, we marched from sundown to sunrise, then resting until midnight. Then we would lie down on the ground, with a saddle for a pillow and a rousing fire down on the ground of fence rails at our feet, sleep sweetly, if it did not rain, for the nights were cold, until sunrise. "For weariness can snore upon the flint, when rusty sloth finds the down pillow hard."

When on our long night marches, tired and sleepy, we often were diverted by the antics or our Regimental Adjutant. He was a short fellow, with abbreviated legs and rode a big horse that he could hardly straddle. The adjutant was much disposed to sleep and his efforts to keep awake were amusing. As he nodded his head sunk lower and lower on his chest to be pulled back with a jerk as if he would land it on the tail of the horse. Finally, he would succumb to overpower drowsiness and for a few minutes dream of his Ohio home, a good dinner and a spring mattress, when an alarming lurch in the saddle, or a low drooping limb would almost sweep him off, and arouse to his dreary surroundings, and the banter of his comrades.

I missed fruit very much while in the south. When in Marietta I had some grapes that were fair; apples and peaches were hard and worthless. Pears were never to be had. Persimmons grew in abundance and were regarded by many as a great delicacy. I did not like them. Figs were abundant and if one like yams he could get plenty, and the biggest ever. Irish potatoes were very scarce and very poor.

Hood, by this time, had gone up into Tennessee on his way to Nashville where he met General Thomas and was terribly defeated. But that is another story. Sherman now began to make preparations for his southward campaign through Georgia. On November tenth it may be said to have been begun. The sick and wounded, non-

89

combatants, extra baggage, tents, wagons not actually needed, and everything not required for the future campaign was sent to Chattanooga from Rome. The army was stripped for fighting and marching. The men had worn out their shoes, hundreds of them were barefooted and it was necessary to refit.

About Galesville the country was rich, with immense cornfields, and while on the march we had lived on salt pork and hardtack, we here we subsisted quite luxuriantly off the country. To a farmer who protested against having his fine flock of sheep driven away, it was explained that Hood had broken our railroad communications, that we were a strong hungry crowd that needed plenty of food, that our Uncle Sam was deeply interested in our continued health, that he would soon repair these roads, but in the mean time we must eat, and, though we preferred Northern beef, just at present mutton would have to do. It is doubtful whether he was sufficiently interested in our welfare to be reconciled he saw his flock wending its way to our camp.

For the march about to begin the army was divided into two wings, the right and the left. The right wing, Major General Howard commanding, was composed of two corps, the fifteenth, General Osterhaus commander, and the seventeenth, General Frank P. Blair. My regiment, the thirty ninth Ohio, belonged to the 17th Corps. The Seventeenth Corps was made up of three division; our division, the first, commanded by Brig. Gen. J.A, Mower. The left wing was under the command of Major General W. H. Slocum. The whole army consisted of Infantry 55329, Cavalry 5063, artillery 1812, aggregating 62204, Officers and men. For the campaign each regiment was allowed one wagon and one ambulance.

When I entered the service, each regiment was allowed thirteen wagons, that is, one for each company, two for headquarters, one hospital wagon, and one ambulance. Under Sherman the impedimenta had been gradually cut down, and now not an unnecessary article was to be carried along. The men had no tents other than the shelter, or dog tents as they were called, which were carried on the back. Headquarters had one tent fly. The men were supplied with everything needed in the way of clothing and equipment, and were in splendid condition for a long and swift march.

We had returned from our pursuit of Hood and were at Marietta again in camp, when November 12th, we received marching orders, not as we had expected for the south. But in an opposite direction. It turned out only for a distance of eight miles, and then we proceeded to tear up railroad, our only connecting link with the north. Until midnight the troops were thus engaged, and seventy- five miles of track was destroyed. As far as the eye could reach in either direction the fires of the blazing railroad ties could be seen. Every tie was burnt, and every rail bent. At daylight on Sunday we were again on the march south and made twenty- nine miles. ON Monday we were once more in Atlanta.

That city had been the best depot for war army stores. Mills, foundries, powder works, cannon factories sprang up in a few months from which the Rebel armies were supplied with cannon, rifles, sabers, etc. Granaries had become magazines for army stores.

On the night of the fifteenth there was a grand and awful spectacle. By order, the chief engineer destroyed with powder and fire all the store houses, depot buildings, and machine shops and all other places that could be of use to the Confederate Government. The heavens were one expanse of lurid fire; the air was filled with flying, burning cinder, buildings covering two acres were in ruins. Every moment there was the sharp detonations of exploding shells and powder concealed in the buildings, and sparks and flames would shoot far up into the sky.

About seven A.M of the sixteenth we pulled away from the city; the day was beautifully clear with a bracing air. A band struck up the anthem "John Brown's Body goes marching on" the men caught up the strain and the chorus "Glory! Glory! Hallelujah!" was sung out with fervor never excelled. Our nearest base of supplies was one hundred and fifty miles off, at least. But our real destination was Richmond, Virginia, one thousand miles away, through an enemy's country, and we might, for all we knew, have to fight every mile of the way, ---a bold and hazardous undertaking!

We know now we were going to salt water, either Savannah Geo, Port Royal, South Carolina, or Pensacola, Florida. Soon Atlanta, the deserted city, with its flames and smoke, was lost to view. The men were swinging along in the way bred of hundreds of miles of marching, with a "devil may care" feeling, unmindful of the long miles ahead, and deaths, dangers and wounds they were sure to encounter. Sherman and his Generals alone knew certainly what his plans were. What the rest of us lacked in information we made up in surmise and imagination. All had implicit faith in their leader and felt they could whip anything they might encounter and overcome all obstacles.

Sherman was six feet in height, wiry, muscular, without an ounce of superfluous flesh to spare from his long limbs and body; large beard and mustache, and I never saw him without his big mouth and lips closed on a half-burnt cigar. He was rather carless about his dress and he had an unmilitary custom of wearing low shoes and white stockings showing above and but one spur. I had never seen him otherwise, and years after the war, when recalling the figure of Sherman, these pedal extremities, clad in low shoes and white stockings loomed large in my mental visions.

Then never seeing these peculiarities noted in various descriptions of the man. I began to believe that my mental vision was awry, but lately I ran across, to my relief, a delineation which represented him in the same attire. At this time, he was forty-five years of age, and his face, unduly furrowed with deep lines indicative of care and thought. He habitually shared all the privations on the coarsest fare. His headquarters were no better than ours, and we had but a tent fly that was rarely stretched during the campaign.

We were now going to destroy the Georgia Central R.R. from Atlanta to Savannah; to capture the latter city; and in our transit through the state, to destroy as much as possible of the supplies necessary to the maintenance of the Rebel army. We were going to smash everything in our way; make Georgia howl and cripple confederate resources to our utmost; and overcome the confederacy with our boldness and ability.

Southern newspapers that came into our hands were full of frantic appeals, as the following from General Beauregard, the commander of the department.

"Arise for the defense of your native soil! Rally around your patriotic governor and gallant soldiers. Obstruct and destroy the enemy. Put everything at the disposal of our Generals. Remove all provisions from the path of the invader, and put all obstructions in his way..."

From President Davis also, came frenzied appeals and prophecies of our destruction.

However, the prophecies did not faze us, and the appeals did not result in our starvations. Though everything that was superfluous was left behind and the army stripped from marching and fighting; yet it was necessary to take along two thousand five hundred ambulances with two horses to each. The number of guns reduced to sixty-five and each gun caisson and forge was drawn by a team of six horses. So, that, including horses of Officers and so forth there were about thirty thousand animals to be fed, and it was estimated that Georgia supplied us with forty thousand bushels of corn daily. The wagon trains were divided equally among the four corps so that each had about eight hundred wagons, and these on the march occupied between five and six miles of road.

The army was to march, as far as practicable, by four parallel roads, each corps taking a separate road, spreading over a width of twenty or thirty miles, converging as might be ordered. The separate columns were to start at seven A.M., marching fifteen miles daily. Of course, circumstances might and did often change such specific orders. The artillery and wagons always had the road while the men, with exception of the advance and rear-guards, pursued paths improvised by the side. Each soldier carried forty rounds of ammunition besides his gun, haversack, blanket, canteen, and his half of a dog tent, and for the general benefit, a few carried frying pans, hatchet, etc.

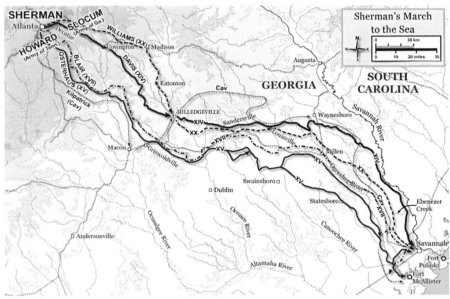

"Map by Hal Jespersen, www.cwmaps.com. Used with permission."

Tuesday, we pulled out of Atlanta, and reached Jackson, fifty miles south, on Thursday afternoon. Jackson had been a pretty and flourishing little town but now its inhabitants had hastily departed, leaving most of their effects behind them, including a great many of their negros who were very anxious to join us. But they were not encouraged to do so as we did not care to have them eat our supplies, though we did take some of the young and hearty men as pioneers. Friday, we crossed the Ocmulgee river on pontoons as the enemy had burnt the bridge. It was expected that we would be attacked in crossing, but the enemy did not materially disturb us. On the next two days we passed through the towns of Hillsboro and Blountsville. Here we were within twenty miles of Macon and about fifteen miles of Milledgeville, the capital of the state.

There we found newspapers from every part of the south and we learned that there was consternation everywhere at our temerity in advancing. Many declared that we were fleeing for our lives and seeking safety at the sea coast. Most of the inhabitants of Milledgeville remained at home but Governor, State Officers and legislature had fled in confusion, some of the Officers gathered in the Hall of Representatives, elected a speaker and constituted themselves the legislature of the state. A proposition was made and debated to repeal the ordinance of secession, and Jeff Davis was put on trial and condemned to be hung on a sour apple tree. We were told in general orders to forage liberally on the country as we went along, -and we surely did. The army wagons carried little in the way of food, --some salt pork, coffee, and crackers.

The skill and success of the men in collection supplies was one of the remarkable features of the march. A company of about fifty men would be detailed each morning from the bridge for this purpose. They would start at daylight, having been informed of the intended day's march, and where we would camp. They would then proceed five or six miles from the route of the command and visit every plantation and farm within range. These foragers would start on foot but never came back that way, about the time of going into camp they would show up on every kind of conveyance; wagons, family carriages, ox teams, filled with sugar cured hams, cornmeal, turkeys, ducks; while the "Bummers", - as they were called, would be astride any four-footed beast that would carry them.

I have seen them come in on mules, cows, horses, oxen, laden from ears to tail. Perhaps the "Bummer" would be seated on an old saddle without girth or stirrup or, more likely a bed-quilt covering the larger part of the mule, or maybe, on quite a handsome saddle cloth across an unwilling cow. Whatever it is he is jolly, satisfied with his spoils and knowing that he will be greeted with applause when his various findings are revealed, such as a basket of fresh eggs on one arm, a ham on the end of his musket, a big piece of honey in his mouth and a jug of sorghum molasses under his other arm. On his head there was always some ridiculously unmilitary gear, - a woman's poke bonnet, an antiquated silk beaver rakishly perched on one side, or a felt hat stuck full of tall feathers, and yards of ribbon trailing behind, and a rug or old carpet over his shoulders while a brace of sheep might lie across his animal in front, or a hog, firmly tied to a mule's tail, is dragged along the road.

Whatever was brought in was turned over to the quarter-master and appropriated for general use. The next morning another detail would start out empty handed and on foot and return as before. It is regarded as a privilege to be detailed on such a party though it was really one of exceeding danger. Spreading out for miles from the marching army, these men frequently ran into the Rebel cavalry and had, when in groups, sever fighting; or, if separate could easily be taken prisoner. But all the same they were a daring set of fellows and never cared about the risk.

On Tuesday, the twenty Second, we started from camp at daylight with veritable snowflakes flying about, the air was keen enough to do justice to a proper New England November day. By noon we reached Gordon a neat town into which we marched with colors flying and band playing, and soldiers dressed in line with bayonets glittering in the sparkling sun. Here we first struck the Georgia Central R.R. which connects Macon with Savannah, to destroy which was one of the objects of the campaign. We rested here one day, and the only day from the time we left Atlanta until we reached Savannah.

For the next few days we made short marches, much of the time spent in tearing up the R.R. In fact, all the way up to the coast the rad was thoroughly destroyed either by our own or other corps. The destruction of the road was complete and was expeditiously done with instruments made for the purpose. A clasp with a long handle and a ring at the top was locked under the rail. Through the ring a long lever was inserted, and the rails ripped from the sleepers. The sleepers were then piled in a heap and set on fire; the rails roasting on top until they began to bend of their own weight. Then, with tongs at each end-they lifted from the blazing pile and each rail wrapped around a neighboring tree or telegraph pole where they remain perhaps to this day. With fifty thousand men are put to such work it does not take ling to demoralize a hundred or two miles of R.R.

As we marched along thousands of negroes joined the column; some carrying household goods, other children in their arms, the older girls and boys plodding by their side. One day a venerable darky, mounted on a mule appeared, and, stowed away behind in pockets or bags made in a blanket, were two pickanninies, one on each side. Next day a mule appeared in the train with two pockets on each side.

Soon, as the fashion grew, old tent fly's or pieces of canvas came into use ten or fifteen pockets and nothing of the mule was visible but head, tail, feet; all else covered by wooly heads, shiny black eyes, gleaming white teeth of little darkies. One day a cow took the place of the mule. If one asked "where are you going Auntie?", he was answered "I'se quine whar yours gwine." The darkies welcomed us with "Bress de Lord, tank the almighty God the Yanks is come!" Again, when a darky was speaking to another who was hesitating about joining us. "Stick in dar! Stick in Dar!" Its all right. We guine along. We're Free!" A day's march varied according to the country we were going through; the rivers to be crossed and the weather or enemy encountered. Always the division having the lead was unencumbered with wagons, and in the rear of the division to be available if necessary.

In the division following, behind each regiment came the pack mules, which we had picked up on the way, laden with all sorts of camp baggage, blankets, pots, pans, needed for cooking, and the lead horses with negro servants. Perhaps the advance has met as was often the case, a squad of Rebel cavalry. They never delayed us much. The flankers, are deployed on a line parallel to the leading troops for several hundred yards, looking for any concealed foe or for any works that may have been thrown up to impede us. If any such appeared a regiment or brigade was thrown out, and it never took long to clear the way.

When a river or creek, too deep to wade or for wagons to get through, was reached the column was halted. The Officer in charge of the pioneer corps goes forward and, using some fence rails or pine saplings, bridges over the place; or, if needed, lays the pontoons. Meanwhile the bugles have sounded, and there is a halt of all the line, and the soldiers lie along the roadside to rest or smoke a pipe or munch a piece of hard-tact. Then the bugles sound "forward" and on the way, they go.

When getting in the vicinity of camp, Officers of the general commanding corps, ride out in advance to select the ground, preferably some location near wood and water. Arriving, the troops file out into the woods and fields, the leading division stopping first, those in the rear marching on yet father, to take their turn in advance the next day. As soon as arms are stacked, the boys attack the fence rails, fires are kindled, coffee prepared and, in this campaign at least, a bountiful supper is provided.

The wagons, in the meantime, are parked and the teamsters feed the animals. By and by the tattoo rings out on the night air, shortly followed by taps, and the soldier wraps himself in slumbering host the picket guard keeps nightly watch.

Then, all too soon, came from the different regiments, far and near, bugle sounds of the reveille, and the beating of drums break the stillness of the morning air. Shouldering campfires are started into new life, company cooks are preparing breakfast and grateful fumes of steaming coffee pots greet the nostrils; the animals are fed and hitched or saddled, the bugle sounds the sick call; but those not fitted for a long campaign having been sent to the rear, there is little response. Knapsacks are strapped on, muskets shouldered, men fall into line, the bugles sound; the men file out, company by company, and the drums and fifes start then again upon the road for another day's march and adventure.

Fifteen miles a day is not much for a single regiment to accomplish, but to move that distance an army corps of fifteen or eighteen thousand men is quite a different proposition. The division which yesterday did the right of the line, today is the rear guard and probably will have a tedious time in reaching camp.

In the best of weather, the country roads are badly cut up by the passing of so many hundred wagons and heavy guns. When it rains, they become well-nigh impassable. Corduroying has to be stored to and quagmires delay. The teams begin to lag as the day advances and the roads are more and more cut up. The heavy batteries become stalled and require the aid of the soldiers to lift the wheels from the deep ruts; halts are frequent and tedious, and all are impatient to get into camp, but it is long after dark before the last team reaches its prescribed place, and the tired soldier rolls himself in his blanket on the ground.

The mule is a much-traduced animal. One could not witness his faithful efforts day after day on long marches on heavy roads without attesting his inestimable virtues. There may be actually no poetry in a mule; he is not a pretty beast, yet it would be difficult to find a more hardy, long winded, strong-legged, uncomplaining creature, then the army mule. There are six before each wagon. On the near one of the pole, -two, big, scrawny long-eared powerful creatures, -sits the teamster with his jerk line, the middle pair is somewhat smaller, while the leaders are always round barreled, bright-eyed and alert little animals. In their bridles the teamster always has a bit of bright ribbon or some tinsel in their harness.

When the wagon is inextricably stuck in the mud, as was often the case, it is interesting to see with what restful patience they stand while some fence rails or saplings are being laid for a more substantial foundation. Then the train guard stack their muskets and plunge into the mud to assist with shoulders at the wheels and body of the wagon. At the word, the mules straighten out their legs, toughen the traces and brace themselves for an untied effort. The driver cracks his whip and dexterously touches up the leaders with his long snake lash, lets out a few startling oaths, - I never knew a teamster who did not swear like a pirate, - and without any fruitless, nervous jerking's or twitching, the six bends to the collars and with combined effort and with a shout from the soldiers, the wheels are moving.

Our march was continued through many towns, over rivers, which we pontooned, and through many creeks which were waded. The river crossings afforded to the enemy advantageous, opportunities for attack, of which they almost invariably availed themselves, but we met with small loss and were not greatly delayed. We went through a beautiful country, passed fine plantations, rich in corn, potatoes, hogs, beef, and Turkeys, from which we drew a plentiful supply. Coffee, salt and a limited supply of hardtack, was all that was given to the men. They lived off the country and fared finely. Our stock was abundantly fed, and greatly improved, as we captured thousands of mules and horses to substitute for worm our animals. The manner of filling the wagons with corn was novel. Without losing their places in the column, the quarter master would be detail a few empty wagons from the train into the fields, hurry them to the full cribs which were built of logs and roofed. The train guard would, with a lever, raise the roof a couple of feet, and the men, laying on their backs, would kick out the corn into the wagons close alongside. Then the teams would resume their places in the column as it came along.

The weather was fine and so mild there ensued no hardships in sleeping in the open. Usually it was as warm as June in New England; rises were in bloom, flowers a plenty, and in the woods abounding in vegetation strange to us of the north. Of course, there were some rainy days and long night marches, but altogether it was a really pleasant campaign. We destroyed on the way immense quantities of cotton and numbers of cotton gins, and many mansions of well-known and prominent Rebels.

Near Sandersville a body of cavalry was seen to set on fire stacks of fodder in compliance with appeals of Rebel leaders to destroy everything in the way of food and forage and thus starve our army in its passage through Georgia. In retaliation, the houses in the neighborhood were burnt, and on entering the town the citizens were told that the same course would be repeated under similar acts on their part. This intention on our part spreading little destruction followed.

One day the foragers brought in an excellent horse which very much admired. I wanted him. An order had been issued from general headquarters that any Officer who desired a horse could have such a one appraised by the quartermaster and could purchase him at the price. I never heard of any Officer paying such price or any other to the quartermaster. Yet, to make my title clear I had the horse appraised and thereafter regarded him, as did others mine. After riding him for a couple of weeks, one morning after a rainy chilly night he was reported missing. A broken halter told the story. He was a high spirted animal, because fractious during the stormy night, and, unseen by the sentinel, had decamped. I was distressed at his loss and sent the orderlies on the search for him.

In a few days it was reported that he was seen in General Blair's train. The next afternoon, my division being on the right of the line and reaching camp early, I took the opportunity to ride to the nearby town were General Blair had taken quarters. Looking over the fifteen or twenty horses, those used by himself and retinue, I found mine, and on returning to camp, I wrote his adjutant General claiming the horse as having been decreed to me after appraisal by order of the quartermaster and asking for an order to resume possession. My plea, as indeed I presumed it would, availed nothing against the covetous possession of a Major General. I was often chagrined by seeing Blair so complacently riding my beautiful horse.

I was never without a good animal to ride, and generally had one for my negro attendant. I had been riding an especially serviceable easy horse for some months, - handsome chestnut mare, - and naturally, had become fond of her, and then she began to show lameness and I had her taken out in the field and shot. As I saw her drop from a musket ball through her head I was pained. She would have come all right with a little rest, -but there was not rest on the march.

On December third we reached Millen on the line of the R.R. All the station houses and the road itself had been destroyed thus far. Here was the prison where thousands of our soldiers had been confined for months past, - a space of ground four or five hundred feet square, enclosed by a stockade, where, without any covering, their blankets having been stolen from them, they were exposed to all the vicissitudes of the weather, with just sufficient food to sustain life. Here seven hundred and fifty of our men died.

Millen was second only to Andersonville in the notoriously inhuman conditions to which prisoners were subject. Some of these prisoners had dug holes in the ground into which they had crept for shelter, we had hoped to release our imprisoned men, but in anticipation of our coming, they had all been taken to Savannah. In the neighborhood was a plantation on which the house, a cotton gin, and stables, were smoldering, and the dead bodies of several hounds that had been used to track escaped prisoners, were seen.

Images above: Exterior and interior views of the Lawton POW stockade showing dead soldiers lying unburied, from the January 7, 1865 issue of Harper's Weekly.

By Saturday, December tenth, we were within ten miles of Savannah and for the first time we began to meet serious opposition. Indeed, since leaving Atlanta, my regiment had been in line of battle but once.

Before reaching this point, we found fresh earth works thrown up. But the forces that had occupied them had prudently, retired as we advance and gradually closed in about the city. While marching along we came upon a gathering of men about an Officer, the adjutant of the first Alabama Cavalry, whose leg had been terribly managed by the explosion of a bomb on which his horse stepped. The horse had been instantly killed. Just then Sherman came up and in Fiery Language vented his anger on Rebels who were guilty of such unmilitary, and unjustifiable act.

We had some fifty prisoners with us and of these the General ordered a number to go forward, with picks to break up the earth and thus explode any remaining torpedoes or to clear the ground of them. These men begged hard to be spared this ordeal, but the General was inexorable and a few pricks of the bayonet in the rear started them along. They moved very cautiously and without further injury, soon had unearthed seven of these murderous implements which I saw lying by the roadside. Every house about there was burned.

Our division, General Mowner's of the Seventeenth Corps, had now come within a few miles of the city and had run against the familiar line of fortification, parapets, etc. All of Sunday the eleventh, we were under fire and lost a number of men. Sunday night the Thirty-ninth was ordered to throw up works on the extreme front. We were so close to the Rebels, that I could distinctly hear loud voices and the rattle of their musketry was plainly heard. By midnight our earthworks were completed. It had begun to rain, but we slept soundly in the open with the very wet blankets for shelter. With morning came shells and bullets pretty thick. We could see the smoke from their canon just in time to duck behind the parapets before the ball came over.

For an hour or two in the morning I was with one of our batteries, detached a little ways from the regiment which was exchanging shots quite regularly with some field guns. We dropped behind the parapet before the shell could reach us. But it was quite an animated duel. While eating lunch one of those balls struck the top of the earth work and a shower of dirt spoiled our repast. Wishing after a while to rejoin the regiment I did some lively sprinting, from one tree to another before reaching it in safety. Towards night our corps, the Seventeenth, was relieved by the Fourteenth and we were held in reserve.

On the sixteenth our division was ordered south to the Altamaha river, about one hundred miles, almost to Florida, to destroy the Gulf R.R. from the Ogeechee to Altamaha rivers. We returned on the twenty first, the day on which the aristocratic city of Savannah fell into the hands of the "" ruthless invader". Before this, Fort McAllister on the Ogeechee had been gallantly taken by assault by the fifteenth Corps under General Hazen and we had come into communication with the fleet and supplies for the army who was down to short rations. We had enough salt pork, but badly needed bread, sugar, and coffee.

The country about Savannah had been stripped by the Rebels of everything eatable for men and horses. My horse, for instance, for two days previous to our going to Altamaha had nothing to eat but green willow leaves, and our regiment went on a foraging expedition with not result but few poor potatoes. By the twenty second, we were comfortably at "Thunderbolt". A pretty seaside resort, (8) a pleasant five-mile ride from the city. From October first until December twentieth, with the exception of one week, we had been continually on the move, and every day in the saddle from daylight until dark. Now we reached the first mail for two months and learned what was going on in the world.

The next day I rode to the city, which after the fall of McAllister, had been quickly evacuated by General Hardee and his troops. Savannah was an attractive City of twenty- five thousand people most of whom remained. They looked rather glum and did not show themselves much or a while, but we had had just such deal with before and knew every feature of their disposition. It was not very long before a meeting of citizens was called by the mayor, at which they expressed their wish to accept the President's amnesty proclamation promising to hear after to be good.

There were many little parks about the city with handsome shade trees, a fine monument to Count Pulaski who was killed in 1779 when an assault was made on the city during the Revolutionary war; it being then held by the English. General G.W. Smith of the Rebel army, who had accompanied Hardee when he evacuated the city, left his wife behind. She was Miss Helen Bassett of New London, an intimate friend of my sister Anna living but a few doors from us in new London.

I paid a visit to Fort Pulaski and Jackson which had been a long-time obstacle to our Gunboats. There were heavy works all about city in which cannons were still remaining. We captured more than two hundred guns, magazines filled with ammunition, thirty-five thousand bales of cotton, steamboats, locomotives, etc. It was delightful to me to get again a sight and smell of salt water, and what was a great treat, we had plenty of oysters. Some of the Officers went oystering one day and returned with thirty bushels, and we had a surfeit of bivalves. There were about "Thunderbolt", beautiful groves of live oaks from the branches of which depended gray funeral moss in great masses which made a most unusual appearance.

After remaining here in camp for ten days, on January third tents were struck and everything was got in readiness to embark on transports for Beaufort Island, South Carolina. The right wing of the army, General Howard, going by water; the left, General Slocum, crossed to the east side of Savannah river and went up by land. It took more than a week to transport our whole corps. Many of our men, never having seen salt water before, were even on this short trip, were terribly sea-sick and declared they would prefer to walk a thousand miles on the worst roads then to spend a single day on the ocean.

Beaufort had been garrisoned by Negro Soldiers. Our white men, in their dirty and somewhat tattered clothes, did not improve by comparison with these darky soldiers in their clean shirts and white gloves. There was a pretty good hotel in the town which we enjoyed very much. Among delicacies we obtained there was butter. The first time in six months I had tasted it. This, in connection with buckwheat cakes and molasses, was real luxury, I think McDowell and I enjoyed this combination three times daily all the time we were there. The Seventeenth Corps remained at Beaufort about a week.

Then, by pontoons, we crossed over to the main land and started for Poctolago, some thirty miles from the coast, on the way to Richmond, Virginia. We had several encounters by the way. All the country from Beaufort to Pocatoalgo was low alluvial land cut up by numberless creeks and sloughs, with innumerable swamps and low extended rice fields crossed by raised dykes or causeways, so that we were traveling through water most of the time, and it was raining continually. Advancing towards Charleston and Savannah R.R. there was a sharp skirmish and, the enemy falling back, we went into camp.

We occupied the Fort at Pocatalago with bands playing and flags flying. As was the case when we left Atlanta, all sick and incompetent soldiers were left behind, and transportation was reduced to the smallest possible. Everything gathered on the trip to Savannah was thrown aside and no tents were permitted. The strength of the army was sixty thousand men and sixty-eight guns. The two thousand five hundred wagons carried ammunition for a great battle; forage for seven days and bread, coffee, sugar and salt for twenty days. We depended largely for fresh meat on beefs on the hoof, and such cattle, hogs, poultry as we expected to gather on our line of march.

We secured many Rebel newspapers when we reached Pocatalago and their statements in regard to our march through Georgia were very amusing to us who were there. According to them our army was terribly harassed, nearly starved, and but a remnant of it remained. They prophesied that what few had survived would soon be exterminated on the sacred soil of South Carolina. Every creek was to be disputed, every plain was to be a battlefield, Yankee corpses were to be strewn on the highway and their blood would redden the whole land. Such harrowing threats and shocking predictions we had heard before and they were now simply diverting.

Our men were imbued with the feeling that South Carolina was the cause of all our troubles; the first to fire on the flag and precipitate the war, and that on it the scourge should fall most heavily, and that they were the ones to apply it.

On the eighteenth, the Thirty ninth with two other regiments, went on a foraging expedition and, of course, I went along. Foraging expeditions were always entertaining. We met the Rebs before we had gone three miles and were skirmishing all day, drove them six miles, then loaded our wagons with corn and returned.

On February 1, 1865, the invasion of South Carolina really began when we cut loose from our base without any uneasy foreboding; and the right wing with the Seventeenth Corps in the lead started for Rivers bridge over the Salkehatchie River, which we reached on the third. The bridge had been cut away and the first division waded the stream, almost shoulder deep, meeting the Rebels defending the passage.

We lost a number of men here and several Officers. Here Wager Swayne, Colonel of the Ohio Regiment in our brigade. And whom we all knew well, lost his leg and I saw him brought up the steep banks of the river on a Stretcher. He was afterward an eminent New York Lawyer. We reached midway on the South Carolina R.R. on the seventh in the midst of a rainstorm and there the command was put at work tearing road., both communication, and for bringing supplies from /Augusta and Northern Georgia to Richmond, and during the next two days fifty miles of it were destroyed.

On both days it was raining hard, and the weather was cold and pitiless. Up to this point at least the country as anything but inviting. We had been floundering through swamps, wading creek and "pulling mud" as the soldiers said, while all the time the rain was pouring down on us until we felt we were amphibious. The population seemed to be made up of poor whites, the so-called "crackers", densely stupid, inert, shiftless, bloodless beings, - the women invariably snuff dippers with black teeth and yellow haggard faces, caring and knowing nothing about the war.

Having damaged the railroad sufficiently, we resumed the march for Orangeburg on the opposite side of the Edisto River. Here we found some of our batteries unlimbered and exchanging shots with a party of the other side. Sherman directed General Blair to send Mower's (our) Division four or five miles below town to affect a crossing. We went down there, and a pontoon was laid over the river, but the bottom on the other side was overflowed from the excessive rains we had encountered the previous week.

Standing at the end of that pontoon and viewing that expense of icy water in the half dusk did not cause the Thirty ninth to blink or hesitate at what was imminent, but surely it did make us a bit chilly knowing that a plunge into those aqueous depths was inevitable. The bugle sounded. "Forward" was the order. The men with their cartridge boxes around their necks and muskets held high, with a shout, leaped in, and the Officers followed. Except the adjutant who was cunning forethought, as he thought, forestalling a wetting took advantage of a snake rail fence nearby along which he slowly and laboriously crawled for a hundred yards, -the cynosure of all eyes. By then the rails precipitately dropped under the water and the Adjutant crestfallen and baffled, to the great enjoyment of the rest of us, and the banter of the bedrenched crowd, always ready for fun, made a reluctant jump and was like the rest of us, - wet.

The footing through the swamp was most uncertain, filled as it was with slippery cypress knees and sunken logs over which many a one had a tumble. While doing my best to avoid falling, a recruit, who had joined us at Pocatlago and was rather fresh to the vicissitudes of a campaign, steeped on my spur, with a jerk to retain my own balance I upset his and down he went backwards. A hasty glance showed but a rifle barrel above the surface of the water. Obstructions at the head of the column caused frequent halts which were utilized, if the opportunity offered, by climbing on any partly submerged logs that happened to be near. Nothing was to be gained by the change except the amusement that each one derived from seeing the other fellows into the water again. We were in the swamp, up to our waists in water for half an hour.

On emerging thoroughly drenched, my first endeavor was to empty my high-topped boots, which were, of course, full of water, and which it was not feasible to take off, because I could not have got them on again, and too, because we were to start at once after the Rebels who had been shooting at us from the side of the river. Accordingly, I inverted myself into as perpendicular a position as possible, which process being repeated a number of times, resulted in draining my boots and drenching the rest of me.
The enemy being driven away, a roaring fire of fence rails made us fairly comfortable and in our yet half dried clothing we laid down about midnight without blankets and slept until morning; When we started for Orangeburg.

When we entered the town several stores and houses were burning. The fire had started from some cotton that had been ignited before our entrance. Orangeburg was a pretty little town, with a population of three thousand, on the north side of the Edisto about twenty-five miles From Columbia; our skirmishers firing into the train as it sped away. Every day, as the army moved along, additions were made to the drove of cattle; for every four-footed beast that our flanking foragers came across was driven in and appropriated for our use.

On our march from Orangeburg we passed through a burning forest of pine woods, and a magnificent spectacle it was. Many of the trees were dead and the dry leaves and pine cones having caught fire, accidentally or otherwise, ignited those, and for miles the woods were ablaze; the flames streaming up to the very tops of trees eighty or ninety feet high.

Alfred Waud, Harpers Weekly, "Sherman's March through South Carolina - Burning of McPhersonville, February 1, 1865". Library of Congress

Our road at times ran alarmingly near the burning forests, and the crash of falling trees. Up-shooting cinders, rolling clouds of pitch black smoke, and really terrific heat itself. There was a pretentious sublimity in the scene of falling, crackling, blazing boughs and leaping flames, as tree after tree succumbed to the torrid heat, and the clouds of stifling sooty smoke enveloped us in gloomy darkness. We were glad enough to finally emerge from such terrifying surrounding into broad daylight and fresh air.

Now we were gradually approaching Columbia, the capital of the state, but not without a good deal of stubborn opposition, and on the sixteenth, we reached the banks of the Congaree River. About midnight, guided by the fires on hill and dales, the Rebels began shelling our camp, wounding and killing many, the big bridge across the Congaree had been burnt, but large a force of our men had crossed the Broad River, seven miles about the city, and the enemy, knowing what was coming to them, prudently withdrew.

The morning of the seventeenth was beautifully clear and pleasantly warm. Across the water, bathed in sunlight laid the city of Columbia A pontoon was being strung to enable our troops to cross, since of the big bridge that spanned the river nothing, but high stone piers remained. Before the pontoon was completed sufficiently for the corps and horses to go over, a couple of Officers and I availed ourselves of the somewhat uncertain footing ad entered the town an hour after our skirmishers got in Generals Wade Hampton and Beauregard got out. An indescribable scene of confusion was presented.

The main street was lined with blazing cotton bales, fired by order of General Wade Hampton. Stores had been broken in and their valuable contents strewed on the sidewalks; fine wines and liquors were in profusion, tobacco which had been selling at $2.00 per plug, was thrown out of the warehouses by the box for everyone to help themselves, articles of household furniture, and merchandise of every description, was cast pell-mell in every direction by a mob left behind by the Rebels.

As we were walking up the street the proprietor of a hotel, before which there was a barrel of whiskey with the head knocked in and from which everybody was invited to drink, accosted us very cordially and invited us in, and as we were looking for diversion, we went. He was extremely conciliatory and cringing, professing to be at heart a Union Man. Recognizing us as Officers, his interest, Rebel as he was, was to win our good will and any influence we might have in protecting his property. Accordingly, everything in the hotel was at our disposal and the best dinner we had enjoyed for a long time, with champagne in abundance, was ours.

Under the guise of Provost Officers, mindful of their protection and freedom for molestation, we went to many private houses, interviewing the ladies there in, and were entertained with their criticisms of the north and everything pertaining to it. They were privileged and induced, indeed, to express their hatred of the Yankees, the final success of secession the inhumanity of the mudsills, all of which was very amusing to us.

Columbia was a handsome city with fine residences and lawns even then filled with flowery shrubs and plants. The arsenal was filled with shells, rifles, and every material of war, and ammunition. The capital was a beautiful building of light granite, but not then completed. Here too was the place for the manufacture of Confederate Money. Bushels of confederate bills, each one representing any sum from a hundred to a thousand dollars were in the streets, for anyone to appropriate. Large crowds of whites and blacks filled the streets which presented an animated appearance. Sentinels were posted, and patrols were about, so that good order prevailed.

Burning of Columbia, South Carolina, Feb. 17, 1865. Alfred Waud. Harpers Weekly (Library of Congress)

About nine P.M. the wind increased to a gale and the smoldering cotton bales, fanned into active flames were flying about in the air, lodging in the trees and falling on the housetops. Soon buildings began to burn, ignited by the scattering cinders, and before long the conflagration was raging in every direction and the whole heavens were lighted up. A detail of soldiers with some citizens and a fire engine were doing their best to girdle and subdue the flames but they got beyond control. By this time my negro, with my horse, found me and I rode out to the regiment, encamped a couple of miles from the city. The wind blew a gale that night and I feared my tent fly would be carried off.

In the morning we marched into the city and a really pitiable scene it presented. The attractive residential district and so many of the houses I had visited the previous day were all burnt to the ground. "Nickerson's Hotel" where we were entertained so lavishly, was in ruins; nearly all the business portion of the city, two churches, and in fact about two thirds of the town had been destroyed. Groups of men, women and children were gathered in the streets and squares, frightened and bewildered hovering over such household goods as they could save; some with only a mattress, a trunk or a bundle of clothes. One building which was not burned, I assumed to be a jail or an asylum.

Columbia, South Carolina (Library of Congress)

On the green square in front was a large group of frightened people, and from the iron barred windows the inmates were thrusting their arms in violent gesticulations, screaming and hurling all sorts of epithets and curses upon us, as with colors flying and bands playing "Hail Columbia", we marched by a violent scene of unrestrained commotion and uproar.

We remained on Columbia two days, tearing up the railroad, destroying the state arsenal, throwing the powder and shells unto the river and demolishing everything that could be of use of the enemy. A number of Officers, who had been captured and confined for many months in the Rebel prison near Columbia, succeeded in escaping during the excitement attending our approach to the city, where secreted by some negroes and came to us, haggard and half-starved but over joyed at their release. They said that their rations consisted of only corn meal and sorghum molasses, and their camp was called "Camp Sorghum".

Destroying the rails (National Archives)

The negroes were the most demonstrative crowd. "Tank de almighty God" one said, "Massa Sherman hab come at last", and one old fat black women exclaimed "I prayed dis long time for yer, Bress de lord; you will hab a place in Heben, You'll go der sure." Before we left the city, five hundred beef cattle were turned over to the mayor to feed the destitute people, and one hundred muskets with which to arm a guard to maintain order after our departure.

On the twentieth of February we were on the road north to Wainsboro, which we reached on the twenty first, destroying the railroad on the way. From here our right wing was turned eastward towards Cheraw and Fayetteville, No. Carolina. It had been raining for several days and the roads were infamous; the creeks were converted into immense swamps; the rivers were overflowed, and the bottom had fallen out of the roads. The wagons went down to their beds and the mules to their bellies; the batteries got stuck in the mud; the men were covered with mud and their clothes wet through, thought starting at daylight we rarely reached camp until long after dark, men and mules quite worn out.

One day my regiment was rear guard for the corps, and, though we started at daylight and marched but ten miles, we did not reach camp until after midnight. A thousand wagons and six times as many animals had preceded us on a country road that was deluged with rain. The whole surface of the country seemed one sheet of water.

Wagons and ambulances were in every condition of helplessness. Some lay entirely on one side buried in mud, another stood very nearly on end as if about to descend head foremost out of sight; while on little hillocks in the swamp the drivers and guards had built fires about which the contents of the wagons had been placed pending a desperate effort to rescue the wearied animals. The teamsters even had to stop swearing, probably because they had exhausted their vocabulary and found themselves unable to do justice to the subject. Many mules were so inextricably engulfed that they were left to die in the pits they had made in their fruitless efforts to free themselves.

It was after such a day that, tired, hungry, wet and cold we had, late that night, reached a dismal camp. I drank my first cup of coffee. Headquarters tent fly's were stretched and pegged down, for it was raining, company quarters had been assigned and knapsacks unslung while cherry fence rail fires had tended somewhat to dispel the gloom and enliven spirits.

Throughout camp cooks were busy, and there could be heard the crackling of coffee berries under the quickly repeated blows of hundreds of musket butts. Soon, fragrant aroma from the steaming coffee filled the air, and, for the first time, appealed to me as supplying just the beverage that would appease some very insistent craving. SO, it was brought to me, -a generous tin cup full. It proved so adequate to my internal need that I directed the darky to bring a second cup. That superfluous cup was quaffed and then it was regretted, and distasteful remembrance lingered long. Fifty years intervened before I drank another cup of coffee.

After this toilsome march, on the next day we reached the Catawba River at Peay's Ferry. Here the regiment swam or waded across the stream, about three hundred feet wide; our horses almost losing their footing at times, where the river was deepest. The Rebel cavalry, meeting us on the other side, a brisk skirmish followed. The region through which the army had been traveling for some days was very sterile and it was difficult to supply the needs of sixty thousand men and ten thousand or more camp followers, and foragers had been out every direction.

One day one of them was found hanging to a tree by the road side with a paper attached, "Death to all foragers!" At another, the cavalry reported that they found twenty-one of our infantry lying dead with their throats cuts. These cases were the cause of some acrimonious letters between Sherman and Wade Hampton.

Now we were off for Cheraw, on the right bank of the Great Pedee River, and the head of steam navigation, - a place of importance as a cotton depot, one hundred and forty-two miles from Charleston. As usual it was raining, and roads were horrible, but, on March second, The Seventeenth corps had got within a dozen miles of the town and found the enemy intrenched on our front.

It was considered very necessary to gain the bridge crossing the Pedee at Cheraw, for swamps spread out for miles below the city and made crossing difficult. After a spirited fight of an hour, the Rebels were driven from their entrenchments and our soldiers were at one end of the bridge when the enemy were leaving the other. But we were too late to save it from flames. A pontoon was laid, and our division was soon across and skirmishing for two miles beyond.

We then learned that, in consequence of our movements and the destruction of the railroad, Charleston had been evacuated by general Hardee, who with his troops, had come to Cheraw to oppose our advance. Cheraw was found to be full to stores and provisions which had been sent from Charleston for safe keeping; the owners not dreaming that we would ever get so far upon their sacred soil. Among other things thus sent was a large quantity of Madeira Wine.

General Blair found, of this wine, eight wagon loads belonging to some of the old aristocratic families of that Rebel city, who never thought that it would be drunk out of tin cps by Yankee soldiers. As much as was wanted came to our headquarters and was appreciated. We captured here twenty-four guns and General Mowers had these guns fired on March fourth in a salute in honor of the second inauguration of Lincoln. There were also found there two thousand muskets and thirty-six hundred barrels of gun powder. The town was very pretty with side streets and avenues bordered with elm trees. There was along with little emigrant train composed of women, children, and a few men, of loyal proclivities.

AMONG THE RUINS OF COLUMBIA, SOUTH CAROLINA.—[Sketched by Theodore R. Davis.]

At Columbia there were two or three families of position who had given proof of their sympathy with the Union cause by assisting prisoners to escape. And, at peril to themselves when we entered the city. The fire had destroyed the houses of such and they were homeless. In this emigrant train was a huge family coach containing ladies with their personal baggage; also, an army wagon loaded with women and children, and wagons filled with negro women with hosts of little curly, bullet headed picaninnies. Here at Cheraw we learned that Jo. Johnston, our old foe, who had been displaced for Hood, had again been placed in command. He was regarded by Sherman as much the most able man he had been obliged to encounter.

On the sixth we resumed our march and started to Fayetteville, the capital of Cumberland County, North Carolina, on the left bank of Cape fear river, at the head of navigation. The four columns of infantry covered a strip of forty miles width; thus, affording to each corps plenty of country from which to forage. We met with but little opposition on the way from the enemy; but, as usual, the roads were abominable as the rain fell persistently.

On the eighth we reached we reached Laurel Hill, the dividing line between North and South Carolina. At one point on the road I saw half a dozen curly headed negros perched on top of a rail fence, singing "I'm glad I'm in the army", which I believe is an old Sunday school hymn, and the soldiers, as they passed by, greeted them with "go it, little ones!", "Bully for you, curly head;" "You're right this time, little one."

At night we encamped in a beautiful grove of pines. The ground was covered with the long spindles from over hanging trees and made a clean, enticing bed, (undisturbed for years" for wearied bodies, of which we gladly availed ourselves. The wind filled the air. We slept all night as on the best beds, but the reveille's awakening disclosed such a grimy set of men that to distinguish Caucasian from the darkest darky in the train was almost impossible. No siren of a pine groove ever allured us, with specious pretext of clean soft beds and aromatic order, to make a camping ground again within her resinous borders.

As we approached Fayetteville, Wade Hampton's and Hardee's forces opposed us and a spirited encounter in the town followed. They were covering the rear of the retreating army which got across the river and succeeded in burning the bridge across the Cape Fear behind them.

Fayetteville was a city of seven thousand inhabitants. The arsenal there, which the U.S. Government had built, had been enlarged by the confederates, who, never thinking that an invading army could get thus far into their domain, had filled it with immense stores of machinery and material, - thousands of muskets and quantities of ammunition. The river was navigable to this point. The mills and various manufactories and steamboat piers gave evidence of considerable commerce. The misused arsenal of Uncle Sam, and all the ammunition and stores were destroyed before we left.

While we were at Laurel Hill on the eighth, we heard that Wilmington at the mouth of the Cape Fear River, had been captured by our troops under Major General Terry. General Sherman, taking advantage of this possible opportunity for getting into communications again with the United States after so long a separation directed one of his spies to secure a boat and float down the river, - ninety miles-, carrying a cipher dispatch to the commanding General. He announced our whereabouts and would relieve the intense anxiety of the government and of the people of the north as to our safety; for. As we knew must have been the case.

There had been all sorts of disquieting surmise and speculations, as well as indubitable stories of defeat and capture during six weeks of our isolation. At the same time that the spy started in the boat another spy on horseback was dispatched with the hope that at least one of them would get through. As a matter of fact, both of the daring fellows made the perilous trip of nearly one hundred miles unseen and safely.

On Sunday morning, March twelfth, (as a hurried letter to my mother of that date states) while our soldiers were quietly resting, the Sabbath stillness was broken by the shrill whistle of an approaching steamer. As if an electric shock had gone through the camp all were on their feet in an instant, cheering, shouting, and cavorting about in the most flagrant manner, as the "red, white, and blue", fluttering from the little vessel's staff, revealed itself, bringing us at last in communication with home and friendly greeting. General Terry had received Sherman's note and had promptly replied; for we had taken Fayetteville but the day before. Letters and newspapers were greedily read, for we knew no more of what had been going on in the north than did they of us. The next morning the gun boat, Eollus, Captain Young, U.S. Navy, came to anchor opposite the tow and the blue jackets of the navy were a welcome sight. A tug boat followed with supplies of sugar, coffee, and bread, but no clothing, of which we were very much in need.

Gunboat Eolus

We remained in Fayetteville three days and then crossed the river on pontoons and started for Goldsboro. From Fayetteville the train of refugees which had followed us from Columbia and what sick and wounded we had been carrying were sent back to Wilmington. The rain had begun again, and we went on, as so many days before, through swamps and mud, the roads almost impassable, requiring repairs at nearly every foot. Fifteen miles beyond, at Averysboro, we came up against the Rebel army intrenched with infantry, artillery and cavalry. Here there was a loss to us of twelve Officers and sixty men killed and a large number wounded. At Bentonville, twenty miles farther on, my division, under General Mower, was in the thick of the fight and the shell and rifle balls came startling close. My regiment lost their twenty-five men.

General Mower was highly thought of by Sherman, who after this battle promoted him to the command of the corps, and said he regarded him as one of the boldest and best fighting men and seemed to be absolutely indifferent to personal danger.

I remember one day in Georgia, when our division was in the lead, a turn in the road brought us under the engulfing fire of the enemy's guns and the command was given to file off the road, continuing the march in the parallel woods. Mower, however, indifferent to the flying shells, continued his course, in the middle of the road as though nothing was happening in which he had any particular interest. There was a saying in the army "that three successive sets of staff Officers were in heaven," He was a New London man and knew my family quite well. After his death, his wife held the position of post mistress at New London for some time.

The Battle of Bentonville, which by the way was the last one for Sherman's Army., was fought on a beautiful spring day, which I distinctly remember as one of two in contrast to the many preceding rainy ones. The air was full of sweet fragrance from the pink and white blossoms of the peach and apple trees. The bees were humming, the birds were singing, and a soft gentle breeze rustling the fresh green leaves of the overhanging boughs.

As I rode along, noting these pleasant indications of opening of spring, I heard the not very distant boom of cannon, - a discordant note in the sweet bird music, - It reminded one of the ugly fact that not far away were thousands of contending men madly earnest in wounding and killing each other. Then, there came to mind a line of the old missionary hymn that my father used to sing Sunday evening when I was a youngster. "Where every prospect pleases and only man is vile."

As I hurried along, occasional musket crack was heard, and I soon came to a thick cane brake, impossible for a horse. I left the animal with the darky, and found the regiment in the line near the edge of some woods. The enemy's skirmishers were four or five hundred yards distant.

Just then a big stag came bounding from the forest some distance to our right coming towards us between the opposing forces. He spreading antlers were held high above his arched neck; his nostrils distended. He quickly turned his head from one side to the other, scenting lurking danger, and wavered in his graceful stride as if uncertain whether to advance or recede. So, he passed down between the lines and out of sight, and not a shot disturbed him.

While the battle was on a horse came running rider less into our lines. He was handsomely caparisoned and with holsters at the saddle bow. He probably belonged to some Rebel field Officer, who had been wounded or killed, and fell from his saddle. The animal was turned over to me, as mine was somewhat jaded, and I rode him to Washington. Our loss at Bentonville was one thousand six hundred and forty-six, and the next day we passed in burring the dead and removing the wounded.

On March twenty- fourth we got into Goldsboro, the goal for which we started from Savannah four hundred and twenty-five miles behind. From the Thirtieth of January until the twenty fourth of March, with the exception of ten days of laying off, we had been on the march; crossed five large navigable rivers, the bridges over which had been burned; traveled through innumerable swamps; waded hundreds of creeks; and when we were not in the water, we were in the mud. The enemy opposed us all the while. We had captured cities, destroyed an immense amount of war materials; torn up hundreds of miles of R.R. which were very essential to the continuance of the car; scattered armies; demoralized the people by our victories and had done more to end the war, and bring back peace than any other army in the country.

We did it all too, at comparative little expense to Uncle Sam, since from Atlanta to Goldsboro we had lived off the country through which we traveled; had captured mules and horses by the thousands to keep our trains moving and had confiscated enough cotton to help materially in paying the old gentleman's bills.

In our campaign the army passed over an average breadth of forty miles of country to Goldsboro, and consumed all the forage, cattle, hogs, sheep, poultry, cured meats, cornmeal on our way, so that it was necessary for the confederate Government to send provisions from other quarters to feed the inhabitants. It caused the abandonment of the whole seacoast from Savannah to Newbern with forts, dock yards, gun boats, etc.

Our appearance as we entered Goldsboro must have been to one unused to the scene, very grotesque. Uncle Sam's blue had long since worn out, in lieu thereof, the men wore clothing of every style and color, - a swallow trailed broad cloth coat of an aristocratic planter with perhaps gray trousers or drawers solus. No shoes and a plug hat would adorn a figure covered with mud, and with face and hands blackened with the smoke of many pine knot fires.

Before we were half through the trip the men's shoes had begun to wear out and when we reached Goldsboro there were two hundred of the men and line Officers of my regiment who had marched bare-footed for days. Their feet were blistered and torn by travelling over corduroy roads and through the woods. In the rear of every regiment were seventy-five to one hundred sore backed skeletons of mules and horses carrying as many sore footed soldiers, ragged and dirty. The good people of the north, judging from outward appearances, would, I think, have been loath to place the country's interests in their hands. When we met General Schofield and his troops who had just come from Wilmington, the tattered clothes and varied costumes of our men were a subject of great merriment to them and we certainly did present a woeful appearance. Such tatterdemalions gained nothing in looks by comparison with these men in trim regulation blue, the Officers in proper military; - paper collars, burnished buttons and blackened boots. But these ragged, bare headed, shoeless, brave, jolly soldiers of Sherman's legions were quite satisfied with themselves and the glory they attained, if they did not have the style.

On the sixth of April we received news of the capture of Richmond and Petersburg with the greatest of delight. The telegram was read to the brigade when out on drill, and the cheering that followed the announcement was immense. The drums rattled, the band struck up there was alternate cheering and music through the day. The day we arrived in Goldsboro witnessed the arrival of the first train of cars from New Bern N.C. The whistle of the locomotive was welcomed with vociferous shouts from the soldiers, for now the army was to be refitted and bare footed men to be shod. Mean-while the army had quietly settled down in its camps about the city upon the hillsides and in pleasant groves.

But we soon tired of camp life and were glad to again on the march to new fields of action and incident. So, on April tenth the army, complete in all respects, started out full of life and in the best spirits for Raleigh, the capital of the state, fifty miles Distance. We marched that day about ten miles, on the road to Smithfield, skirmishing actively with Rebel cavalry all the way, and, on the tenth, we entered the town. The enemy made a desperate effort at defense, erecting barricades and fighting in the streets., but our men steadily advanced and took the place which had been held by Johnston's retreating army, supposed to be thirty thousand strong. They had burnt the bridge over the Neuse river which winds around the edge of the town. The court house and jail stood on the public square and by the side of the jail was that relic of the past, the public stocks, which our soldiers took down and burnt.

On the thirteenth we had the news of the surrender of Lee's army to Grant which was announced. The men gave cheer after cheer in which Officers and everybody else joined and then they yelled and yelled until they waked the echoes for miles around. The bands played "Hail Columbia" and all the other patriotic tunes, while in the "intervals, drums and fifes throughout the corps rattled and blew the loudest. That night the army halted about fifteen miles from Raleigh. Raleigh had the honor of Andrew Johnson elected Vice-president and succeeding very unworthy Abraham Lincoln.

The next day we entered the city, Johnston having retreated. It was a beautiful town of ten or twelve thousand people with houses, wide lawns, roses and flowers in profusion. The most prominent building, of course, was the state house of light granite, on which was raised again the national flag.   As governor Vance had run away from the state mansion. General Sherman took possession of it for his headquarters. We were encamped a short distance from town. The weather was very warm but by a lavish use of arbors and a scanty use of clothes we kept fairly comfortable.

General Johnston had retreated rapidly across the Neuse, burning the bridge, and, having the R.R. to lighten his train, could retreat faster than we could follow. On the morning of the fifteenth we broke camp as usual to continue the pursuit of Johnston who was fifteen miles ahead of us. The rain was descending in a deluge, the roads were in a horrible condition and a trying day for men and mules was in prospective. The advance had got out several miles, - my regiment was more fortunate and had hardly left camp, - when cheer upon cheer came rolling back to us. The column was halted and presently it was announced that Johnston had requested a temporary suspension of hostilities. A tumultuous time followed and in spite of the mud and rain every sort of antic was indulged in. General Sherman had received from Johnston a message asking for an armistice, and that action might be taken towards a surrender of his forces. An interview between the two Generals followed five miles from Durham Station. Here Sherman met for the time in their lives though they had been exchanging shots since May 1863.

Just as Sherman's car was about to start for the conference a telegram was handed to him from Stanton, the secretary of war, announcing the assassination of President Lincoln and the attempt on the life of Secretary Seward and his son. Not daring that such a terrible news should be divulged to the army during his absence, lest, by some overt of a Rebel citizen or at the instigations of some impetuous soldier, swift retaliation should be urged and perhaps the city laid to ashes, the order communicating the tragedy was withheld until the following day. The universal feeling was one of horror, a desire for revenge and a hope that no project for surrender would be entertained, but that the army might advance on the foe and fight it out. The troops were now inactive, awaiting events.

The terms proposed by Sherman were disapproved at Washington. The armistice came to an end and hostilities were ordered to be resumed after forty-eight hours truce. In the meantime, General Grant had come to Raleigh with a letter from Secretary Stanton. New terms of surrender were suggested and complied with Johnston and the war was ended. Johnston surrendered thirty-one thousand men, one hundred and eight pieces of artillery. Fifteen thousand small arms. Most of the men had stayed away with guns, horses, mules and wagons.

The city of Raleigh swarmed with Johnston's soldiers and they were passing our camp continually. Their Officers, according to these deserters, making no effort to detain them, apparently regarding their cause defunct. We were reviewed by LT. Gen. Grant and then orders were promulgated that we should march, under our respective commanders by easy stages to Richmond. It was getting very warm for campaigning. We had a very easy march a few days before and yet in the division three men fell dead, supposedly from the effects of the sun. One from my regiment fell in the rank and died in a few minutes. We left Raleigh on April Thirtieth on a three hundred mile to Richmond, and reached Petersburg about the May ninth.

Here, twenty-two miles to Richmond, on Sunday April second, Grant fought his last battle, closing in on Lee and breaking his lines. Where upon Lee sent a courier to Jeff Davis, who was at the time attending services in St. Paul's church. His dispatch said, "My line is broken in three places and Richmond must be evacuated." The city had quite a metropolitan appearance, and, for us, who for eighteen months had seen nothing of dry goods and groceries, it was quite novel. As usual, the Yankees had filled the stores and the people were reveling in good things from the north. I suppose however, the advent of Sherman's army being its "First Appearance on the boards" in the east was a s much an object of interest to the inhabitants as their city was to us' At least so I judged by the curiosity evinced, not, in this case, confined to

128

Yankees, and the questions asked.

A couple of days later we were encamped at Manchester, on the opposite side of the James River from Richmond. A pontoon bridge connected to two places, as the Rebels had burnt the old one. About the first object of interest on reaching the other side was the so-called "Castle-Thunder" a former prison for our soldiers. It was by no means the style of building its pretentious name would signify, but a common brick three storied edifice. Deserters, negros and Rebels occupied the dirty building, their legs dangling from the windows between the bars.

Two or three hundred yards farther on was Libby Prison, notorious in history as the place selected by the confederate authorities for the imprisonment and starvation of captured Union Officers. I went over the detested place which Union Officers entered with very different emotions than they would have a short time before.

To prevent the U.S. from gaining possession of a lot of tobacco and cotton, the confederates started a fire and thirty squares in the business portion of the city were swept clean by the flames. Banks, mills, foundries and churches were burnt up in the heart of the city. The capital building was a dirty dilapidated affair with rather pretty ground about it and some fine status.

Jeff Davis lived some little distance in a house presented to him by the citizens. The streets were full of a strange mixture of Union and Rebel Officers, all in their respective uniform. The flag of the Union was floating over the city, and the troops of the Union were patrolling the streets. Lee's army had melted away and the power of the Rebellion was broken. We remained at Richmond a week or more and then camped in the Vicinity of Alexandria.
One day I rode into the city and hunted up my Rebellious brother-in-law, Billy Wattles, who, like all the rest of his confederate brethren, was not at all reconciled conditions as they were. I believe that Wattles had been on Jeff Davis staff in some legal capacity, where he was an exceedingly bright lawyer. My sister, Harriett, had sometime before

taken refuge with my mother in New London.

By order of the War department, a grand review, by the President and Cabinet, of all armies then near Washington was to take place. General Meade's Forces on May twenty third, General Sherman's on the twenty fourth. Accordingly, on the afternoon and night of the twenty third, we, that is, Sherman's army consisting of the Seventeenth, fifteenth, fourteenth, and twentieth Corps, crossed over the long bridge from Alexandria and bivouacked in the neighborhood of neighborhood of the capital. At nine, A.M. of the twenty fourth, the signal gun boomed, and hardly had the smoke cleared before the bugles blared the "Forward", bands clashed, and the long column started with, Sherman and a brilliant staff, himself, with more than usual care, dressed befitting his rank and the occasion, at its head.

The Grand Review of the Armies (Library of Congress)

A short mile's march up Pennsylvania Avenue, its sidewalks jammed with approving, cheering crowds, brought us to the reviewing station directly in front of the White House. Extensive stands had been erected on both sides of the avenue and these were filled with spectators in holiday dress, and Officers in bright uniforms. On the reviewing stand were the President and his cabinet, the Secretary of War, Lt General Grant, General Meade, and all the notables in Civic and military life.

Past these came seventy thousand soldiers in broad fronted column, Sherman's stern bronzed veterans of bone, muscle and skin, swinging along. Their tattered battle flags fluttering victoriously over their heads in the full pride of achievement, ranks in close ranks and magnificent array. The musket, glittering in the right sun of the beautiful day, seemed to one looking down the line like one welded mass of steel, so perfectly were they aligned, so uniform the step, and all eyes directly to the front; a mighty host which looked and felt as if they might defy the world. Our division, as well as each of the others, was proceeded by its Corps of Black Pioneers with pick and spade on shoulder keeping perfect step and distance.

In rear were six ambulances, and to enliven the scene, pack mules laden with the "Bummers "spoils and the foragers exactions of hams, crowing game cocks, squawking chickens and a grinning pickanniny astride. For seven hours that serried host of warriors filed by with even step and firm tread while the glittering of thousands of muskets and sabers.

The polished brass cannons, the hundreds of bullets ridden banners presented a scene splendid and imposing. It was the last act in the wonderful drama of those gallant corps, and amid the thundering plaudits of thousands of enthusiastic spectators this army of seventy thousand veterans paid its last marching salute and then broke ranks. We remained encamped about Washington the following ten days. The city full of soldiers; all ranks were represented from an Assistant Surgeon to a Lt. General. Indeed, Generals seemed to be in the majority; greater in number than privates. I was fortunate in meeting a Yale classmate and unfortunate in not meeting him the day previous too our leaving the City.

We went by cars to Parkesburg on the Ohio River and from there took boat to Louisville, Ky. At Louisville the regiment was mustered out of service. To muster out a large army and make the necessary mustering rolls is no trifling job.

By the time we got back to the Ohio River my regiment had made quite an extensive circuit of states, a pretty long walk, to say the least, and fighting for the greater portion of the distance. From Cincinnati down the Ohio and Tennessee Rivers through Tennessee and Alabama, through the heart of Georgia nearly to Florida, up the center of North and South Carolina and Virginia. With the exception of a few hours sail from Savannah to Newbern, South Carolina, the men had marched every foot of the way, one thousand, four hundred and eighty miles. From Louisville we took the boat to Cincinnati to disband. On reaching the levee there we filed out in due time, nine hundred men and Officers.

This was the home city of the regiment and we received a hearty welcome. When we reached the street a brass band and a tumultuous crowd awaited us. The streets were lined with a cheering lot of men, women and children, and every window had a half dozen heads peering out; all wildly excited and uproarious. This, quite different from the Washington review, was a real home coming; the regiment being very largely made up of Cincinnati men or from those living in that vicinity, so that nearly everyone had friends, acquaintances of families to greet him. So tattered flags were again unfurled, the bands played, the crowd cheered, and handkerchiefs fluttered, but the men failed this time to keep eyes directly to the front. The line often wavered as some woman would dart out from the clamoring crowd to cling, sobbing to the husband whom she had not seen for four or five years of anxious waiting, or as some comrade would spring from the ranks to clasp his mother, or some girl with beaming face would leap from the throng to give and receive an eager kiss from her long absent sweetheart. Such things were happening all along the line and everyone was joyful. The fellows who went from home gay, fresh and youthful, returned stern, bronzed, and mature.

The man whose love of danger and adventure had been a strong and compelling passion came back to hang up his gun and cheerfully take up the steady grind of earning his daily bread. Wonderful to relate, that army, which had had years of bloody and destructive fighting, melted away and every man who had wielded sword or musket, quietly went home to accustomed work. Peace had come. "Grim visage war had smooth his wrinkled front." The sword was turned into the plough share and the spear into the pruning hook.

I have written this simple narrative for my grandchildren Sally and Bobby, whom I dearly- love and in whose affectionate remembrance I hope to live

"Signed"

Pierre Starr Hartford, 1912

Pierre Starr's Civil War Letters

You have read Pierre's 1912 narrative and experienced his Civil War journey. The narrative was written late in his life and many may say that it is not of much use as a research or academic work. So, this section is the letters of Pierre and the letters of George Cadman, with added letters from other members of the 39th Ohio Infantry. These additional letters will add proof of the importance of Pierre's narrative even after all the years that have passed.

His journey was etched into his mind.

Corinth miss. July 4th, 1862,

My Dear Mother,

Here I am in Corinth of Historic Fame. But before I say anything of this place or of my future movements I have better tell you how I got here. I wrote you from Buffalo on Sunday. The following morning, I started for Cincinnati, and after traveling all day and night reached that city early Tuesday morning. On going to the Quartermasters found that no boat left for Pittsburg landing (at which place I was ordered to report) till Wednesday Evening. So, I remained in C. nearly two days and this had an opportunity of seeing to a large degree the Queen City of the West. I say to a limited degree because it was so intensely hot that I was almost impossible to work about much.

Well on Wednesday evening on the Steamer Nashville I started down the Ohio for Tennessee River and arrived at Pittsburg Landing the following Sunday morning. Yesterday- The sail down the river was very pleasant. the scenery on the Tenn. I think, much the prettier will Though the Ohio is rather the larger still not so much so as I anticipated, for both it is perfectly wild, we could sail 20 or 30 miles without seeing an habitation. In comparison with our Eastern river this struck me particularly. The water in both rivers though more so in the Tenn. Is very dirty-about the color of clay, and as I was obliged to drink it, I assure you I was pretty will disgusted with it.

Before reaching my destination the battle began, one of the soldiers on board of whom there were a number, being shot through the head by a Kentucky Rebel, above the landings in Kentucky at which we stopped, I was looking at the man at the time the rascal jumped on his horse and was off before anyone had time to interfere.

We passed Fort Henry of course, it is now quite despicable and not at all formable in appearance. On the boat I made several pleasant acquaintances. Reaching Pittsburg I found no Hospitals there, the Medical Director to whom I was to report, having removed to Corinth, so in company with one of my friends of the Steamboat and a you soldier whom

136

I met here, we procured an ambulance a pair of horses and about 5 P.M. started for Corinth we passed over the battlefield of Shiloh. on our way the splintered trees, the cannon balls remaining of them, still the great majority having been taken away by curiosity seekers.

The graves of the dead, the ovens (earthen) for baking bread. The remains of tents and camp fires- and the fields several miles completely cleared of grass & shrubbery- all attested to the presence of a large army & hard fighting. The distance from Pittsburg to Corinth is 28 miles. We were seven hours making it, from this you can imagine the condition of the roads. Corduroys do not suit me at all. Finally, we reached C (Corinth). Now the question was could we find any place to sleep or anything to eat?

After going to the Hotel, and every other house nearby in town which there are perhaps 50 or more, we gave it up, and camped out in the street, sleeping in our ambulance-houseless & supper less. About daylight the fife and drum, in connection with the fuss prevented my sleeping anymore and we started for breakfast. An apology which we obtained at the Hotel.

Everything here is of course of the U.S.A. Government trains fill the roads, and we found soldiers everywhere last night patrolling the streets and lying about everywhere in the streets. However, came in to take to greet them regiments and so had to sleep anywhere.

The morning unshaved and unwashed they were swarming everywhere after breakfast. I reported. I reported to McDougall (The Medical Director) in accordance with a request that I made when I am ordered to report to the medical director of the Army of Miss. The surgeon general of the 4th Division of that army came with me in the boat from Cincinnati and in the Ambulance from Corinth. He wants me to get into his division and I think I can.

I started with him this afternoon for the Med. Directors head Quarters- about 15 miles south. SO, I have given you a very limited space my moving here. It is not so hot here as I anticipated, though it is rather boiling in the sun. I am writing this on the top of a cigar box on the piazza of the

Hotel. There is nothing like civilized a communication here. It is a miserable little village, dusty and dirty. There are but few troops in town. Halleck's headquarters are here. There are some 40,000 the other side of the town. I can not yet tell you my address-but will write as soon as I find it out. If these lead pencil marks are not all rubbed out, I wish you would send this letter to Jed. I told him I would write but have neither the time or accommodation at present. I intended to have written Jack too, but it was impossible- I am well-in good spirits-have had a pleasant trip-and like the anticipation.

> Love to Jed, Emma & others
> Your Affectionate Son
> Pierre

Steamship Nashville Library of Congress

Camp Clear Creek;

Camp Clear Creek Miss. '62

39th O.V.I

July 24th

My Dear Mother,

Here I am a last, I hope fixed in a regiment. I wrote you from Corinth
last week Monday. Monday afternoon in accordance with my orders I
proceeded an ambulance and started for Gen. Rosecrans Head
Quarters, about four miles south of Corinth, he reported to Dr. Throll,
the medical director, by him I was ordered to report to the
Commanding Officer of the 11th Ohio Battery for duty which I did that
same evening. The battery was composed by about 150 men. They had
no surgeon then so that I was the only medical Officer. I did not like
the position very much, as the battery was remote from any regiment, I
had little society and no medical Officer with whom I could consult in
case. I wished to do. So, I determined if possible to get my orders
changed for some regiment and after staying there about a week I had
an opportunity to do so, and was ordered to the 39th reg. Ohio Vol.
where I now am. I like the regiment very much & the Officers with
whom I am brought in contact, that is those who are on the Col. Staff
to which I belong and with whom I mess.

We number about 700 men, and have the reputation as I learned before
I came here of being a crack regiment of the west. A fine band
accompanied us, the surgeon of the regiment having been away I have
had the care of the whole for a few days. This morning I had about 60
sick to attend to. There are some 25 in the hospital tents. I expect soon
however to be relieved of a part of the care. We have a very pretty
encampment about 7 miles S.E. of Corinth. I have had an opportunity
of seeing the much talked of fortifications about here, and before I

return expect to see much more, including perhaps some variable warfare.

We do not know of course how long we shall stay here, it may be several months and again we may be under away to-morrow. I have had an opportunity of becoming somewhat used to camp life. With the exception of two or three I have slept every night on the ground in my blanket, Last night I did the same. I hope to be able to raise a cot before long. [one night when I was at the battery, it rained very hard, and, I had an opportunity of seeing how much more I could stand than I thought I could. I got pretty well saturated, as I slept on the ground, but still slept first rate the next morning] The weather has been pretty warm, the terminate often being over 100 in the shade, but I do not seem to feel the heat as much as in Hartford. We have a fine breeze every day and the evenings are really cool- a double blanket being no more comfortable every night since I have been here.

We get Cincinnati and St Louis papers which are three days old. SO that we are in a great measure enlightened of affairs in the North. I am very desire of hearing from home, not having a letter from anybody since I left. I am in good health, never better in my life. A good many of the luxuries of home are and of course deprived of and some of what we regarded as necessities, but still get along nicely

Foraging parties are sent out after food frequently and we live very well. One of our Negros went out yesterday, after vegetables for our table, among the sicesh in this part of the country, he brought back enough of everything and with a grin on his face, said that "he's expense for the day was 30 cts.

It seems such a long time before a letter can get home and an answer returned that it is almost disheartening to write. I hope you will make the interval as short as possible.

Your affectionate son,
Pierre

Starr July 30, 1862
Camp Clear Creek;

Dear Jack,

By an unevaluable connection of circumstances, contrary to my expectations I omitted seeing you before I started on my Southern Journey, and since I am here the next best thing, I think is to write you. It seemed that I arrived in Hartford after my examination in New York, the same evening on which you left Wilmington. That was a disappointment to me and no doubt also to you, if as you intended you traveled up to 14th St. the next morning to breakfast with me. When I left you, you remember, it was my intention to enter the Navy. Arriving in N.Y. however and going up to see my Tutor. He informed me that there was a board of examination sitting there at the time of those intending to enter the Army. And he felt the case before me in such light, that I immediately changed my plans and joined the "military".

I stopped a day in Hartford after my examination, nearly two days in N.L. and by boat went to N.Y. received my orders. Saturday Morning to report at Pittsburg Landing Tenn. And the same afternoon started for Buffalo. SO, I had no time to come over to Newark. After an eight-days travelling I arrived at Pittsburg Landing. But the surgeon to who I was to report had moved his headquarters to Corinth Miss. So in company of two other, on Sunday Evening we started for C (Corinth) 28 miles distance. Our road led through the battle of Shiloh, so I had an opportunity of seeing where our troops came so near being rushed into the Tenn. River.

About midnight we arrived at Corinth, after ineffective attempts to bet anything to eat or better place in which to sleep, we hauled up on the square of Corinth, having a lot of Government wagons, soldiers, ETC and Inquired for "Balmy Sleep" and very soon in spite to me our old bedroom, we were oblivious to all

In the morning I reported myself and staying all day in Corinth, started again in an ambulance to report for duty. For duty to the 11th Ohio Battery, thou I was broken in to camp life, not being supplied

with Col. I had to make one of the ground. This was all very in dry weather for a change, but one night when it rained tremendously and meandering through my blanket and under my back. Then was decidedly more romance than comfort, and I could not appreciate what I so often heat that "A soldiers life is always gay" Bread varied sometimes with pork for a treat,. formed or breakfast dinner & supper There being no other medical man there I had charge of the battery after a week's experience there I was fortunate enough to be received and was ordered to my present quarters.

Our regiment numbered about 700 men, the officers on the Col. Staff to which I belong are fine fellows, our mess is tip top, for by means of foraging parties we manage to get from the secesh about here everything we want in the way of necessity and luxuries. Among other things we have just received a lot of peaches and other fruits. A fine band being connected to the regiment, we have the pleasure of their music every evening. This s somewhat a different mode of living from what I have been accustomed to and yet it is formerly belonging to the secesh in my house it is not to be sure very elaborately furnished to which I have been fortunate enough to raise often sleeping till a couple of nights since on the ground, a box which is my dwelling case, and some meal sacks for a carpet, comprised with my valise its embellishment an artifical tower of branches in front form a shade and with its surrounding scenery of hills and woods and snowy tents it is by no means an unpleasant picture.

We are not lacking contrabands, each one of the staff being supplied with that useful article as a servant tomorrow I am going to get a horse for my own use and see something more of secesh country all together we are very comfortably off. The weather instant of being as less in July than I have last month. The nights are very cool, then has been, one hardly in which it was not necessary to sleep under two blankets to be comfortable. My pay at present $125.00 per month. Besides a horse with trappings & keeping provided. I want to hear how you have succeeded in your business prospects. U haven't yet received a letter since I left home, when my direction gets north I hope they will pile in. I am rather doubtful to sending this to Newark.

Yours Truly Pierre

39ᵗʰ Reg. Ohio Vol. 1ˢᵗ Brigade
2ⁿᵈ Division-Army of the Miss. Is my direction
let me hear from you

Camp Cedar Creek, Miss.
Aug. 10ᵗʰ ,1862

your letter was received this morning and I hasten to answer it, since by the time this reaches you. I will have been about three weeks since you have heard from me, as it takes at least 16 days for a letter to come and go. Yours was the first letter to come and go. Yours was the first letter I had received since I left home, and I assure you I was very glad to hear from the North. We got here only Cincinnati and St Louis papers, there days old and those irregulars ably, and at 10 cts. A piece, neither of them is larger than the Hartford Courier. By the way the complementary notice you speak of in the Hartford paper is really alarming. One of the Sub-editors is an old friend and college class mate of mine and I suppose that accounts for it. Since I have been here I have written Jed, jack and the Dr. It is very great pleasure, away out here to get a letter. They are so scarce and far between.

The weather in N.L. would no doubt be regarded as excruciatingly hot, but we manage to get along here without much trouble, since we dress to suit the weather and not papering. The evenings are right cool, we have not had a warm night yet. Much cooler in that respect than summer evenings in Hartford.

The enemy are supposed to be about 8 miles from here. Guerrillas are much nearer than that. Cannon are booming now within distance and surmise are safe in regard to the cause. I am not inclined to be blood thirsty but should like to see some fighting and the rebels whipped, instead of lying here apparently doing nothing. Of course, we have no idea how long we shall remain here but if you put on your letters "to follow the army" they will reach me sometime. So, you need not wait every time tell you have from me before you write.

Yesterday we had another Asst. Surgeon come to Reg. in will both remain here for the present. I have had the whole Reg. to take care of as our surgeon in the Brigade Surgeon and is time is mostly taken up with other business. I have had also considerable writing to do in the way of discharge papers ETC.

Camp life in summer is very comfortable, I sleep as soundly in my tent (I have now raised a cot. Blankets, bug fly net.) as I were doing any were. The morning call is at sunrise when the companies are drilled, but we, that is the Col. And Staff get up for breakfast about 7, we dine at 3 O'clock, and have supper at 8 P.M. You say both of my letters were received. I wrote you from Buffalo, a short letter; from Corinth, and one from here, did you receive all three?

Yesterday afternoon I went to Corinth to make one or two purchases. The Rebel fortifications which started along the road and strengthened and improved for future use if necessary. Columbians and Rifle Pits are at every turn in the road near Corinth and we are continually passing government wagons and horses. We came out in the evening it was beautiful moonlit night, and the camp fires all around us and made the scene beautiful.

We have quite a pretty encampment here, the ground varies between hill and dole, and the white tents seen through the woods look very romantic, about evening the bands tow or three of the different Regiments around here, in connection and ours, stricken up and their effect is fine. I fear however in a short time we shall be deprived of all of our bands except one. Which is to be the brigade band and will be stationed at headquarters.

Entrenchment seems to be the order now in governments express. I hope you at the North will soon raise the 300,000 men, and at the same time have soon enough to fill up the old regiments before making new ones, under some Green Commanders. I still keep well, never was better in my life then I have been out here. —may it so continue, for this is a hard place to be sick in. I have had but one death in the hospital since coming here-please remember that a letter is a great acquisition here and write
144

accordingly. I wish you would ask Jed to send some Hartford papers now
and then

> With much love
> Your Affectionate Son,
> Pierre

39th Ret. Ohio Vol.
1st Brigade,
2nd Division,
Army of the Miss.

Memphis Tenn. Aug. 23rd, 1862

My Dear mother,

It seems a long time since I have heard from home and I really am
beginning to get anxious but trust that nothing unpleasant has
prevented your writing. About two weeks since I forward to you by
Adams Express two hundred dollars $200.00 to be deposed of as you
may think proper. I might have sent a larger sum if I had not passion
for my horse out of the sum of I received, and as It had been so long
since I last was paid. I had more to pay out than I ought to have
should. The regiment has not even yet been paid. I succeeded in
getting my money because I was detailed to the U.S.3rd Cavalry in
which I have been serving for the last two weeks. This morning
however I returned to my regiment. Of course, you will notify me
when you receive the money, which should have reached you before
this.

> Hoping to hear soon,
> Your affectionate Son,

Iuka Miss

Aug. 24, 1862,

My Dear mother,

You have no doubt expected a letter from me before this and I had intended to write but have not had a will intended time to do it so. About three days since we received orders to march to I-V-Ka (as it is written by the aborigines) and I will myself to proceed by cars. I had to take charge of everything as our surgeon has resigned on account of sickness and the Capt. In a German who speaks quite untellable. At a half an hour notice we struck our hospital tents to take out of town with baggage and sick and was at the depot, that is to say an open field without a house in sight. I got them with the two sick men, hospital stores tents etc.

About 5 o'clock in the afternoon the cars were expected every minute. But they did not appear, and it began to grow dark, so I ordered the tents put up, the sick cared for and we made our home for the night. The new day we waited till three o'clock where at last the train arrived. As the brigade had gone from that part of the country, and the secesh abounded there, in the course of 12 Or 24 hours we could have very been likely have been in their hands. So, we were not at all sorry to leave.

Luka is about 25 miles East of Corinth, near the boarder line of Miss. It is (or rather was) the stylish watering of this part of the south, a second Saratoga for Southern Snobs. It is a very pretty little village, abounds in two Sulphur and Alum Springs, has two large hotels for summer patronage, and a number of handsome mansions. It is quite an improvement on other parts of the country which I had seen. It is said to be the most healthy place as well as cooler in the states we have a most delightful breeze here in our camp- which is just on the border of the town- all the time, and if a little salt were intermingled it would almost be N.L. Since I arrived I have been sleeping most of my time at the "Iuka Springs Hotel" which has been converted into a Military Hospital, a great change from last summer when it was crowded with Southern Belles and beaux. In the large square on the first floor, perhaps 75 feet square, where the light fantastic was worth to be tripped, I deposited my sick "Mudsills" On the evening that I reached there, 500 sick occupied the house. The next day my regiment reached here and a couple of days after I managed to get all the sick in the field again and for myself I was glad enough to get out of a house and into my tent on the field again.

I came on the cars with a surgeon of the regular army, who is to take charge of the hospital, he wanted to stay with him as an assistant, but I preferred remaining with the 39th. I have however to attend to their men everyday tell relieved by others who are to be regularly approved there. There are I said to be many pretty rides about here, as would very likely be the case in such a watering place, but the secsh are altogether too inviting to be pleasant and if is not at all safe to go more than a mile or two from the cams in any direction.

　　We had a supply train captured a day or two since several men shot by guerrillas and other news incidents which bring forcibly to our minds the conviction that we are in an enemy's country, and the propinquity of the Rebels. Speaking of rides, I have got a fine horse of my own now, and my riding experience in here fore comes very nicely into play, as I ride more or less every day, as of course one never thinks of getting about the country in any other way than on horseback. I have written you a letter and some papers from Jed and also a letter from Jack. Please tell them that I will answer them as soon as I get time. This is considered an important point in a military point of view, and it is thought will play a part before the war is over.

I am glad people north are waking up to the idea that this is a real live war and no play work and that if the country is to be saved they have got to fight. My direction is the same as here to fore, and always will be whatever may go. I like this life first rate for a change. Everything is very high- Milk per Qt. 25 cts. -eggs per doz. About 50 cts. -Butter per pound, little chickens 75 cts. etc.

As all are secesh about here of course they get as much as they can out of us. Saw an order from the Provost Marshall, however this morning regulating the prices, so now they can't check us more, That the law allows-which is certainly enough to satisfy any rascal. By later order we can now send out parties who take corn, potatoes, Etc. from the Rebels when they meet them which is certainly no more then proper.

In haste,
Your affectionate son, Pierre

Iuka Miss. Sept. 6th 62
Dear Mother,

Both of your letters arrived by the same mail to day. Somehow, they managed to get through in a most unaccountable short time. The one dated 31st was only seven days coming. Your anxiety about me and my horse would be very funny very laughable did I not think that you really meant what you wrote. I do not suppose you are very well posted in war matters, yet perhaps you have heard or read of such things as a picket guard and a camp guard at all events, wherever a town is taken possession of or a country occupied by the troops to prevent the highness of enemies or the egress, this is of course the case here.

Our pickets encircle a space of two or three miles in diameter within which guerrillas or any other armed men do not or cannot come and by one which it is not safe to go any distance, nor can a consummate fool as needlessly to throw sufficient their hands or be shot by them knowing where they are and the danger of going beyond the lines of our army.

So, don't try to conjure of any more such needless stories of anxiety. You seem surprised to learn that a surgeon needs a horse, you are mistaken if you imagine that a surgeon walks wherever the regiment is in the march, he has duty to attend to which require him even in his great convenience did not call for it. Your deduction that because I have a horse that I am have received any pay is without foundation. I
148

have in addition to my pay of $125.00 per month, a horse furnished me by the government. I have not as yet drawn my pay because I have not needed it before. I do now however and shall draw it in a day or two. I wish there was some way of getting a part of it North, but I do not know of any at present.

We remain at Iuka from which I wrote you last, we expect to move somewhere shortly. Four days ago, just as we were sitting down to dinner our orderly brought orders for us to get ready to march immediately accordingly tent were struck, baggage packed, and teams loaded ready for a start. We waited in that uncertain state for a couple of days getting along the best we could, until we concluded that the necessity for moving had passed, and that no more orders are coming, and we venture to put up our tents again and live as usual. I am still kept busy at the hospital, though I live in camp.

There are about 900 patients there now. Contraband are coming in every day in larger numbers, they are some 300 or more of them. They are kept at work, draining trenches and working roads and if we fortify here they will do the digging. I rode down this afternoon to see a crowd of about 100 who came in yesterday. They are a most motley group of uncles, aunties and little picannies. I don't believe they are as well off as if they were on the plantations. Anyone body can have one who chores. They all appear like happy in the ignorance of the pasture.

It is just two months yesterday since I started for Tennessee. I am very glad have done what I have and am will suited with my position. My health has been first-rate ever since I came down and I have passed a most pleasant summer. The thick under cloth if which I brought I have worn every day, and think I have been more comfortable as regard than if I had been in Hartford. You ask me if there is a Chaplin in our regiment, there is not, there was one sometime since, but he resigned, I do not know of but one regiment about here which has one and is home at present. I am glad to hear there is some hopes of N.L. having the Marry Face, who knew but there is ambivalent future for her, yet. I am sorry that your taxes are so large and your fund no more. I can lend you if you will like to borrow. Jed, I wish you is into in much danger.

Drafting seems to be postponed in all states and I suppose it has been in H.(Hartford). I wrote him since coming here, All I have received two or three batches of papers which was very acceptable, I need to write Jack in a few days. The flickering flame of my tallow dip which has got quite low in its socket, warns me to stop and the end of the page has reached,

Your affectionate Son,   Pierre

Near San Jacinto
Sept. 22, 1862 26th Ill. Reg.

My dear mother,

A friend and I went to the battlefield. We spent a couple of hours there. By this time all the dead have been buried exempt for a few whom were the hill where they fell. Long trenches are filled with the dead and heaps of sand thrown up attest to the numbers of unknown who have been thrown in the same ditch. Dead horses are all over the place. The trees were splintered and split and it seemed as if every leaf was pierced. We marched again and slept between rows in a corn field and the next morning our clothes were saturated. I have not changed my clothes for a whole week. General Stanley of West Point commands our division and Rosecrans commands the whole of the Mississippi.

You Afft. Son
Pierre

Near Jacinto- Sept. 22nd
Hd. Quarters 26th Ill. Reg. 62

My Dear Mother,

I wrote you a few hurried lines from near Corinth as I had not written for some time and did not know when I should have another opportunity. About two weeks since I was ordered to report to the 26th Ill. For duty. They being almost without medical service and the 39th seems the only one that could spend a Surgeon in our division. The

Medical director has provided to return to return me to the 39th as soon as possible and I hope I am back in my old quarters. The 26th is well known as a fine regiment but I do not feel as much at home here. But I must not dwell long on this for I have a good deal to write about.

We left Iuka in somewhat of a hurry. I remained a day after the regiment to look after some hospital items, tents % Etc. Friday evening I left I had expected to remain tell Saturday, but a few moments before the cars left for Corinth. I managed as a special favor to have some of my hospital goods put on the train and as some friends of mine were going down I concluded to go also leaving my hospital steward with a couple of men to look after the rest of the things. Now this rather impromptu department of mine was quite lucky for it. I had not gone there, I should have had to have done one of them things, either to walk 20 miles, been taken prisoner or perhaps been shot. For that evening there was an attack on the town by the Rebs, they were repulsed however by our troops.

The next day however Price attacked our overwhelming force was about to come against them but before he had an opportunity, our force, which consisted only of two regiments and some cavalry (Had been left more of a rear guard to forces which had gone away the other day) decamped for Corinth. Some of our men were taken prisoners, and 25 or 30 were killed & wounded. The rails were torn up & the bridges burnt. On Saturday the train was fired into. On Sunday the surgeon of our Division and myself started on the train which was to try to get to Iuka. About two hundred soldiers were on the train.

We succeeded in getting the town of Burnsville, 7 miles from Iuka, for the train could not go. I had the pleasure of seeing all the secish their taken prisoner and when I left there with their houses in flames. We lost all the stores which were left in Iuka. My regiment was encamped about four miles from Corinth, I however remained in the town for the succeeding week. Thus the regiment was ordered to march, taking five days rations and leaving tents and baggage of every description. Thursday at about 2 a.m. They started. I stopped to take the sick into town, and in company with a surgeon friend of mine, we took a pair of horses, an ambulance and driver and the next day and started after. We did not know where they had gone but as it was generally expected that there would be a fight, so we determined to find them if possible.

We first made for Jacinto. On our way we stopped at our encampment and there I wrote you a few lines, arrived during the afternoon but the Division had left, on its way towards Iuka, near which there was known to be a large Rebel forces under Gen. Price. We hurried on after them, and in a little while began to hear cannonading and to pass currier doting along the road with dispatches at every five miles along the road there were relays of horses and from the curriers we learned there was a big fight in progress. We hurried along but it grew dark, we missed the road and had to put in for the night by the road side in our ambulance.

The next morning, we started early on the right road this time and had gone about 3 miles when we reached the hospital, where the wounded had been brought from the battlefield. It was an old broken down house with log stables & sheds, then were completely filled with wounded and dead that one could hardly get through them. There were probably between three hundred there, but I was too busy to count them. There were a number of surgeons there and I was asked to stop and assist them in putting the wounded in to ambulances and having them carried to Iuka, which was now retaken by our forces.

The battle began on Friday afternoon 19th Sept. and lasted two hours and a half when it became too dark to distinguish the enemy. The Rebels were badly whipped, our troops remaining in possessing of the field while the Rebels skedaddled during the night having leaving their dead and wounded on the field. Seven hundred and more of them dead and wounded were found by our men the next day on the field, among them was Gen. Little. Price was in command on their side- Rosecrans on ours. The only I think we have to regret is regard of the victory is that Price ran away.

All Saturday I worked very hard getting after the wounded. Some were treably cut up and mangled. There were three lying close together and when I asked them were they were wounded, they raised their blankets and I found that the left leg of each was taken off above the knee. The same cannon ball did the work for each of them. But there is no use in going over the mournful story told so often of ghastly wounds and horrible suffering, such as I saw during that day. We attended to their wounds before they could move them. A stream of ambulances was coming and going from Iuka all day, and by evening we got all away. From Friday morning about 9 o'clock till Saturday evening though working all Saturday.

I had nothing to eat but two or three hard biscuits. Saturday evening having got away the wounded I started for Iuka, and on the way passed on part of the battlefield. The dead were lying by the road side yet unburied, gun-cartridge boxes, swords, coats hats Etc. were lying ever way in profusion. I had no opportunity then as it was too dark of going over the field. Before I got to Iuka, I met this surgeon with whom I had started from Corinth, he also had been at work in the hospital in Iuka, he had not yet found the Division to which we belonged. I left my ambulance and joined him, and we started again in pursuit. We did not find them that night and slept in our ambulance on the field.

The next morning, we found them. They had been in pursuit of Price but could not catch him. The Army encamped for a few hours to rest and in the meantime a friend and myself took horses and went over the battlefield about five miles distance. We spent a couple of hours there by this time all the dead had been buried except a few whom they were burying by the road where they fell.

Long trenches were filled with the dead and heaps of freshly thrown up earth attested to the number of unknown ones who had fallen and had been thrown unrecognizable into the same ditch. Dead horses were scattered all over the field, and in one place where the 11th Ohio Battery (which you remember her, I attended for a short time). They lay in heap as I counted them, 22 horses. This battery was cut terribly, every one of their horses was killed and their guns fell into the enemies' hands, after losing a great many men and have every one of their Officers severely wounded and one of them killed. These guns however were all recaptured and are still in our hands.

The trees were splintered and cut by the balls and it seemed as if nearly everyone was pruned. there was one oak tree in which were counted fifty rifle balls, arms and accouterments were gathered in heaps and the will know "butternut" coats of the sesish were thrown under the guts of our horses.   Hundreds of dollars in Confederate money was found by the soldiers in the boxes of the dead.

But I must say I shan't get anything - by the time we got back to camp the troops were drawn up in line ready to march and off we started. We marched till about 9 P.M. and then stopped in a corn field. I had not had that day not a particle of breakfast or of dinner, nothing to eat but one awful hard cracker, and had no supper till at night after marching, we had some moten. As I said before the regiment was ordered to leave behind tents & baggage so I with others laid down between two rows of corn in my blankets and slept like a rock. Everything was saturated with dew in the morning, but it didn't seem to do the slightest harm.

At 4 A.M. we were ordered to march again, and breakfast less we started and continued until about 9 a.m. When we stopped between some earthworks where we are now remaining, it is surmised that we are to say here several days in watch for the Rebels if they dare attack us, but of course we don't know anything about it. I received your letter yesterday on the march.

Writing is a very difficult thing here, on the ground minus tents, Camo stools and everything else but what nature offers. I do not know that I can find ink enough in camp to direct it. Of my health I cans say it is first rate, never was better. I would like to get to Corinth were my baggage is, for I haven't been so saturated that I could take off my clothes or boots for about a week- much less put anything clean, such is army life, sometimes quite luxurious, as others quite the contrary.

You asked who is the Genl. of our Regiment, a Regiment is commanded by a Col. Not a Gen. General Stanley - a West Pointer commands the Division, and Gen. Rosecrans the whole army of the Mississippi. Don't be anxious if you don't hear from me. I can not write regularly. My direction is 26th Reg. Ill. Vol.

2nd Brigade   2nd Division
                        Army of the Miss.
            From your affectionate son, Pierre

Head qtrs. 26th Ill. Near Corinth,
Sept. 25th, 1862

Dear Jed,

We got lost going to the battlefield and slept in the ambulance. The next morning we took the right road and came to the battlefield. The battlefield was strewn with wounded and in all there were 200 or 300. Arms and legs shot away they were lying in the sun many of them uncared for. Many of them were shot through the head and their shattered skulls and limbs presented a horrible spectacle. They were shot in all imaginable parts of the body and one poor fellow had been shot in the back of the head and the ball came out of his eyeball and the organ was hanging by a shred of kind and blood running down his cheek.
                        Pierre

DEFENSE OF BATTERY ROBINETT BY THE OHIO BRIGADE. BATTLE OF CORINTH, MISS., OCTOBER 4TH, 1862.
Sketched by D. Auld, 43d O. V. I.

43d O. V. I.
Changing front forward on 1st Co., crushing the right flank of the Confederate columns.

63d O. V. I.
Being cut to pieces but holding their line.

27th O. V. I.
Capturing flag of 9th Texas.

39th O. V. I. In reserve.

13

Camp near Corinth Miss.
Headquarters 39th Ohio Oct. 14th 62

My dear mother,

As you have no doubt heard of the big fight we have had here perhaps you have been anxious to hear that I am all right. I wrote you last at Rhenzi. I believe for s0me time before and ever since that time we have been continuously on the march. I dated my last letter at Head Qtrs. Of the 26th Ill., but a day after I wrote, I was transferred as I anticipated I would be back to the 39th and am once more at home. I left Rhenzi with the 39th on the 1st Oct.(crossed Out) 29th Sept.. That night we encamped within five miles of Corinth. The next afternoon I went into Corinth to see after some four men that had been left there intending to return to camp the next day. In the morning however I found that the regiment had orders to move and had left for I knew not where. I had plenty to do however in Corinth for the combined forces of Earl Van Dorn & John Villipigue were on the way to Corinth determined to make a grand effort for its capture.

On the afternoon of Friday their advance forces began to meet with ours, who were gradually driven in towards the town. The wounded then began to arrive and the large depot filled with them and also the two hotels in the place. Among the wounded were two of our generals- viz- Hageman and Oglesby- the former I saw breath his last in the evening. Gen, Oglesby was alive when I last heard of him. Towards evening the fighting got quite close to us, and the cannonading and musketry was too evident to be very an living, particularly as it was evident that we were getting the worse of the fight.

I could see the Rebs just outside of our works and our massed columns rushing forward to meet them with flags flying and drums beating. The cheers of our men and of the Rebels were distantly heard as either one or the other made a successful charge. Night brought an end to the contest for the present. We had nothing over which we could be jubilant, all put rather despaired here, as they gathered in crowds about the Hospital and other parts of the town narrating the incidents of the day and anticipating those of the morrow. All were serious for they knew that tomorrow would be the decisive battle and without we succeeded better than we had to day, we would be badly whipped and prisoners or worse the next night.

I had been working very hard all the afternoon and evening attending to the wounded of whom there were many hundreds and put us almost used up. About midnight with a couple of friends I went to a private house to get a nap, for I knew I should have to work hard the next day. The next morning at four O'clock we were awoke by the heavy booming of cannon and immediately it became evident that the town was being shelled by the enemy.

It was a little before daybreak and we sat the window a few minutes looking at the firing before going downtown. It was a most grand sight.

For some little time their guns were not answered by ours, but then our guns got into position. Their shells would come over us with a most unearthly whiz, peculiar for them, and them burst with a terrible explosion. Several come most uncomfortably near our heads and we would encroach to avoid them. Several buildings in town were struck. The Hotel (turned into a Hospital) to which we were going, was struck a few minutes before we reached there by a shell, the victims was stretched across the doorway when the shell entered. Mangled and dead, many were wounded. The other hospital was also struck by a shell.

Our batteries had now however, it having become day light, silenced the Rebel battery and our infantry had taken possession of the guns. Some of the wounded had the precious night been removed a little way past town. There was a hill there until about 8 O'clock, I suppose (though I haven't a very definite Idea of the time) and then the cannonading on our side began. The enemy had only one battery and that had been taken by us.

It is supposed the enemy numbered something like 40,000 like all events it was their grand army of the West. The combined force of Genl. Price, Van Dorn & Villepigue, which has been forming here for so long a time and was the pride of the Rebels. We had nothing like that numbers of men but possessed the advantage of artillery. The battle about nine O'clock became most terrific.

The cannons were blazing all on our right and left was a most continuous roar. The musketry crack could be hear very close wherein the noise of the cannon allowed it, and we could see the Rebels swarming in all around us and making the most desperate charge in solid columns, while our cannon balls were fairly make them dance as they ploughed their ranks and whole companies seemed to go down together. The firing kept getting closer, the enemy were in the town, and got into General Rosecrans quarters, the cavalry was rushing from one side of town to another, commissary trains were on the move to a place of safety and everywhere was the most intense excitement.

The firing seemed to be redoubled in intensity, the artillery was perfectly awful, and again I rode very near to our fighting lines, and the ground seemed to almost tremble. The result seemed to tremble in the balance, every horse in town seemed to be on the run and it looked like a prairie.

We received an order from the Genl. Saying that we must remove our hospital farther out of town, and feeling rather sad we began to comply, but had hardly started to do so when we received another order saying- the enemy had been repulsed, the hospital safe in its present position, we were victorious, the Rebels were running and now I suppose The fight ended about noon Saturday Oct. 8th. It was not known then that the enemy had retired finally. I was not aware till then of the position of the 39th. It had not been actively in the fight but was held as a reserve and when I found them they were drawn up in double line of battle expecting the enemy every moment.

We now held the ground for a long distance which had been in possession of the enemy and their dead and wounded were then inside our lines. Our Col. Was thrown from his horse at the first volley and very severely injured about his head, he went home this morning. We had but a few of the 39th killed and wounded.

As soon as the enemy was known to have retreated a friend and myself took an ambulance and went on the battlefield after the wounded. There were awful sights, the dead and the wounded, friends and enemies, mangled and them in the most invaluably shape, some without heads, others armless or with legs torn off, others were entirely torn into. There were secish who bore the marks of cannon balls. Our men were killed by the muskets.

The wounded were almost without numbers in heaps around the field for two or three miles. The Rebels casualties of from 6 to 8000 killed and wounded. It certainly amounts to that for I saw myself almost many number of them. That was a day of great excitement and I shall not soon forget it. The next day I was glad to get orders to join the Reg. which was going in pursuit of Price fleeing forces. About 8 A.M.

159

Sunday Oct. 15th we all started in pursuit. There was a division or two ahead of us in the pursuit of a different road. We left everything in the shape of baggage. The men had neither tents, knapsacks, or blanket, not a single thing in addition.

We were yet. We were victorious after a fleeing enemy and didn't care for a little inconvenience.   For about the first two miles of our march we were going over the battlefield of the two proceeding days. Another surgeon and myself rode into the woods and at nearly every step our horses would snort at the dead and mangled body of secish soldiers, splintered trees, fragments of shells, torn and bloody clothing, etc- etc were proof of a hard fought battle.

Wed. kept on our march and in a few hours evidence signed of Prices hasty flight. Tents, hams. Wagons, flour, cooking utensils, camp stool, ammunition wagons, caissons, etc. etc. was turned along the road in utter confusion. Hospitals filled with stash, Rebel surgeons having been left in charge were at intervals in the work. The surgeons were friendly and talkative I divided a batch of papers which I had just received from Jed with one of them. In one of the hospitals were three wounded, Rebel Col. Two of them had a leg amputated. We acknowledge a dreadful whipping, they could not object.

In a little while we met a body of about 300 men sent in by Genl. Price under a Col. With a flag of truce to bury the dead. The number sent shows he had a realizing sense of his loss. For a week we marched in pursuit, tired, hungry, & dusty. For many as 24 hours I had nothing in the world to eat but hard crackers. We would lie down in our blankets, supported at nine o'clock and about midnight be again on the march.

I never thought I could be so dirty as I was on that trip. It hadn't rained for weeks. Thousands had just traveled over the road and the dust was awful, still we plodded on, hot, hungry, and tired. I was nearly exhausted and just as if I could hardly sit on my horse an hour longer. I did not take off my boots, fairly the trip of a week, and in addition to having our rest wholly broken up, we could get nothing to eat but hard crackers & pork, while hardly during the day would we

160

stop long enough to fry the Pork, so we had to subsist on crackers, as all were too tired at night to try to cook anything.

On Friday after we started we had a rain storm. We were on our way back, and the rear guard to along train. It poured in torrents for hours, and we all got soaked to the skin. The wagons got stuck in the mud, and for an hour at a time we would stand by drenched to the skin and shivering with the cold. I don't know how it was, but I got through it alive.

And Sunday we got back to Corinth, passed in review before Rosecrans and are now recuperating in camp once more. Old soldiers say that is the hardest march they have taken yet. I certainly can't since anything worse.

I received your last letter, directed to the 26th Ill. Yesterday and also one from Jed with some papers. Please tell him that I take great pleasure reading the papers which he sends. I suppose you are at Newington and will direct this accordingly. My direction is so as referred Regt 39th Ohio etc. I would like much to be in H. a few days-so Jed sends papers quite regularly, so you need not trouble yourself about it. How is Jack, I have been intending to write him but have had no time, Yet. It seems like being in a first-class hotel on the most extravagant scale, just to be in camp to sleep in a tent, and have the privilege of washing one's face, brushing one's teeth and having a good dinner. Give my love Anna & Jed & the little ones. I will write Jed soon.

Your affectionate son,
Pierre

I will try to send you a paper containing a letter concerning the fight & I would like to have it preserved.

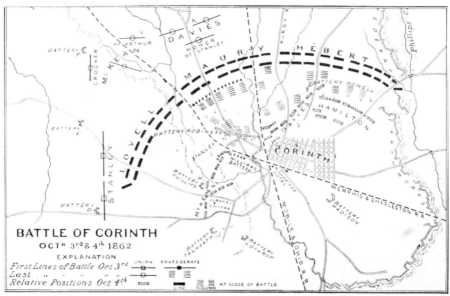

BATTLE OF CORINTH
OCTⁿ 3ʳᵈ & 4ᵗʰ 1862
EXPLANATION
First Lines of Battle Oct. 3ʳᵈ
Last " " " "
Relative Positions Oct. 4ᵗʰ

REVISED AS TO POSITIONS OF THE OHIO BRIGADE BY MAJ. CHAS. H. SMITH AND DAVID AULD.

Corinth Miss. Nov. 5ᵗʰ 1862

My Dear Mother,

Your two letters were received, the last one Yesterday. I was very sorry to hear that you were so unfortunate as to have the varioloid brought into the house and truly necessarily confined to it. I sincerely hope that nothing more serious will occur than a few wearisome days without your customary walks and society. I feel decidedly lonely at present myself and it happens in this way.

We had been here in Corinth about three weeks and as there was a chance of our remaining some time. We had floored over our tents, built brick chimneys, dug drains and made all things both comfortable and stylish for camp life. But alas for our expectations we had hardly got fine before we got orders to March. I was suffering at the time and had been for several days before with an inflammation in the side of my face and ear which totally incapacitated me for duty. Accordingly, I determined to remain, moreover the morning the Reg. started north (Sunday last) I received an order detailing me, with another surgeon to take charge of the Division Hospital during the absence of the troops, so here I am. My face has got well, and I would like very much now to be on the march but can't leave. It is quite lonely to be without the Reg. I am sorry you found Jed in his unusually "hard up condition." I had hoped with you that after the last ----------- he would be at least beyond want.

In regard to my clothes you can make what selections you deem best. I don't remember exactly what I have got. I brought in with me when I left home a fine thick pair of gray pants and vest. I have never taken them. I have never taken them out of my vales, neither shall I as long as I stay in the army. I wish very much I could get them to Jed. If the express cost would not be too exorbitant I would send them, at all events I will enquire how much it will cost. And perhaps send them.

In regard to your proposition for a horse, it seems to me that $150.00 is too much to give for a horse for his use, I were to buy a horse that he would spoil in a very short time. Again, I don't see why others should own and he use him, better give him the horse out & out as it would be exactly as will for us and certainly much pleasant for him to be using his own beast. Supposing I should ever want a horse for my business, such as one as could be suitable for farm work would not do for me.

In regard to my finances they stand as follows. Since I have been in the Army. I have recd' from the government pay from July 5th to Aug. 31st -$233.00 of this sum I have now a little more the $100.00 left, and government owes me now something over $250.00. I did not intent to draw any more pay until my present stock was out, and it may last for a couple of months. Yet in the case I could draw $500.00. It is difficult to get money home. The only safe way is to send by some reliable person who is going. The express will not quartermaster it, and it is not safe to send a large sum from here in a letter.

I have only been four months as yet in the army. So I think it best not to make any calculations as yet about it. Courtship and marriage am

163

not in my line of business just now. I had always supposed your carryovers to ones marrying with nothing to live on, and consequently you project of my employing my time in the country and managing as I would have hardly anything else to do struck me as rather rich. A poverty stricken professional man is, I think, the sadist of all and the most pitiful. I am sorry for Delran, he was made a great mistake doubtless and I think he is fully aware of it and sorry for it.

The medicines that I gave you for cons tininess our Sulphur and nut veronica, the latter you took at night. Were there three different kinds? I think not but am not certain. Wrote Jack a long letter some days since, as I had not written him for a long time. I directed to No. 11 Academy St. was that right.

I suppose our weather is somewhat different. Yours just now. I am sitting in my tent without any fire, the wind blowing in and it is quite comfortably warm. For a couple of days sometime ago it was nasty cold, the water froze one night in our tents, and in the morning, I found about an inch of snow on the ground. I came to the conclusion that the "Sunny" South was a myth and thought we would have to winter up north to keep warm. Now however the days are quite warm often uncomfortably so. The nights are cool and a fire necessary for comfort.

Where we shall remain during the winter, or whether we shall march I can't say. It probably depends somewhat on the success of this expedition that has just gone off. I expect we will stay in or about Corinth, though many think we will get to Vicksburg or Mobile, I should very much like to get in some new quarter of Mississippi. I expect the Reg. Back, or that we will be ordered to it in about a week. Everything is covered with dust here, it not having rained for nearly a month. It is impossible to keep anything like clean. I hope to hear in your next that you are well and out of your jail. Mrs. Brown I trust will recover.

Your affectionate Son,

Pierre

Camp near Lagrange Tenn.
Nov. 17, 1862

My dear mother,

Yours was duly received on yesterday and I take occasion to answer it to-day. Again, our position is changed and this time we are in Tenn. Only across the lines however but a short distance from Miss. We had expected to go into winter quarters at Corinth, accordingly we by tearing down a few houses, we procured boards enough to floor over our tents and make things very comfortable. The Col. Had a large brick fire place built in the rear of his tent and we were accustomed to being very luxurious, but alas! For all plans in the army the regiment was ordered off.

When I wrote last I was still at Corinth, being ordered to remain in charge of the hospital there and not knowing whether I should remain there for the Reg or I should go to it. The day after I wrote you however, I received an order to rejoin the Reg. at Grand Junction Tenn. Which I was very glad to do. Took the cars to Jackson Tenn. A place of considerable size and very pretty. We got there at noon and remained until the next morning where we took the cars for Grand Junction, then sending for ambulances we reached the regiment that evening. We remained there two or three days and then moved day before yesterday to our present camping ground.

Our brigade is now the very advance of our army of our army In this direction. Nothing being between us and the Rebels who are supposed to be some 40,000 or 50,000 strong about 20 mile from here. So indeed it was stated by a deserter who came into our camp last night. I was very glad in a paper which I received from Jed to learn that they Navy Yard was going to be located at New London. It is pleasant to think that N.L. may have been designated for a place of some importance after all I sincerely hope it is so. Probably may now be worth something, and town hill lots be as valuable as they were ten years ago.

I can hardly imagine here that is near Dec. The weather is delightfully warm, and It takes but very little execution to bring out the preparation. Over coat are never put on except perhaps in the evening and one less about out of doors is if it were summer. A day or two since I saw a Rose Bush just budding in a Yard of a secesh, all this while you in U.S. an probably having cutting north winds., had frozen ground etc. I do not envy you your weather. I should not have supposed you would have had so much trouble about the trunk any man with strong fingers can open it. I do not understand what Jed means by saying that the Gray shirt not answer at all . If it is not strong or thick enough I have nothing in the trunk or elsewhere that is.

I am very glad you have been so fortunate in you small pox adventure. I think the family have a good teal to congratulate themselves in a getting off so cheaply. I had a letter from Jack the other day. He said nothing about his business, so I suppose it continued the same. I am glad he is ----- of -----winter clothes. McClellan's removal took us out here a good deal by surprise, at the same time we were not sorry, we feel wishing at least to run the risk of getting someone who will put things through in a somewhat livelier style. We are all full glad that we have . The at last got clear of Corinth. There is no probability that we will get back there again for a long time, If ever.

Lagrange is a very pretty place indeed. I went over there yesterday. The houses are well built and tasty. The place abundant in trees. It is probably of 7 or 8000 inhabitants, will a laid out, has a large University there. It has not that very old or poor appearance that most southern towns have, that I have been in. But most of them loo as neat thrifty and will to do as our New England towns. About a week ago I had a severe attack of chills and fever which confined me to my bed for two or three days. I have got will over that and am now all right again. I have, I think been very fortunate as regards to my health out here, having with that exception not been sick again.

> With much love,
> Your affectionate son,
> Pierre

Columbus Ohio,
House of representatives Dec. 12th 62

My Dear Mother

You will doubtless be greatly surprised at the date of my letter and wonder what has brought me out of Rebellion, and so comparatively near home. Perhaps also you will be none the less taken by surprise when I tell you the reason of my having left the Army of the Miss. And coming here which I will proceed to do. For some time I have reached dissatisfied with the contract service in which you know I have been, from the fact that I could not fuel myself settled with any regiment though I have been by far the greater part of the time with the 39th . Yet I would like at any time to be transferred, and in fact the last three weeks I was in that service. I did duty with the 27th Ohio having been transferred to it. More over Contract Surgeons were gradually being replaced by regular assistants so that I was in a position to have my contract awarded at any time. The medical director saw fit, or an assistant should be appointed from the State of Ohio to take my place.

In view of these facts I made up my mind to break up my contract, which I did on the 1st Dec., come on to Ohio, try to pass the examination before the medical board of examiners for commissioning Asst. Surg., and if possible be commissioned to the 39th Ohio. In all this I have succeeded admirably, and in a day or two will receive my commission from the Governor Tod, as Asst. Surg., with rank of Captain. The written examination came off yesterday afternoon, and the oral one this morning I am happy to say I got through both all right. I had very complimentary letters from the Col. Of the 39th asking that I might be ordered to his regiment, and also from the Medical Director and our Division Surgeon. I am writing in the House of Representatives of the State Capital at the desk of probably some eventual proponent of laws.

One examination was held here, and it is now just over, and as I had not written you for some time and did not wish to say anything about my leaving Miss. Till I had passed the examination. I thought I would take the first opportunity of letting you know of the circumstances. I left the army on the 1st Dec. about 7 miles south of Holly Springs and but a few miles from the Tallahatchie's River, which if you had the papers you will see that it was heavily fortified, and a fight was excepted then. Our regiment with two or three others made a reconnaissance to the river the day before I left, and we had quite a skirmish with the enemy. I reached Cincinnati Thursday night, remained there until Monday last when I came to Columbus, I shall leave here the latter part of the week, stop in Cincinnati a day or two to get some things for the regiment and then return to the army.

I am very sorry not to be able to come east, but it is impossible though It seems comparatively speaking so near home, but I could not go home before examination, not having time and now I have orders immediately to rejoin the regiment. So, it must be put for some time to come. You said you did not anticipate seeing me for a year. I trust by the end of that time I will be able to get home. The direction will be as before for my letters only instead of "2nd Division" write "Ross Division" The no. of our division having been changed. We are in Gen. Grants army so when you see its movements recorded in the papers you may know that my regiment is along. I do not suppose we can get much farther South this winter, as the rainy season seems to have begun, and the roads when I left were being badly cut up. The railroad bridges have also been all burnt by the Rebels and it will take some time to replace them.

It is rather odd that I should receive a commission from the State of Ohio. I have certainly got out of my bearings a good deal, but I have made some good friends out here and while I remain in the army proper to stay where I am. I have not heard from you for some time but suppose this is a letter for me at the regiment. I hope you will approve what I have done, the course seemed to me the best one I could purpose, it is pleasant to have a commission.

> Your affectionate son,
> Pierre

Columbus Ky. Dec. 30th 1862
Dear Jed,

A longtime since, I received a letter from you. The answer to which has been unavoidably delayed until the present time., and now much to my disgust I have considerable more lonesome than is pleasant. I suppose you have heard through mother of my having gone to Ohio, passed an examination and got a commission and appointment to the 39th. I am very much pleased with the issue of the affair. I had been thinking for some time that I should have to leave the contract service and perhaps come home, for although the Col. Wished me very much to go to Ohio and obtain the position of Asst. Surg. Of the Reg. but there was no opening which I could fill as the regular asst., since there had been one commission to fill the place that I was occupying as contract asst. and when he came I should have to leave. But fortunately for me our surgeon was transferred at the Cols. Request to a German Regiment (he the surgeon was a German) there was then a position to fill his place, and I was strongly recommended for the vacancy thus created and I obtained it. The pay is now $113.00 per month, not quite as much as I have been received, but still I guess I can live on it.

I left the regiment on the 1st Dec. reached Cincinnati on the 5th, remained till the 8th, then went to Columbus to the examination which took place on the 10th & 11th then returned to Cincinnati and remained there till the 20th, at the end of that time the 175.00 per month with which I left the Reg. had disappeared with the exception of about $10.00 and I considered it expedient to be moving back before I completely suspended. My transportation was allowed me both ways by the government and as I expected to makes all the connections I thought I could get through without any difficulties as regard to missing. I left Connecticut on Saturday and was in rout the following Friday before reaching Columbus Ky.

I disembarked there with $5.00 in my pocket hoping to meet the cars and go the rest of my journey immediately which was yet a good many hundred miles, but alas the villainous guerrillas had discomposed my plans by tearing up the Rail Road for some fifty miles. They were then within some few miles of the town in some fever and all sorts of numbers were flying about as to be an attack in the town; all the government stores were on the bank of the river, ready to be shipped at a moment's notice to Cairo and general excitement was in commons. To my dismay I was told by to quartermaster of transportation that the road would not be open for a week or two. What I was to do in the meantime having but $4.00 left after having paid for my nights lodging and breakfast bill, was a stunning question for me. Something must be done, and I wandered about for a long time hoping to meet with someone too good to be true, and I didn't credit it.

Holiday work has not been a very brilliant in for me, you can well believe. Christmas, I spent coming down the Ohio, and New Year's I suppose must be passed in this miserable hole. When I left Cincinnati, I expected to be with the Reg. by Christmas, and am doomed to be woefully disappointed. Uncle Sam owes me a lot, but it can't be got at present. Under all the circumstances I might just as will have taken a trip to Cincinnati, when I shall have another opportunity now I have no idea, a commission is not so easy thrown our as a contract. I have now no desire to leave the service, and am very well satisfied - that is if I can ever reach the Reg. again. It is of course much pleasanter to be commissioned not only because one cannot be ordered in that case to any other Reg. but the rank (Captain) is more real and natural on a perfectly equal footing with all the other asst. Surg. In the army, of which by the way, I shouldn't wonder I was about the youngest. Thou that I have met an elderly and married man mostly none as young as myself.

I wish I could enjoy the sledding which you or rather the Hartforders and I suppose now reveling in. It is almost impossible for me to believe that it can be winter. So different it is from anything I have experienced in these months before. It is warm now here as it is in Hartford on most June days. I have not worn an overcoat since I have been here, and in the middle of the day hardly need a fire. I think more over it is warmer here now than is usual at this time of year.

Please excuse the poor appearance of this letter: writing on one's knee with a poor pen and a half dozen people talking is neither conducive to legible penmanship or to an interesting letter. If I am not in time to wish you a merry Christmas I wish a pleasant New Year. I hope to have the pleasure of reading some Hartford Papers when I get to the Reg. with much love to Anna and the Children.

Your affectionate brother, Pierre

P.S. When you write (which I hope you will do soon) direct instead of 2nd Division-Ross Div. in other respects the same

Head Qrs. 39th O.V.I
Camp near Corinth Miss.
Feb. 23rd 1863

Dear Jed.,

You still owe me a long letter, but supposing as a matter of course you will write me twice in return. I send you a few lines to accompany the enclosed "Cartes" I had them taken a few days since, and send them now for fear that they will all go to my friends in the Regiment before I can send any home so take the first opportunity. Corinth is not prolific in artists and these will not compare very favorably with those taken in the States but I send you the best I can.

There is nothing new here. I believe my last to you was dated at Columbus. I managed to reach my Reg. finally, after much tribulation and walking some eight miles through the swamp. I found them in Corinth , having just returned from a long and very hard march getting into a fight and capturing from Forrest's Cavalry. Some four hundred horses and as many prisoners. The excitement of this affair I missed though I got a horse from the spoils, which I now ride.

We shall probably have to stay in Corinth for some time to come, as a garrison to the place, though I wish it were otherwise, and I could see some more active service. Town has been very strongly fortified since the battle here and a few thousand men are considered capable of holding it against a larger force. We recd. Orders to be ready at a moment's notice to start for Memphis, but after the rest of our division had gone the order as far as our brigade was concerned was countermanded, and here we remained. SO probably we will not be engaged in the affairs at Vicksburg. Everything is quite here, Standard rumors now and then they find they find their way through camps, but they are no longer regarded. A foraging trip made into the country for a few days at a time comprise our only movement, however there is little to do.

This camp life is a terribly lazy one, nothing in the work to do but to read, ride and smoke. We have very few sick. In fact our Reg. has always been noted as bringing the heal think in the division, and entering a lighten sick list, though no longer names of men than any other in the Western Service.

For the last three weeks I have been in charge of the Small Pox Hospital at this post, a day or two since I worked lived and appointed Post Surgeon. It is regarded as a very good position though I preferred being with the regard manager to get the order changed, though a nice house is provided to me in town if I took the position. When in charge of the Small Pox Hospital I had a few quarters in what was formally the "Corinth Female Seminary" a large and handsome brick building with fine grounds & my hospital bring in a house outside the breast works.

On my return to the Reg. after my trip to Cincinnati. I found a short letter from you, wondering at my dilemma. You must have recd. Shortly after a long letter from Columbus. I have written Tyler, Dr. jack & Jacob but have not as yet have anything hardly one. Please stir this up. I have not been able to learn whether or not the Nay Jaida is definitely fixed me in your next. How does the farm pay now. I wish you had heard the opportunity of getting horses that I have had lately are right fine animals too. I got back to the Reg. about the 10th Jan., having left it on 1st Dec. if I had intended to have been absent so long I certainly should have come up to New England. I suppose you have enjoyed fine sleeping this winter. The grass has been green here all winter, and we can often see roses in bloom in the jugs.

Some days have quite cold though none of the water has frozen, more than a ¼ of an inch, while most of them have been almost too warm for exception

Please Kiss the children.
Yesterday was Washington's Birthday - was the occasion of celebrated speechifying and by drum

> Yours affectionate Brother,
> Pierre

Head Qtrs. 39th O.V.I. Corinth Miss.
March 21st ,1863

My dear mother,

Your note was recd. Evening before last, and by the same mail one from Jack and also a couple of papers from Jed. Quite a windfall for me. You have no idea how pleasant it is to receive such out here in the wilderness. As you will note we are still at Corinth and her there are all the indications of our staying, and the boys have built themselves log cabins or houses to live in. They bring cooler in summer and are much dryer than are the tents. The Major and I who occupy the same tent and going to have one built for our tent in a few days as our tent leaks badly.

We have been having some very heavy rains and many a night I have been soaked with rain pouring down on my face and blankets, not a pleasant intrusion into ones dreams, and in days something I should certainly have regarded it as the five runner of almost certain death, but now I merely draw my rubber blanket over me and sleep quietly through the rain and never yet have had even a cod to remind me of the incident, however it might be regarded not to sleep in the rain and accordingly we are going to change when we can do it at well or not. It certainly seems very odd to have come down to a log cabin, but they are really quite luxurious in our pursuit I take of affairs.

To prove to you I am well, hearty, and living well, let me tell you that I was weighed the other day and I brought the notch up to 140 lbs. manly 15 lbs. more than I ever weight before. I sent you my photograph an week or two since, if you have not received it I will send you another, as you did not mention it in your letter. I also sent one to Jed which I have not heard from yet. I hope Jack will manage to get back to N.L. When he does I shall not suppose you have lately thought of summer in new England, but her we have had some very warm weather.

Early in this month the thermometer was up to 104 in the sun and over 80 in the shade. As that very, time I received a letter from Jack say they were just having the heaviest snow storm of the season- quite a contrast. Here the apple and peach trees are in full bloom, and the grapes grew as fat it has been all winter. I dread a long hot summer here, and hope we shall before long move from the suburbs of Corinth into some fresher locality, as this has been the camping of thousands and thousands of troops for the last 12 months-both Rebels and Union- you can imagine, having been the scene of a most engaging battle, and the burying place of thousands of soldiers, horses, and mules that it is not a delectable place for a summer residence, but of course the call rests with the powers that be.

Our regiment is and always has been remarkably healthy and we number over 750 men for duty, a larger number than any other can show in this army. Affairs at Vicksburg appear to be advancing but you a probably get later news the we do here though the Cincinnati and St. Louis papers.

We have just sent out an expedition into the country for things for our mess. We got 4 dozen chickens, eggs Etc. and are now living light. We have paid for potatoes $4.50 per bushel-butter 60 cts. Per pint, but there are sutler prices who charge what they please. There is no reason for such prices, for when the commissary has the articles we get them quite reasonably.

The chitters appear to be endeavoring to create all the trouble possible. I wish, with advantage to Iourssey pecurally we could turn them out, and the men for them disadvantage, it would be the better. We are now permanently detached from our division and now you will address:

> 39th Reg. Ohio Vol. Inf.
> Fullers Brigade
> Corinth Miss.
> Your Affectinate,
> Pierre

Head Qus. 39th O.V.I Corinth Miss.
April 9th, 1863

My Dear Mother,

Yours, was recd. Last evening acknowledging the receipt of my picture etc. We are remarkably fortunate in regard to our letters reaching their proper destination. I believe most of them have as yet was carried through. I know of many Officers here, whose letters have done so. I am now living in a house, a log one to be sure, which of course city folks would turn up their noses at, but we think it very comfortable, not to say luxurious and as to style it surpasses anything in this neighborhood. So, we envy nobody's granite residences and spurns anything in the shape of a house not made of logs. It sheds the rain and protects us from the sun which is all that is regarded in this country as essential.

A secish saw mill furnished the lumber for our floors and other necessary fixtures, such as tables and bunks to sleep on. We have a porch extending in front some six or eight feet and our house presents a very attractive cozy appearance. We are going to turf it amount and set out trees and then I should like my friends in the east to come out and look at us.

Day before yesterday there was a celebration here of the battle of Shiloh, the through command of Infantry, Cavalry and Artillery was out and presented a very fine appearance of war torn virtues. An oration was delivered by Col. Bane, who lost his right arm in the battle. A fine band played, and we popped in river before Gen. Dodge, who is in command at this post. There is to be a raid, it is said, down south by a couple of brigades from this command, with or not our brigade will be one of them is in doubt. I rather hope we will go for the sake of a little excitement for one gets quite tired of camp life with hardly nothing to do.

The weather is getting quite warm and the dust very plenty, and this Summer we I expect will be a rather hard one, more do than last when we were encamped near in the woods, out of the dust. And where trees were plenty. But we came here in January, not expecting to remain but a short time and the greater part of the trees were cut down for fire wood.

Adeline Imlay, I suppose is now a young lady of just about the interesting age. I used to think that was when she was about eight years old, but doubtful I should alter my opinion if I were to see her now. As I am her Uncle I suppose I can send my love to the Young lady of sweet sixteen without impropriety. I would like to see her if she has a photograph of herself, please ask her to send it to me.

I certain by hope Jack will find something to do in N.L. (New London) when I have you. When I heard you were there this May late then I thought there was a great probability of it. The chances seems to be less now but I have no doubt he will finally get back there and then I shall be glad to hear of you going to house Kenkins again, but as things are at present- I do not see how you can be much better find.

I received a long letter from Jed a Fridays mail. He tells me of the change in his family arrangements and appraised my confidant of his future prospects- they are a little unlooping" as you say. Though I cannot say but that they are perfectly warranted. I have seen his

176

"fondest hopes decay" I often that I am not quite so certain as he appears to be in regard to these free feelings. He says that he desired $600.00 and with that seems he thinks he will be impending gain in that case. I wish most hastily you could let him hear it, and if give for your orphan children. So, as far as I am concerned I am willing to be left out of consideration. He says he has had between $5000 & 6000 and offers .06 pr. Ct. on the $600, why not let him hear it as you would make an interest and where else a good security.

Refugees come in here every day with a pitiful story of hardships and want following afflictions and comfort. Surly the Rebellion cannot be endured much longer by the southerners, when every blessing man in the north is making money though he does grumble over a little tax as if the country is not worth it. I shall feel most heartily ashamed of Connecticut is she allows Tom Seymore(12) to be elected Gov. by set of miserable crave heartful copperheads. It is to be hopeful the constituents will take the most of that stripe, and make them fight, since they don't know how to act like men at home. You speak about sending me the N.Y Papers. I am much obliged, but we get the Cincinnati and Memphis papers, which contain all essential news of the N.Y papers and much fresher. If you will have sent your own dailies, I would like it much- I think you speak of having sent me Some N.Y. papers, I never received them. Jed said that he mailed me, Harpers Illustrated it would never reached me.

I am very glad I am not like Frank Perkins, at home daily doing nothing and I have no doubt he dislikes it as much as I should. I suppose after Billy's death, he feels obliged to his entering the army. You ask what I think about coming home? I can't say that as, yet I have thought anything about it. I don't think it is honorable for anyone to rejoin the circle when this is no special reason or his doing so, and I don't know of any one in a better position when he is in the army as a volunteer and his interests and his payments of fourteen suffers Somewhat in consequence but that is inevitable. For the present I think it better dispense thoughts of my return. I should certainly prefer to be gaining a practice and practice at home, but I am not losing any time here as many are who have entirely given up their profession to join the army. But it is getting almost too much to see what I am writing so I will close, with much love

> Your Affectionate Son,
> Pierre'

Monday April 20th ,1863,

I intended to have sent the fore going long ago. But did not have the opportunity. One now persists itself and I will avail myself of it. On the morning of the 14th our unusual preoccupied avocations were interrupted upon by receipt of an order to have all trains harnessed and the men ready to move. The enemy being a few miles off, of course all was busily and excitement for a time. Blankets were hurriedly rolled up and strapped in our saddles, and a few rations put in our haversacks. In a few minutes we got orders to form in line and move out and in less than 15 minutes from the receipt of the first order we were on the march. Artillery, Cavalry, and Infantry were all on the move.

You can hardly imagine the fine excitement of such a scattering. From a scene of Holiday Parade, but I can answer you it was intensely interesting, as the cavalry-1000 or more, strong galloped by us, the infantry cheering thousand, they are responding and the field pieces rumbling along with their six horses apiece. But after all the results of the march was nothing for we only went out about five miles and returned. Then had brisk skirmish and a few killed, but I was not the object though to follow them on the next morning the expedition which I have already spoken of started.

They numbered about 6,000 men and the object was to go to Florence on the Tenn. River about 60 miles east of here and destroy the bridges expanding across the river there, thus cutting off communications between Vicksburg and Chattanooga and preventing the transport of Rebel troops from one point to another in case of attacks. It is expected if our expedition is successful that then Rosecrans will advance from

Murfreesboro with his immense force, and then communications West being cut off. If they get away at all they will go East instead of reinforcing Vicksburg.

This expedition as I have said started of the 15th yesterday we heard from them. Gen. Dodge had met the Rebels about 30 miles from here, advantaged generally posted, he engaged them and with a loss of about 30 killed and wounded and our sides and a couple of company taken prisoners. They drove them 15 miles to Corinth- here the Rebels received reinforcements of 4,000 men and Gen. Dodge fell back to his trains, some two miles his rear. Then he sent a dispatch to here on ordering the Ohio Brigade to reinforce him immediately. We got an order about midnight and my reg. with the rest of the brigade started early this morning.

Much to my regrets had to remain in charge of the hospital and have remained with one or two Officers in a deserted camp lonely and whether our reg. will ever return of course we have but little idea. It seems a pity that just as we had very fine houses for our accommodation that we should be ordered to move, but such is war. We are about a mile from Corinth and have been expecting all day to receive orders to move inside the works. Having no fighting men here and only pickets and outposts having all been removed, a dozen guerrillas could capture our whole command.

All the baggage has been left here. Affairs are begun to look after what lively and perhaps we are now going to have such a peaceful summer after all. All the Corps that have been in Corinth for the last month have gone away, a few have come down from Jackson, Tenn. To take their place, but yet there are very few detailed here to resist an attack. Gen. Oglesby came in town this morning. Everything being boxed ready to be moved at any moment. It was with difficulty I could find anything to write on or with. We are very anxious to ascertain about the fight which is doubtless going on near, and also what's to be our destination. But as communications can be carried on with the telegraph or railroad, it is not expected we will know for some days. I shall go to the Reg. as soon as I possibly can.

Yours,
Pierre

We were to have been paid off today but it has now postponed

Corinth Miss. April 26th, 1863

My dear mother,

I do not know how I can better show my affection of the promptness
with which you answered my last, then by replying with the same
dispatch. I am now alone, in almost desolate Camp. But two or three
Officers and about fifty men remaining from the regiment, which
marched from here a week ago today into Atlanta to reinforce. Gen.
Dodge who sends them fighting the Rebels. I remained to take charge
of those sick in quarters, and hospitals whom it was necessary to leave
behind. In the meantime it is extremely, dull, the Camp in its presents
a notable contrast to its appearance when the brigade when with its
two or three thousand men- making quite a good sized town.

I have heard today that we can expect them back about a week. As the
weather has been very rainy since they left and they took neither tents
or baggage with them, I suppose I ought to congratulate myself that I
was or did to remain and what it my log house instead of sleeping on
the ground in the wet. The two papers which you sent me were duly
received. I hope M.B. will succeed in his efforts for the Navy Yard,
certainly he has as much at stake as any one, and will no doubt will
work heartily for it, but you have a very powerful antagonist in Penn.
I am sorry you see no more to encourage you in Jed's affairs. I can't
pretend to judge of certainty of his expectations from his own
arrangements as regards my advancing him the money he desires. I
haven't got it.

Although I have been in the service about ten months, I have not
received pay as yet but five. I have enough however for my wants out

here, and am perfectly willing Uncle Sam should keep it for the present as I consider him a very safe banker. You seem to want to know something of my associates here, my mess is composed of five besides myself. The Col.-Lt Col. Major- Surgeon and adjutant of them the first four are all graduates of Literary College (the Col. And Surgeon are from Dartmouth (College) and are professional men. Prefect gentleman and first-rate Society. I doubt if it were possible to find in the service a regiment whose field Officers are of a better class than ours. They are men whose society would be an acquisition at home, and not like those whom one is an Officer necessary thrown in the army and therefore endured I congratulated myself in being so fortunate in companions.

No reading matters as relates to medicine- I am also favored in comparison with the great majority of Reg. as we have quite a good surgeon. The greater part of our medical books, the Surgeon and myself obtained from the deserted, medicines from two or three remaining southerners M.Ds. and other literary productions are also not so scarce as night be anticipated-More, good-bad- and indifferent float around the camp and are present from one to the other as common property till read by all.

As the town of Corinth it is a dirty depleted place, with who one time there might have (have) been originally pretty and neat and home like long since crushed out of it by thousands of Soldiers- Rebel and Union- who have over-run it and apparently have emaciated one another in the endeavors to make it as uninviting as possible to thin successions. When the Rebels evacuated last spring they burnt a number of houses, and of course our men have no regard for the property left behind.

The town originally might have had a population of about 2000 and as a point of intersection of Charleston and Memphis, and Miss. Central, Mobile & Ohio R.R.s & has been of importance in a military point of view. There are hardly half a dozen of the original families here, the private homes are all taken as hospitals or used for some other gov. purpose. Everything that pertains to a pretty country town-such as trees, Strawberry-flowers and grass has long since departed. Then are a few pretty places however still left-used as the headquarters of General Officers.

There were two churches here, one of which is now converted into a prison, the other into a magazine and arsenal- thou hotels – one retains its former character, the other is a hospital. The stores which there were a goodly number are occupied as sutler shops. There is not a fine building in the place if I except perhaps the female seminary-now a hospital, when as I wrote you, I was working for some little time, it and one of the churches are the only brick buildings here.

I can hardly say within the town was regularly laid out. At all events, now streets are where ever they have been found convenient. The whole town is encircled with a formidable earth breastwork and with many minor works- the whole mounting about 100 heavy guns, while for 5 or 6 miles in every direction are the fortifications, rifle pits- and embankments of Beauregard defenses and of our forces to capture the place. The fires woods are all cut down about us for miles, making a formidable abatis works of a will approach of the enemy. Graves of these fallen in battle or overcome by disease are in profusion everywhere around and high mounds when numbers have been entwined together show where the bullets rained the thickest.

No fact Corinth is not attractive place, the bottom falls out of the roads in winter and the dust is knee deep in summer and it is here to choose which is pleasanter. Our picket lines are so contracted here lately that rides over the bartered tracks are getting quite monotonous and seldom go out of camp. I am glad to hear you intend a trip to N.Y. I certainly hope you will go and stay as long as you please, regardless of a few dollars expend more or less. I do not know of anyone who has a better right to do so than yourself, and think all would be glad if you indulge in a change of life for as lone a time as would be agreeable. If you could pay a visit to Anna so much better, though as you say it is almost too long a trip for you to take alone.

Your affectionate Son
Pierre,
As you somewhat jumbled the last address, I will give it to you now in full,   Asst. Surg. 39th Reg. Ohio. Vol. , Fullers Brigade, Corinth Miss.

Head Qtrs., 39th O.V.I
May 10th, 1863

My Dear Mother,

I have been expecting letters for several days from some one of my correspondents, but not having as yet been the happy receipt of any. I will in a rather blue mood write you, my reliable correspondent. We are under marching orders- or rather should say riding orders for we go by rail-for Memphis Tenn. I will not put this in the mail until we are about starting in order that you may know that we have really gone. We received orders this morning to be ready to move at a moment's notice and are prepared accordingly- so if you receive this letter you may know that we have left Corinth. The presumption is that we are to take the place at Memphis of troops who have been ordered to some other point- but the fact is we don't know anything about it.

Military life is very uncertain, we had anticipated remaining here for the rest of the summer, when suddenly we are ordered to move at any moment to no-body knows when. We have a very pleasant camp here comfortable houses and are rather both to leave them. If we once get out of Corinth. I hope we will never return. I wrote you some day since-an answer to which letter I have not yet recd.-saying that I was left in almost deserted Camp. The Reg. returned some few days after. They went rite near the Alabama on a Rail which was very destructive to the enemy's possession in that part of the Country. Hundreds of head of stock was taken, and numerous houses burnt out property of all kinds destroyed among the buildings burnt was the "Alabama Military Institute" and fine residences of the Ardent scesh.

Thousands of darkies came streaming back with our forces-of all sizes of sexes eager to be free, and after all I very much doubt if they were being as comfortable and as happy as in their plantation houses. But they have an idea that within the lines of our any flow milk and honey, and that thing advert will be warmly welcomed by every Northern Soldier. I do not know how many there are in and about Corinth- certainty. Many thousands. An effort is being made to form a regiment of them. I witnessed them drilling the other day, it is to say the least-capable of great improvement. We are here ineludibly anxious about the fighting going on in Virginia. The news in regard to which we are just receiving.

All feel that it will be awfully depressing if we whipped there again and pray that Hooker may escape the name that seems to have hether to hung over the Army of the Potomac. The news from Vicksburg seem to be very promising of good results to our side. Rosecrans in east Tenn. Is also regarded as soon whip the Rebels, whenever he chooses to open the ball. We have great confidence in Rosecrans under whom we served some months and fought and concurred in two battles. I am well and healthy and while I remain so am glad to be in the field. The direction of my letters need not be altered.

> Hope to hear from you soon,
> Your affectionate son,
> Pierre

May 11th Sunday morning

We leave this morning at 8 A.M.

Head Qtrs. 39th O.V.I.
Memphis Tenn.
May 17th 1863,

My dear mother,

I recd. Yours yesterday last Sunday I wrote you that we were under marching orders. Four Companies of my Regiment left on Sunday evening for Memphis with the Lt. Col McDowell and myself went, leaving the other field and staff Officers to come on with the remainder of the Reg. in a couple of days. We left Corinth about 6 O'clock in the afternoon May 12. The train carrying besides our four companies, a company of artillery with all their guns, horses, wagons etc.   A freight car was the best accommodation we could obtain for ourselves, on the floor if which we slept very comfortably that night- for I have got used to hard beds- rolled up in our blankets.

We reached Memphis about six O'clock the following morning. As we neared the city we passed numbers of very fine mansions with extended and handsome grounds belonging wealth and refinement- a very pleasing contrast with what I have been accustomed to us in the past of our country. Having disembarked a staff Officer of Gen. Feitch conducted us to our company grounds for the time. Near our camp was a very handsome house with extension and finely cultivated grounds for the lady and gents of which the Col. And Myself had the good fortune to be introduced and were cordially invited to make their house our headquarters till the rest of our Regiment arrived, as we were without tents and baggage. The offer was of course all the more thankfully received.

So the upside of the affair was that we became the inmates of one of the finest houses of Memphis. The gentleman was an old and wealthy resident of this city. The wife quite young and dashing, both very hospitable more on their account. I think than ours- a federal Officer in these times being not protected in a Southerners house. At any rate

I had the pleasure of sleeping for the first time in six months on a most luxurious bed, in an elegant furnished house. With hardly an exception all the residents sympathized with the south- their brothers and relatives all being in the Southern Army. The lady we stayed -for instance-had two brothers in the Secsh army and thought arousing neutrality of cousins was altogether Secsh, as was made very evident by conversing with her.

In a couple of days the reminder of our forces reached here, and we moved our camp, the former position being too contracted for our 750 men. We are now about ½ mile from the city in a most beautiful woods called "Prairie Grove" Since we have been here we have obtained new tents for the whole command and their snowy whiteness in this fine grove marks our encampment as pretty as can well be imagined.

The country around is very fine-naturally   rich and well cultivated. The land is finely diversified with hills and valleys and beautiful country residences of Southern Merchants and scattered about numerously. The rides of course very delightful quiet, different from Corinth. When I went our mainly because I thought it my duty to take exercise the city is quite handsome one of about 40,000 inhabitants and has been one of the greatest cotton markets of the south. King Cotton is distinct here now however yet good deal of businesses of various kinds is carried in and the streets were of a most busy appearance excluding like our Northern Cities. We felt rather sorry to leave our comfortable houses in Corinth, but after all I think I am about as well off in a tent, certainly I consider it no hardship to live in one most.

The weather delightful, it has not as yet got too warm for comfort here in the woods and in the morning or late in the afternoon riding is very pleasant. We were ordered here to take the place of the 4th Division, which has gone to Vicksburg, the presumption is that we are to remain some little time. I do not like the idea of giving away my clothes because they are almost all new and if clothing is anything like as high in the east as it is here out here. I would like to be spared the expense of starting over again in that line. I received a letter form Jack two or three days since, also one from Jed.

The market in town is a great luxury to us. We are now able to get many things that we had not seen since summer before last. We have a fine Cow which supplies us with all the milk we want. I give you an idea of prices here, let me tell you that milk sells for $1.00 per gallon- we are offered the other day without any encouragement on our part as we had not Idea of selling-$125.00 for our cow in gold. The joke of it is that we bought the ow when we were down in Miss on a march for $20.00 confederate bill, which was taken by one of our boys on the battlefield of Corinth-and which bill cost us $1.50 of U.S. money. We can now easily get our animal as many dollars as she cost us cents. My direction will now be "Memphis-Tenn." instead of Corinth Miss." In other respects, the same.

Your affectionate son,
Pierre-

I enclosed another of my photographs as you desire-   Give my love to Anna- P.

Qtrs. 39th Reg. Ohio Vol.
Memphis Tenn. May 28th /63

Dear Jack,

I have the pleasure of dating my letter from some other point than "Corinth Miss." Unexpectedly we received an order the first of the present month to move immediately by rail to Memphis, Tenn., in accordance with which here we are in a most delightful camp a short distance from the city. The movements of an army in the field an most unloved, for we had just finished our stylish house of logs, and made up our minds to while away the summer in as cool and expeditious a way as possible in a dull town, when ordered to pack our duds and depart for unknown places-our expectations was that we were destined for Vicksburg but it turns out that for the present at least we are to remain here until next fall.

We are most delightfully encamped, and have the view of a fine city & amuse ourselves with a most pleasing contrast to Corinth, the interesting points of which had got most unromantically State after a few months residence there. I hope we shall not be encamped in that historic place again.

The Lt. Col. And myself preceded the regiment by a couple of days and "Saw the Elephant" caged in this city in all its phases. We were introduced into the family of one of the "upper lives" who had a splendid place near our camp and most cordially urged to take up our quarters in the mansion out of regard I imagine for their own protection, than any special of hospitality toward Federal Officers, since they or at least the gay young mistress, were a dedicated Sesech, she having three brothers in the Southern Army.

At all events we were much pleasure to accept the offer of a luxurious bed and to feast our eyes once more on the elegancies of a civilized life. I don't imagine however that I in my rough suit of Soldier Clothes, heavy high topped boots, with pants inside as dirty as it is possible to be after an all-night ride and sleeping on the floor of a freight car, and having not an article of baggage with which to make a change or to improve one's toilet added much to the appearance of the afore said civilization. As you say we are about having warm times in the west, not at this particular point, but a little farther down the river.

Great movements are on the Espies. Grant has completely wasted Vicksburg and it is a fore gone conclusion that it will be ours very shortly. He has had some severe fights but has whipped the Rebels badly. Some hundreds of the wounded have come up the river and are in the city-thousands are expected shortly. I wish we could have something glorious form they army of the Potomac. Instead of the continuous defeats that invariably attend every grand movement there. Why is it the eastern troops can't whip them once at least.

The last letter from mother announced her intention of going to N.Y. to see you. I wrote her day before yesterday, we also have the pleasure now of riding down Street and looking at the pretty faces, probably they do not view us as with as much gratification as we do them, since they are Sesech and vanquished. You indicated the mildness of the weather with you by saying that an overcoat has been Super fluous. With us an overcoat has been necessary only on exceptional days throughout the whole winter, and now the weather is, some days, extremely oppressive. When the evenings are delightfully cool and refreshing.

We usually lie about the camp during the day amusing ourselves by playing cards-reading, talking, etc. till about 5 P.M. when our horses are Saddled and two or three of us ride into the city. Travel about town till dark, play a few games of billiards and then return to camp. We have a very pleasant crowd here at headquarters, all pleasant, well-educated young fellows and time passes accordingly. Since we have come to the city we have been enjoying all the early vegetables such as you get two or three months later. You ask if I am coming north this summer. I can't see any prospect of a leave of absence and reframe from worrying myself with useless wishes.

Your fraternally,

Pierre

39th Reg. Ohio Vol.
Memphis, Tenn.

It really makes little difference when you direct my letters-the station of every Reg. being known at Cairo - about all that is necessary is the number of the Regiment.

St. Cloud Hotel

Nashville Tenn. June 20th 1863

My Dear Mother,

I received your letter dated June 10th, the day on which I mailed my last to you and in which I told you I had orders for my regiment. I left Sulphur Branch yesterday and to-morrow start for the front. I send you by express $100.00 which will settle up the bond business and $50.00 over which you can do what you please with. It is intolerably hot. The perspiration is pouring off my face while I write- I am well. I doubt understand what you meant by saying that my letter troubled you and that you wished I were at home without referred to my health. I had a few chills, but they don't amount to very much and one can't even get sick enough with them to obtain a sick leave.

I haven't had a shake for some time and all right, so you need not give yourself any uneasiness on that account. Love to Anna and the Children.

> Your affectionate Son,
> Pierre

Head Qtrs. 39th Ohio Inf.
Memphis Tenn. July 1st 63

My dear Mother,

The heading of my letter shows to you my safe arrival at the old regiment. I left Hartford as you remember on Sunday night and reached New York early Monday morning in time to take the seven O'clock train to Cincinnati. When I reached Columbus-Ohio I met one of our Captains-he told me the detachment reached there the morning before and had rec'd a furlough of five days- with orders to meet in Cincinnati on the following Saturday (this was Tuesday) of course this was terrible reflections to me- since I might just as well have remained in Hartford four days longer than I did instead of hurrying off so preapactably, but of course it was impossible to foresee such a change of affairs.

As it would not pay to return I continued my journey to Cincinnati reaching there Tuesday afternoon and remaining until early Sunday morning following when the men having returned we took a steamer and started down the river reaching Memphis Sunday evening being just a week in the trip. I have had a very pleasant trip indeed, the only drawback being the knowledge that I might just as will have been home a week as a couple of days instead of boarding in Cincinnati; however, I met two of my old compatriots in that city, and the time passed pleasantly enough, I found two letters from you here on my arrival. One of them acknowledging the $100.00. My first saving doesn't sum to have amounted to much. It is very warm and sultry here. We are in hopes that we will be allowed to remain here all summer now, it is getting much too hot to move. My flying visit home seems like a dream. I now expected and so will. I don't expect to get away again until the regiment is mustered out of service, which will be in about one year from this. Before I left Hartford, I had a beautiful sword given me by my friends Tyler and Callender- it is a beautiful affair. It is recently that I saw you that I have nothing in particular to communicate. I took it for granted you would like to be appraised of my safe arrival.

Your Affectionate Son,
Pierre

Head Qtrs. 39th Ohio Reg.
Memphis Tenn. July 19th ,63

My Dear Brother,

Yours was duly received a day or two since and in order to keep up my habit of punctually in answering your letters I write now though really having nothing to communicate beyond the simple fact that I am swell, and still in Memphis.

I notice by your letter that you had at ready received the news of the Capture of Vicksburg, hence was a season of great rejoicing when the order arrived. We were all confident here that Grant would take the place, as I expressed myself when North, still I was a relief to know that I was actually in our possession. Port Hudson has also fallen into the Hands of Bank's which leaves the Miss. River open to its mouth. The other days when riding down to the river.

I saw several boats with their canvas slung. "For New Preclude "hung out for the first time since the war begun. We have taken in this army in the last two months over 40,000 prisoners and immense numbers of cannons and small arms. Meade has also I suppose taken a large number and under such drafts it does not seem possible that the Confederacy ever can hold out much longer. We are all very much disappointed that Meade allowed Lee to escape, it is the old story of moving "just too late" We had every encouragement in believing that Lees entire army would be captured, and it might have been as will or not, it seems to me with the immense army that was at Meade's disposal.

John Morgan's cavalry raid into Southern Indiana and Ohio is now amusing us. The fact of his going with a few miles of the city of Cincinnati and completely enduring it, is sufficiently and edacious warrant his escape. Which I have no doubt he will affect. I don't suppose however you have as much of this affair East as we do here, who receive only the Cincinnati papers. From the accounts we receive I should judge that the New Yorkers were having a very lively time. The riot is a disgrace to the city that it would be a much greater one to the whole country if the draft were not most rigidly enforced.

It seems to me I should take more pride in living under Confederate Rule, thanks to be under a government too timid or too weak to carry out, under every contingency, what else is doomed by the great majority of the people vital to it continuance and strength. It is disgraceful to see a city like N.Y. over run by a mob which a little resolution and a few grape shot could see its beginnings easily have put an end to it, and it is disheartening to soldiers in the field to see the sneaks and cowards at home endeavor- at would seem almost with successes to prevent the fulfillments of laws which ought to have been carried out long ago, and which are necessary access a time of hostility in anything like a reasonable time.

I am glad to hear that Gen. Newton is gaining much honor. He certainly now has a fine opportunity as corps commander in the Army of The Potomac. We are expecting to be paid now every day when we are I shall transmit what I can- and you will please invest it as you think best. The weather to-day has been very hot- but for three or four days previous it has been remarkably cool, in fact almost cold-such changes I imagine are anything but healthy, though it doesn't seem to affect me. - for about a week after my return, however I fell anything but all right. I wrote to Jack some days since and intend to do likewise to Jed in a day or two.

Head Qtrs. 39th Ohio Inf.

With much love,

Your affectionate son,
Pierre

Starr July 20th ,1863,

My Dear Mother,

At last I can address you again from the Regiment. You, I suppose received my last letter dated at Columbus Ky. Appraising you of my arrival that far, and my inability to proceed farther just then. I remained in Columbus about a week after I wrote you and then being thoroughly disgusted with staying there doing nothing I determined to leave.

The railroad had not yet been completely repaired, their remaining about 8 miles of it still over which the cars could not run, and which were said to be given up to guerillas. The great difficulty was in getting my baggage from one end of the break to the other, however I determined to try.

In company with another officer I started. The cars ran about 30 miles when we were stopped by a burnt bridge, and now came over time to foot it. I managed to get hold of a contraband and impressed him into my service, by putting my valise on his shoulder, which was more than I could probably carry and ordering him to travel, while I toted my carpet bag. There were quite a number of officers along, each carrying his own baggage.

Creeks had to be crossed on most treacherous rolling logs or by boldly wading through the water in many cases quite deep. In the end it was almost immaterial which course was pursued.
We had to travel along by the side of the railroad, the trains having stopped in the middle of the woods, not near any road. The portion in we had to walk was through low swampy fields over which the cars had gone on trestle work for the greater part, which abounded in bridges over numerous creeks and little streams, all this wood works the rebels had burnt, and the consequences was we had to walk through mud and water, seeking nearly knee deep at every step for about 8 miles.
ended in a mis-step on the slipping logs and a slide into the water. However, at length, just after dark, awfully tired, through wet and desperately hungry we got to the completed portion of the road when we could again take the cars and completer our journey to Jackson Tenn. about 50 miles distance.

I had had nothing to eat but a little dry bread since eating breakfast and the prospect was not good for supper, first were butt and pork fried. We had not stopped near any town but in the most if a barren wood, lying out in which on a cold night without any blankets did not appear desirable, though if I had had my blankets I could have got along very well. So, I thought if I could, I would get better quarters a with intention I scraped acquaintance with some Engineer officers, who were then repairing the Railroad and got the privilege of sleeping in a car, and passed the night quite comfortably, all the rest-built fires and laid out in the words all night.
194

The next day about noon the cars in which we were to go to Jackson when we arrived about dusk. I was wholly ignorant as to where my Regiment was, but on jumping from the cars at J. much to my gratification I met my Lieut. Col. From the last two weeks and was there at Corinth, it had had a fight with the Cavalry about here and had captured some 400 men and as many horses. They had been without tents or shelter of any kind and had to lay out in the rain at night, in fact had had the hardest campaign the Regiment had ever been on. I concluded I had been quite lucky in escaping it.

I remained in Jackson a couple of days and arrived in camp n the 11th of this month having been absent nearly six weeks, I was very glad to get back to my old friends and the Regiment though sorry to be in Corinth- a place I do not like.

 I had been here two or three days when one evening we got an order to go our as guard to a forage train into the country. It had been raining and snowing for two or three days and was very cold, but of course we had to go though the prospect was hard. One doctor remained with the sick in camp and went with the regiment, we went without tents or baggage except our blankets.

We started at about daybreak, it was very cold and snowing hard, the people here say they have not known such weather for many years. It was so cold to ride my horse and I walked nearly all day. About dark we halted in a field where the soldiers were bivouac, and they soon built for them self-comfortable large first-rate fires of the fence rails, nearby there was a very neat house owned by a secesh and occupied by himself and two daughters.

We – that is to say the Col. And staff- much preferred sleeping in a house where we could, so we called upon the occupants and made known our intensions of honoring them by making their house our headquarters. It was a bitter pill, no doubt for them to give Union officers a good supper and comfortable quarters, while the soldiers were burning their fences and our horses eating their corn, but it had to be swallowed and they did it with frigid pitifulness.

The next day we started again early and from the full corn cribs of the secessionist thereabouts we got nearly 2000 bushels of corn, all we could carry and started towards camp again. That night we got as far back as our quarters of the preceding night. At our request our very kind southern friends again provided us with a hot supper and good quarters. It was the most comfortable thing I think I have ever experienced for a long while to get before the fire of big roaring logs on those two cold nights instead of bivouacking outside as we had expected to do.

By the next evening we had got back to Corinth having been away from camp three days. I should have written you before this if I had not been away on that trip. We have received orders to be ready to move by cars, at a moments notice, and expect to start for Memphis Tenn. In a day or two, further then that I do not know where we are going.

I found on my return here ten letters from you. We have not received the mail now for about ten days, during that time I have not even seen a newspaper. I got a letter from Jed the day of my arrival here dated away back in Dec. I wrote him while in Columbus and expect an answer as soon as the mail can get running again.

You can imagine that I am very desirous of having what is going on in the world not having seen a paper so long. A lot of H (Hartford) papers I rec'd from Jed with his letter. The weather here has been awful for the last week, rainy or snowing all the time, it is raining now. The camp looks anything but pleasant and navigation is particularly difficult through the mud.

You say Frank Perkins has returned, I was rather surprised to hear it. I suppose again he has nothing to do with me, all you know about him. I was very glad to see in a paper that N.L. was lively with men working at the Navy Yard, that of course must now be a fixed fact.

I am well and fat, we have a cow belonging to our mess, and I am furnished daily with milk. I have been in a good many rather rough places,
196

but it does not appear to have done me any hurt. Please give me all the N.L. news. With much love

Aug. 6th 63

Dear Jack,

Yours was duly received a few days since. We still continue inhabitants of Memphis, sitting on our back sides and holding the place at all hazards. This is very comfortable soldering, but yet not exactly according with my views. Perhaps it is as well however while the weather continues so hot. When It gets cooler however I hope we shall go campaigning again. This mode of life is almost too lazy for comfort. We are getting thinned out here at head-quarters pretty extensively. Our Lt. Col. Is away on sick leave. The surgeon left some days since, on leave of absences, for New England (he is a New Hampshire man) and today the Col. Started for Cincinnati under orders for the purpose of getting some drafted men to fill us up to the maximum number. We are yet about the largest regiment in the department having over 700 men on the ground, while we have a number on detached service-footing up an aggregate of over 800 - this is regarded as extraordinary for a Reg. which has been two years in the service.

Judging from the papers you certainly you bravely did have quite a warlike time in N.Y. for a few days. If in addition to not taking of your clothes for four nights, you had slept on the ground- perhaps in the rain to give a little more zest to it and marched through the days under a boiling sun with nothing to eat but fat pork and hard crackers you could more fully appreciate the fun of soldiering. The only vacation in our usual routine service. I wrote last was a trip of a few days into its country after guerrillas. Twelve of them are now inmates of the military prison as the result of our march.

We are getting short of money down here. Uncle Samuel, has not found us with a sight of a paymaster for over five months and in consequence greenbacks are a curiosity, not so much as a five-cent shin-plaster has been in my pocket for many days. On going down to the levee today to see the Colonel off I gave my horse to a darkey to hold during my absences after a half hour spent on board the boat, the said contraband (expectant of small change) on being relieved from duty-considered himself rather bold when I informed him of my lack of that article and doubtless thought it a clear case of impressment rite the service. Everything here is above usually high, and it takes a much of money to live.

Ice! For us long without which this hot weather it would seem almost impossible to get along. We have been getting for our mess at the rate of eight cents per pound and using from twenty to thirty lbs. every day. This appeared a little steep, however when we came to settle our bills for the month and we concluded to shut down on such an expensive luxury. We are fortunate in having a delightful shady camp on the most elevated spot in the vicinity of Memphis and dressed in "dis habell" we can keep from melting. I very rarely have the will towards evening there take a ride to the city and spend an hour or two very pleasantly one way or another. I bought a very nice mare a few weeks ago and take a good deal of pleasure in riding her.

We had a grand review here yesterday in which was seen your humble Servant appeared in gorgeous array nearly a dozen of our men were sun struck during the short time we were out. The heat was intolerable. I was amused to leave the names of the lucky individuals of New London, who drew prizes in the draft lottery from those you mentioned. I imagine the government will draw more in the shape of money than as soldiers. What are you going to do about it If you are elected? Us government makes it optional- I think you had better endeavor to raise the $300.00. I am glad here that the thing is not going to be made a farce of this time as it was the last. I have not heard anything from mother for a long time though I wrote her a good while since my return. I have been sorry that I went North when I did for, though no one knew it then. I could now get a leave and be at home a much longer time. Since the fall of Vicksburg the Gen. has been granting absences quite liberally to Officers and men, two of the former being away in time all the time and of the latter five percent of
198

the whole command in a 25 day furlough a new batch going as soon as the preceding returns.

I was talking yesterday with an Officer from the army of the Potomac, who had been in Gen. Newtons Division. He not knowing that N. was any connection of mine, spoke of him in the highest terms, as a trained, talented and popular Officer. Who knows but he may take his turn at the command of that army? It has been the graveyard of so many, Military reputations, however that I think must be anything but a desirable place, though the one in command at the last fight will have an everlasting fame whether he earns it or not.

Your affectionate Bro.
Pierre

Head Qtrs. 39th O.V. I
Memphis Tenn. Aug. 23rd, 1863

My Dear mother,

It seems a long time since I have heard from home and I really am beginning to get anxious but trust that nothing unpleasant has prevented your writing. About two weeks since I forward to you by Adams Express two hundred dollars $200.00 to be deposed of as you may think proper. I might have sent a larger sum if I had not passion for my horse out of the sum of I received, and as It had been so long since I last was paid. I had more to pay out than I ought to have should. The regiment has not even yet been paid. I succeeded in getting my money because I was detailed to the U.S.3rd Cavalry in which I have been serving for the last two weeks. This morning however I returned to my regiment. Of course, you will notify me when you receive the money, which should have reached you before this.

Hoping to hear soon,
Your affectionate Son,

Iuka Miss

Aug. 24, 1863,

My Dear mother,

You have no doubt expected a letter from me before this and I had intended to write but have not had a will intended time to do it so. About three days since we received orders to march to I-V-Ka (as it is written by the aborigines) and I will myself to proceed by cars. I had to take charge of everything as our surgeon has resigned on account of sickness and the Capt. In a German who speaks quite untellable.

At a half an hour notice we struck our hospital tents to take out of town with baggage and sick and was at the depot, that is to say an open field without a house in sight. I got them with the to sick men, hospital stores tents etc.

About 5 o'clock in the afternoon the cars were expected every minute. But they did not appear, and it began to grow dark, so I ordered the tents put up, the sick cared for and we made our home for the night. The new day we waited till three o'clock where at last the train arrived. As the brigade had gone from that part of the country, and the secesh abounded there, in the course of 12 0r 24 hours we could have very been likely have been in their hands. So, we were not at all sorry to leave.

Iuka is about 25 miles East of Corinth, near the boarder line of Miss. It is (or rather was) the stylish watering of this part of the south, a second Saratoga for Southern Snobs. It is a very pretty little village, abounds in two Sulphur and Alum Springs, has two large hotels for summer patronage, and a number of handsome mansions. It is quite an improvement on other parts of the country which I had seen. It is said to be the most healthy place as well as cooler in the states we have a most delightful breeze here in our camp- which is just on the border of the town- all the time, and if a little salt were intermingled it would almost be N.L.

Since I arrived I have been sleeping most of my time at the "Iuka Springs Hotel" which has been converted into a Military Hospital, a great change from last summer when it was crowded with Southern Belles and beaux.

In the large square on the first floor, perhaps 75 feet square, where the light fantastic was worth to be tripped, I deposited my sick "Mudsills" On the evening that I reached there, 500 sick occupied the house. The next day my regiment reached here and a couple of days after I managed to get all the sick in the field again and for my self I was glad enough to get out of a house and into my tent on the field again.

I came on the cars with a surgeon of the regular army, who is to take charge of the hospital, he wanted to start with him as an assistant, but I preferred remaining with the 39th. I have however to attend to their men everyday tell relieved by others who are to be regularly approved there. There are I said to be many pretty rides about here, as would very likely be the case in such a watering place, but the secsh are altogether too inviting to be pleasant and if is not at all safe to go more then a mile or two from the cams in any direction.

We had a supply train captured a day or two since several men shot by guerrillas and other news incidents which bring forcibly to our minds the conviction that we are in an enemy's country, and the propinquity of the rebels. Speaking of rides, I have got a fine horse of my own now, and my riding experience in here fore comes very nicely into play, as I ride more or less every day, as of course one never thinks of getting about the country in any other way than on horseback.

I have written you a letter and some papers from Jed and also a letter from Jack. Please tell them that I will answer them as soon as I get time. This is considered an important point in a military point of view, and it is thought will play a part before the war is over.

am glad people north are waking up to the idea that this is a real live war and no play work and that if the country is to be saved they have got to fight. My direction is the same as here to fore, and always will be what

201

ever may go. I like this life first rate for a change. Everything is very high- Milk per Qt. 25 cts. -eggs per doz. About 50 cts. -Butter per pound, little chickens 75 cts. etc.

As all are secesh about here of course they get as much as they can out of us. Saw an order from the Provost Marshall, however this morning regulating the prices, so now they can't check us more, That the law allows-which is certainly enough to satisfly any rascal. By later order we can now send out parties who take corn, potatoes, Etc. from the rebels when they meet them which is certainly no more then proper.

> In haste,
> Your affectionate son,
> Pierre

Iuka Miss
Aug. 24, 1863,

My Dear mother,

You have no doubt expected a letter from me before this and I had intended to write but have not had a will intended time to do it so. About three days since we received orders to march to I-V-Ka (as it is written by the aborigines) and I will myself to proceed by cars. I had to take charge of everything as our surgeon has resigned on account of sickness and the Capt. In a German who speaks quite untellable. At a half an hour notice we struck our hospital tents to take out of town with baggage and sick and was at the depot, that is to say an open field without a house in sight. I got them with the two sick men, hospital stores tents etc.

About 5 o'clock in the afternoon the cars were expected every minute. But they did not appear, and it began to grow dark, so I ordered the tents put up, the sick cared for and we made our home for the night. The new day we waited till three o'clock where at last the train arrived. As the brigade had gone from that part of the country, and the secesh abounded there, in the course of 12 0r 24 hours we could have very been likely have been in their hands. So, we were not at all sorry to leave.

Luka is about 25 miles East of Corinth, near the boarder line of Miss. It is (or rather was) the stylish watering of this part of the south, a second Saratoga for Southern Snobs. It is a very pretty little village, abounds in two Sulphur and Alum Springs, has two large hotels for summer patronage, and a number of handsome mansions. It is quite an improvement on other parts of the country which I had seen. It is said to be the most healthy place as well as cooler in the states we have a most delightful breeze here in our camp- which is just on the border of the town- all the time, and if a little salt were intermingled it would almost be N.L. Since I arrived I have been sleeping most of my time at the "Iuka Springs Hotel" which has been converted into a Military Hospital, a great change from last summer when it was crowded with Southern Belles and beaux. In the large square on the first floor, perhaps 75 feet square, where the light fantastic was worth to be tripped, I deposited my sick "Mudsills" On the evening that I reached there, 500 sick occupied the house. The next day my regiment reached here and a couple of days after I managed to get all the sick in the field again and for myself I was glad enough to get out of a house and into my tent on the field again.

I came on the cars with a surgeon of the regular army, who is to take charge of the hospital, he wanted to stay with him as an assistant, but I preferred remaining with the 39th. I have however to attend to their men everyday tell relieved by others who are to be regularly approved there. There are I said to be many pretty rides about here, as would very likely be the case in such a watering place, but the secsh are altogether too inviting to be pleasant and if is not at all safe to go more than a mile or two from the cams in any direction.

We had a supply train captured a day or two since several men shot by guerrillas and other news incidents which bring forcibly to our minds the conviction that we are in an enemy's country, and the propinquity

of the Rebels. Speaking of rides, I have got a fine horse of my own now, and my Headquarters 3rd U.S. Cavy.
Memphis Tenn. Sept. 5th, 1863,

My dear Mother,

I have been anxiously expecting a letter from you every day for the past four calls and have written I think three times since I have heard from home last. I have been accustomed to hearing so regularly that this long delay troubles me a good deal. About three weeks since I sent to you by Adams Express two hundred dollars $200.00 which I should be glad to hear had safely arrived at its destination. I received a letter a day or two since from Jack in where he said that he had been to M.D. and expressed great pleasure from his visit. He said that all were well which I was very glad to hear, for I had begun to think that the contrary must be the fact. You will see by the heading of this that my quarters have been changed. I was detailed there on four weeks since to take charge of this regiment of regular cavalry. I have very pleasant quarters and associates and like my position much, though I consider it pleasant to be always with my own regiment. Do let me hear from you soon,

your affectionate son,
Pierre

Head Quarters 3rd U.S. Cavy.
Memphis Tenn.
Sept. 7, 63

Dear Jack,

Yours, was recd. Some days since. I have been quite unwell for about the last two weeks and in fact feel anything but strong yet.   I do not remember the last time I wrote you last. I was with the 3rd Cavalry. I have been in charge of it about a month now having been detailed from my own regiment. The regiment returns to training every week at the Carlisle Barracks to recruit, in which case I should be correspondingly near home. I recd a letter here the other day from which I suppose Hal Lact has been drafted as he was after 2 trips to way off Corinth.

I wish you would send me in your next letter a "Black silk necktie ½ inch caviled, tell me what you pay, and I will return by the next mail., they charge too steep here for such articles for much particulars. Please also enquire for price per yard of gold and for staff Officer's pants, they charge here $1.50 per yard which you see is pretty dear. It takes 2 ½ yds. I believe for a pair of pants. If you can get it at a reasonable price and can send it by mail I would be much obliged if you would do so.

Today we are having a storm and it is quite cool. We have been having it very hot. The latter part of last month we had some rain and cold able weather from the sun South in August. Overcoats were in demand. Stores were put up in some tents and Officers modeled around the place as if they were in the midst of a New England winter. I am sorry to learn that Mrs. Brown intending to leave the house-keeping alone. If you say you made a short visit to N.L. it must have been a pleasant cheery one from mother. I believe you are the only one in the family who has been taking to N.L.
I certainly have not, I likely to go there in a while and look at the old place and should be very sorry to see it in straight hands. But as to living there I know I should now be content. I hope mother is not making any plans for my practicing in N.L. for I fear I shall have to disappoint her. If mother could be more distasteful to me. Please let me hear from you some in regard to the neck tie and soon.

We are leading a quite monotonous life here. I hardly ever go into the city, in fact have not put string enough together for a horse lately.

> Your affectionate bro.
> Pierre

These next two letters were written on the same pages. Pierre's to his mother and then Jared sent the letter and info to his mother.

Sept. 63
Head Qtrs. 39th O.V.I
Memphis, Tenn.

My dear mother,

I wrote a few days since and now do so again to inform you of my where about. The 3rd Cavalry was transferred from the Corps in which I am to another and ordered to Chattanooga. The Officers seemed very desiring that I should go with that command and I should go with that command and I should have liked the campaign but the Medical Director did not want me to go out of his corps and so I returned once more to my own Regiment. I wish we could be on the move again, being tired of remaining in Memphis, probably now we will remain all winter. I wish I could spend it in Connecticut instead of here.

My horse which you will remember I told you in my last was stolen, though diligently searched after has not been found. That is the worst of buying horses here, they are such a very many miserable vagabonds abounding here who make it their business of stealing horses, put them in some cellar, brand them- cut their manes and having disguised them as much as possible, sutler them, cheaply, to anyone who will buy. It is in this manner I imagine that mine has gone.

It is quite cool here. I have no doubt as much so as in N.H. we have a fire going in our tent all day with an exception of an hour or two at noon, and in the morning, it has been right cold, we have had frost several times. By piling down an old house we have now procured bricks and are going to build a big old country fire-places for our comfort. In your next address to me at the 39th Ohio Inf. Fullers Brigade. I afraid you are having a very lousy and unpleasant time now at home since Mrs. Browns departure. I hope you could be able to make some pleasant arrangements before the winter is over. I don't see that there is any chance of my being company for you, as I cannot anticipate any chance of a leave this winter----------

Your affectionate son,
Pierre

Newington Nov. 1st ,1863
Dear mother,

Pierre's letter reached us yesterday afternoon. We are all well and not
having of importance has happened since you left. I have been shut up
in the house a couple of days from Cherry's stepping on my foot but
have been out to Church to day. I hope you and your baggage reached
N. London safety? Love from all,

Your affectionately, Jared

Friday Oct. 29th

Iuka Miss. 63

My dear mother,

Though, having no letter from you to answer still I suppose you might
like to hear of our movements, so will make the most of this
opportunity as I do not anticipate another soon. A week from last
Sunday at daylight the Reg. in accordance with orders recd. The
previous evening bundled up bag and baggage and started on its
predestination. After a six-day's march we reached.

Corinth - it looked as familiar and unattractive as ever. Our stay there
was limited to about 24 hours where we were ordered off again-this
time on cars to Burnsville is a miserable little village which boast
having sent out two full companies of guerrillas though it does not
seem as if there could ever have been more than 300 inhabitants there.
There we remained three days and then again eastward look our way-
a short march to I-V-Ka our old summoning ground, we arrived here
yesterday noon and anticipate leaving tomorrow morning. Now you
probably would like to know what all this is preparing to, will their it
is just the beginning of a large march of 150 miles to Stevenson

Alabama to cooperate with General Sherman in the operations against Bragg's Army.

Major Gen. Sherman controls as we are being in his department though we are under the movement command of Gen. Dodge, who command the divisions of which our brigade formed a part. Thus, you see there is a probability of our having an action campaign just what we all desire for we all got pretty tired of our City Camp Memphis.

I had much rather be encamped in the woods miles from anybody than near a city for the rest of our time in the service, and I would prefer to either, an active campaign such as there is a prospect of our now entering, but don't be surprised if in the uncertainly of military affaires the whole programmed is changed. Guerillas are flocking all around us, ready to gobble up any stray sheep, this morning we had quite a skirmish with them, they are coming up and firing on our pickets about ¼ mile from camp. When I wrote last I dated from 3rd Cavy., I believe Lolos informed you in that letter of the loss of my horse.

I am now lackey in being able to answer his most unexpected recovery. She had been gone about two weeks eluding every effort on my part to find her, Failure in this I was about to buy another, when one day our Lt. Col. Was riding up to town and he thought he recognized my horse with a secesh (at least a Citizen) upon her. He immediately jumped from the ambulance in which he was riding and started on a run down the middle of the street, seized the man by the bridle and ordered the citizen to the provost Marshalls for examination on the charge of horse-stealing. He made all sorts of protests laments but the Col. Was immovable and lodged him safely in the hands of the guard and himself proceeded in triumph to camp with the mare in tow, much to my astonishment and gratification, the next day I went down and I made my charges against the prisoner, the examination was to be continued the next day when we were ordered to move, and so ended the case as far as I was concerned.

It is a longtime coming I have heard from anyone Your last I suppose was directed to me at 3rd U.S. Cavalry. And will take some time to get to me. I think I ought to have recd. One before this however. I shall be glad to learn that you have made some pleasant arrangements for the winter, in your last you were in doubt what to. Divert you next to 39th Ohio, Fullers Brigade ETC.

The quantity of camp equipment is again curtailed for this march. The numbers of our tents cut down, and all sorts of baggage reduced. I cut my baggage down one valise and now carry two. Finally, we have cast our cots and now look to the ground for a bed. So, that we will never be without one. This is rather different from the way which I was brought up but have got astonishing well used to it and sleep as soundly as ever I did in my comfortable bed at home. The only disagreeable time was when it rained when we were very often get flooded. We are now having a most uncomfortable cold rain, which betook us a tough march to- numerous as we go we spend a day sending to the rear all who are to unwell to make a march of 150 or 75 miles. I will let you know of our progress whenever I have an opportunity.
Yours affectionately Pierre

This in one continuous letter
Nov. 5th, 1863

My Dear mother,

Our communications with the rear and consequently with the North being cut off I can't expect to get any letters from you and probably the next best thing Is to write to you, though when this epistle will reach its destination if ever. I have not the slightest idea. I wrote you a few days since from Iuka, on the day following that which I indicated we packed our wagons and started for the Tenn. Rivers which we struck Eastport Tenn.

After a short March of two miles. Arriving there we expected to cross the river at once, but in this we were disappointed thu being about 15,000 men already there waiting. So, we were marched down to the banks of the rivers and encamped there in the mud for a couple of days. The most disagreeable location it has ever yet bee my fortune to encamp in was this. Nothing but soft black mud into which ones' camp stool would suck half a foot when sit upon, was beneath us and around us, covered with reeds as high as ones' heads. Finally, the other commands-those of Brig. Generals Blair and Osterhaus-having crossed we obtained possession of the transports and in a few hours our Brigade consisting of four regiments and two batteries numbering in all 2500 men were in Alabama.

We then marched into the country about a couple of miles and pitched our tents and are now in waiting for about 8000 more troops to get across with whom we are to make our advance to Stevenson about 100 miles distance. I have now explained were we are and so made up for the want of a heading for this letter.

As I said before our communications with the rear are cut-off, or rather given up by us, all the troops on the line of the road between here and Corinth being withdrawn and no trains running. It is the intention as we proceed to drop all communication and live on the country which is said to be very rich, in fact we begin to see already something different from the barren waste which we have been accustomed to in our peregrinations about Miss.

Wild turkeys and all kinds of grain all in great abundance, two or three deer have been shot and hogs are rooting around in the woods in hundreds. We also have no trouble in getting fodder for our horses and mules for which we have about 100 head.

Of one thing however, this country is decidedly destitute as Young and able-bodied men. It is rare ever to meet with one of the male gender under any circumstances and if you do he is sure to be old and decrepit, on the shady side of sixty at least the young fellows are guerillas, however around in the woods keeping very shy of any undesirable number but certain to shoot or gobble up any stragglers from the command.

We have not received a mail or papers for some days and in times like these a newspaper is almost a necessity of life to say nothing of ever having from home. If we get a mail or a paper under two weeks I think we shall be extremely fortunate. For the last few days it has been uncomfortably warm here, quite a contrast I have no doubt to your New England November weather, to day we have been having a warm rain and congratulate ourselves that it has come when we are in camp instead of yesterday when we were crossing the river.

It is about a month or six weeks since I heard from you I hope the next mail, whenever it does come may bring me a letter.

Continued Nov. 7th Saturday

I write the preceding evening before last, not having a chance to send it as yet I will add a few lines. About 11 o'clock in the morning of the 6th we got orders to march and in about an hour were on the read. Yesterday afternoon we came 10 miles to our present encampment and are waiting to day for the remainder of Gen. Dodges command to cross the river and join us, though we may get orders to move any moment.

We have not met with any force of the enemy and very likely will not. A regiment which went on the day before us lost 18 men by guerrillas. We have been more fortunate thus far. As we get into the country we continue to find a very rich and as our armies have not before been in this portion we have no trouble in getting forage for horses and food for men.

The weather is delightful, comfortably warm without an overcoat. I hope it will continue so to the end of our trip which thus far has been a very pleasant one. We must generally get orders to move at daylight and the time that intervenes between breakfast at half past four or five O'clock and reaching camp about Six in the afternoon together with riding all day and having nothing but a hard cracker to munch gives us all a most glorious appetite.

We are fortunate in having a most excellent cook and being well provided with good things in the eating line and getting plenty of chickens to ECT. On the road the tin meals which we do get are heartily enjoyed. We have this instant got orders to move instantly

Prospect Tenn. Nov. 14, 1863

As my letter was cut abruptly short on the morning of the 7th and I have had no opportunity of sending it since I will now begin a 2nd volume. On the morning of the 7th a few minutes after receipt of the order to move our tents were struck and we were on the road and that afternoon marched about twelve miles and camped that night in the woods. The next morning at sevenish started again and marched all day and so have continued each day until yesterday when we reached this point which there is a probability of our remaining some weeks.

I said in the first part of my letter that we were destined for Stevenson Ala. That was the intension when we started on this expedition, but dispatches were received from Gen. Sherman when on our way to that point which altered our course and here we are at Prospect Tenn., a little station in the extreme southern portion of Middle of the state. If you look on the map you will find in southern part of Tenn.

Pulaski (Tenn) - quite a good-sized town with three or four churches, a large court-house and quite a number of fine residences, the largest place we have passed through since leaving Memphis. It is on the line of the Nashville and Decatur R.R. Said R.R. however has not been in operation for the last 12 months. About fourteen miles South of Pulaski is Prospect also on on the line of the R.R. Our Brigade is stationed here while Gen. Dodge's force is at Pulaski. The cooks appointed to this Brigade is to open the road from this point to Athens distance of fifteen miles.

It is estimated that the time necessary accomplish this repairing of burnt bridges and destroyed culverts will take at least a month. So, we are beginning to consider ourselves settled here on in this region for that length of time. The object of opening the R.R. to Decatur is to bring supplies from Nashville to the former point (which is above the Shoals and navigable to transport.) and from thence by the Tenn. Rover to our army at Chattanooga. This advocating the necessity of have to guarding the whole line of R.R. from Nashville to Chattanooga. SO, although we are not to take part, at least for the present, in the fighting operations, we are still to take an important part in the operations going on in this portion of the country.

I have not seen a paper for over two weeks and since blissful of remains of everything that is going on in the world, Military or Civil. It would give me great pleasure to ascertain whether Charleston was taken yet, or if Meade with the Army of the Potomac had whipped anybody or was still holding Washington "at all Hazards" whether Bragg had been whipped or Grant crushed, or the Navy Yard established at New London. The R.R. news from Nashville to Columbia, the only main communication is a wagon train, by this we may since occasionally receive mail, but nothing can be depended on until we get the R.R. finished and then we will probably move from here ourselves.

The weather still continues comfortably warm and pleasant. I had the pleasure of once on the march-sleeping in a house and on a feather bed. The contrast was great but did not improve my sleeping most soundly. I should have done the same however if I had been on the ground.

This march has been through the finest country I have seen in the south, every night we have driven in plenty of beef for the mill and we have had chicken, turkey, lamb etc. in abundance. This is decidedly different from the parts of Miss we have campaigned in when we have been weeks with hardly anything but salt pork and hard crackers.

Sunday morning Nov. 15th

I have an opportunity of sending my letter at last by Gen. Dodge who with his staff go to Pulaski in a few minutes. He brought a mail and in it a letter from Jack. I haven't, a minute to add more and I don't think it is necessary in consideration of the length to which my letter has already reached I hope to hear from you soon.

Your affectionate Son,
Pierre

Head Qtrs. 39th Ohio Inf.
Athens Ala. Feb. 25th, 1864

My dear mother,

I wrote you from Cincinnati a short letter informing you of my arrival
there and my intended departure for the Regiment which we are
unfortunate enough to miss as it left Cincinnati about twelve hours
before we reached them. We reached Louisville early Monday
morning, remained there that day and the following morning at 7
o'clock started by cars to Nashville arriving there about 6 a.m.

We made our way to one of the hotels all of which are filled to capacity
and finally succeeded in getting a most indifferent room for the night.
We anticipated meeting the regiment here, but it had not yet arrived.
After waiting a couple of days, it finally came and on the third day we
left with the regiment for our old camping ground-Prospect- we
reached Pulaski- 14 miles north of Prospect and the Hd. Qtrs. Of Gen.
Dodge early Sunday Morning. While there we got orders to move on to
Athens, Alabama-sixteen miles south of Prospect. We traveled as far as
Pulaski in the cars from there we marched to this place.

Athens is a very pretty village of about 1500 inhabitants with a very
large population of handsome houses and grounds, and a large Female
Seminary site in operation, and the while a very desirable place in
which to be located and vastly preferable to Prospect. Our Col. is
commanding the post. It is pleasant after all to get back to the regiment
in the old routine of camp life.

We are at present occupying for Headquarters what was formerly a
school house, a very pretty gothic building, which answers our
purpose very well, though the floors are nine of the steepest too steep

upon as I know from experience. In a few days we intend to take possession of a few brick houses near us. The present occupants intending to leave. I found my lens all night and with my new equipment make the most stylish appearance of anybody about here.

My poor contraband by the time I reached Pulaski, when he had been sent to the hospital, was dead and buried. It seems that on his return with my horse - when I left for the north, the weather being very cold he froze both of his feet, one of them being gangrenous and separated from the leg near the ankle, while the flesh all came off from the other, and in consequence he died. He might have saved himself if he had chosen to walk as he was advised to do by those who were with him, but he was either too lazy or his feet were so blistered from his previous march that he was unable to do so.

The Rail-Road is now in running order from Nashville here, but the cars have as yet run no farther than Prospect and we received neither a mail or a newspaper since we have been here. As yet we have had not opportunity to send any letters away, but I suppose there will be a chance soon and I wish in anticipation of it. There are some very pretty homes around here and good roads, but one can hardly get out of the town, but a sentinel bars the road. Yesterday Co. McDowell and I succeeded in obtaining a buggy and harness and now we instead of ride on horseback, which is rather a pleasant change as we have to ride horseback so much. The weather is and has been ever since we have been in this part of the country-perfectly delightful.

I am well with the exception of a most disagreeable cold, our regiment now numbers nearly 900 men. Many of where at home took occasion to get a wife, on the strength I suppose of them by bounties, perhaps that is the best way to save it after all. I don't know how long we shall remain here, it is thought that before long we shall move farther South to Decatur. I hope in your next letter to learn that Anna is with you and that your home is not so desolate as it has been here for. Col. McDowell desires to be remembered to you- With much love

Your Affectionate Son,

Pierre
Direct 39th Reg. Ohio Inf.
Dodges Command
(via Nashville)

Head Qtrs. 39th Ohio Inf.
Athens Ala. Sunday Feb. 28th 64

Dear Jack,

Once more we have got back to the old routine of Camp Life. The only position now in which I feel really at home. I was very sorry not to be able to stop sufficiently long in N.Y.   to see you, but it was impossible as it was, I was behind time and did not reach the Regiment before they reached Nashville. When I left you, I found Mother at the New Haven House. As Mrs. Steadman and daughters were there show was apparently very pleasantly situated but you know she never is really satisfied away from New London and that was the case now, accordingly she proposed after staying a couple of days in N.H. that we should go home.

In four days I had seen enough of N.S. to satisfy me for as many years and went to Hartford. I procured board for mother at the Allyn House and the next day she came up. She didn't like the hotel much and after spending a few days there went out to Newington and there remained until I left for the Army. A day or two after I reached Hartford Lt. Col. McDowell came in to see me, I went with him to Poughkeepsie for a few days, there he returned to Hartford and remains until our furlough was up. Our orders were to report to Cincinnati on the 10th Feb., but we did not leave H. till the night of the 9th took the morning train for Baltimore-as Col. Wanted to see his sister who was staying there-remained there that night. Started for Cincinnati in the morning. As the trains were nearly all behind time we did not reach our destination until 3 A.M. on Saturday the 13th. Reading the paper at breakfast the first thing that attracted my attention was the announcement that the 39th had left for the seat of war the day previous.

We were decidedly chop-follow- we had counted on their remaining in the city for some time but a dispatch from Gen. Dodge hurried their departure and we were just too late to join them, however we concluded that as they went down the river on boats we could catch them by going through Nashville on the cars. Accordingly, the next day- Sunday we took the Packet for Louisville, remained there Monday and Tuesday morning started again by cars for Nashville reaching there in the evening. Our regiment had not arrived. So, we put up at one of the fashionable but admirable hotels of the city and awaited its coming. Three days after it came and the next morning we took the cars for Pulaski, from there we took up our line of march for Athens Alabama. We have been about a week it is generally thought that we shall be moved farther south in a few days. This is a very pleasant location and we have no desire to move.

The enemy is in considerable force the other side of the Tenn. River and their pickets all skirmishing with ours nearly every day, except when they make a mutual agreement not to shoot one another. This is a very stylish town of about 1500 inhabitants eventually a place considerable wealth. The Stars and Strips were nailed to the flag staff of the Court House and kept floating there for some time after the secession of Alabama, but there was little use in a few holding out and I suppose there are but a little not Union fleeing here now, though there are many who have not committed themselves to either side and are only desirous to see peace on any terms.

On my return I found that my contraband servant had none died. It seems that on his return to camp with my horse from the point at which we took the cars on our way north, he froze both of his feet-as negro he preferred riding to walking under any circumstance. One of his feet feel off near the ankle and he died. He was a young fellow of about 18 and very bright.

We have confiscated a buggy and harness and enjoy driving everyday as we have plenty of horses and good roads. I expect my stock will be increased in a few weeks by the addition of a cot. My mare having

217

greatly increased in size, I fear she has been indulging in "Corn-oats"

The cars have just begun running through here from Nashville and we hope now to get a mail and newspapers of which desirable articles we have literally been deprived. I had a fine time when at the North and regarded excluding that the time was so short. I didn't expect to leave again till I quit the service. Money goes altogether too fast when I am away from the Regiment and my savings have played themselves out. I did not ask much about Jed's affairs and he didn't volunteer anything. He has not as yet sold his tobacco crops.

New London ever looking terribly dull. The Navy Yard is its only salvation and fine cheer is mighty slim. Since my return I have been getting fat. Yesterday we sent a foraging party into the country and got a lot of Chickens, turkeys, eggs, Etc., we keep two cows. Have got a new mess kit and live ourselves and can entertain our friends in a style rarely for seen in camp. I have never found our mess equaled in any other regiment and I have been at a good many. I have not heard from home since I left. Anna was expected soon, I hope to learn that she is there. Let me hear from you soon

Your affectionate Brother Pierre.

Please send me when you write a black silk neck-tie- not over an inch wide.   Direct- 39th Reg. Ohio Inf. Dodge's Command (Via Nashville) Tenn.

Head Quarters 3rd Alabama Reg. (African Decent)
Sulphur Branch Trestle, Alabama March 21st, 1864

My Dear Mother,

I have not yet received an answer to my last but thinking that its delay might be owing to my change of location for a time, and you might be anxious, as you say sometimes getting regard to me. I'll write though having noted in particular to communicate. Last week our Regiment received orders to march to Decatur. Just previous to their going however I got orders - not very agreeable - to report for duty to the Commanding Officer of the 3rd Alabama. The medical director, who gave the order told me that the Surgeon in charge was sick and as there was a great deal to do, he thought it best to send someone to his assistance for a few days, providing very soon to return me to my own regiment.

I have been here now a little over a week. How much longer I shall have to stay I cannot tell. This regiment is guarding the rail now at this point, when there is a long and very high trestle, which the Rebs would no doubt be very glad of an opportunity to destroy and thus put an end to our communications to Nashville, all of which would no doubt be very pleasant to them but quite the contrary to us. I have received letters from no one since I wrote you last and have heard no new of any kind. We can't even get the papers regularly here.

I saw by the orders from Sherman's Headquarters that Gen. Newton is ordered to report to Gen. McPherson for duty, to what he have been assigned I have not learned. I am anxious to learn how Anna and the Children are getting on and hope I shall receive a letter from you soon informing me. We are settled down on a very high destitute and uninviting looking hill, overlooking the Railroad which the only thing left to convince us that we are still within the bounds of civilization. I was right sorry to leave our Comfortable School House at Athens, and still more to be separated from my Regiment, but am in hopes it will be but for a short time.

I wish you would send me some postage Stamps. I mentioned it in my last but suppose you forgot it. I can't get any here and my last goes on this letter. The Sutler ought to keep them but he does not. You have better continue to direct your letter as before and if I am not at the Regiment they will send them to me. On reading this over I don't wonder that you find it often difficult to make my letters out. I try to write slow, but my pen runs away with me and I forget that you will have a hard task to decipher my meaning. Give much love to Anna and the Children,

Your Affectionate Son,
Pierre

Head Quarters 39th Reg. O.V.I.
Ala. March 22nd ,1864

My Dear Mother,

I have nothing new to write about, not even my health varies enough to alter the old story. I received a letter from you dated March 10th. You must have had one from me since.

This morning at awaking I found myself almost in a snow drift. OUT-Col. McDowell and my-bunk is alongside of a window divided of sash. Last night it snowed very hard and this morning we were almost convinced that we were in the artic region instead of the forbad sunny South by finding our blankets covered with snow to a considerable depth. It really would be good sleighing if we only had the means to enjoy it. You see we are still in Athens. The rest of our brigade is about 20 miles south of here in not a very delectable situation, consequently we are very glad to remain where we are as long as the command has not active duties to perform.

I was much pleased to learn that you had heard from Anna and that she intended some to go to housekeeping in N.L. If she is with you now give my love to herself and children. I hope she will not find the place to dull to be endurable after her varied persistence. The people here have treated us very kindly. We accept their favors, when agreeable, without asking ourselves whether they offer them out of love to us or themselves. I think they are more anxious to preserve their own property uninjured than to conduce to our happiness.

I have received numerous invitations to be present at matinees at the female seminary, but as I am usually occupied at that time. I have never accepted. The teachers are in great dread list we should take their building for a general Hospital. It is being talked of, but the matter is not yet decided. If it is thought best for the command however it will certainly be taken possession of without regard to the education interest of the community- though I know of none in greater need of such institutions. But everything must be secondary to the good of the army, consequently the churches are being taken to serve commissary goods in.

We are all in great need of the paymaster, one trip. Night lightened our Pockets to an alarming degree, and no one has come a long from Uncle Sam with a safe full of greenbacks to replenish them. Whenever he does you shall hear from me. I wish the next time you write you would send me some postage stamps, we cannot procure any here, and they are a great convenience when I want to write you.   With much love,

>
> Your affectionate Son.
> Pierre

Head Quarters 39th Ohio Inf.
Athens, Ala.
Sunday April 10th 64

My dear mother,

I was greatly surprised at receiving a letter from you a day or two since. So long a time had intervened since I heard before that I had begun to imagine all sorts of horrible things being the case as you are leaving my letter so long unanswered. As it is you and Anna a sufficiently unfortunate. I think in having no servants and having to endure other inconveniences while the children are sick. I trust that by this time they are out of danger and that you are more comfortably settled.

As you maintain in your last, Gen. Newton is ordered to the west. I saw in the Cincinnati paper a few days since that he was mentioned as being in that City. I hope to have the pleasure of meeting him before long. By the way I notice that his mane has been withdrawn by president for the position of Major General. I was very sorry to learn that such was the case. Do you know if any of the particulars concerning it? Everyone that I have heard speak of him. After serving in the Army of the Potomac, have gave him a fine reputation. If the communications that I speak of be true I am certain it is the work of politicians who, having their own pets to promote, have no scruples in tearing down our country men to make more room for their compatriots.

During the evening of the day on which I wrote you last we received orders to march immediately to Decature-18 miles South. The enemy were reported advancing in that place in considerable force and a fight was anticipated. Accordingly, we started about 10 o'clock in the evening and arrived in the banks of the Tenn. River opposite Decatur about 5 a.m. We rested until daylight then crossed the river on pontoon bridge and took position in front of the town. All part of the program was fully carried out, but the enemies was not there failing to appear. The next day we returned to Athens, and here we have been quietly encamped since. We are expecting to move farther south in a few days.

I received a letter from Jack by the same mail that brought yours and was very glad to learn that his pay has been increased. I wish it could be doubled. I know he deserves it a good deal more than I do mine. He said that he had sent me a U.S. paper containing an account of the visit of the naval Committee but to that place, but I never received it. In regard to the installment which you are deserve in receiving to make that affaire of the bond screening. We have had no pay since last January and my trip north took all that I then got, consequently I can do nothing until the paymaster come around, though I am as anxious to send money home as you are to receive it. Give my love to Anna and the children. I looked forward to meeting them when I come home last, it would have added a great deal to the pleasure if my visit could I have done so.

You wish to know the name of our Chaplin. It is Rossiter- of Heron, Ohio. He had a fine position of the Presbyterian Church. We like him very much. He is the exception to Army Chaplains. Many truly of them bring their profession into disrespect- according to my experience, by their ignorance and conduct generally. So, Hattie

222

wants to leave the sacred soil and be comfortable among the Yankee tribes. I am very sorry indeed for her in dividedly and would do anything in the world for her but am glad the Southern people all suffering- the more and the harder the better. Perhaps after all they well think they were pretty comfortable when approached by mudsills and be thankful if they can get back and receive a few crumbs from Uncle Sam's Table. Desertion from the Rebel army are coming into Decatur at the of thirty per day.

Your affectionate son,
Pierre

Head Quarters 3rd Ala.
Sulphur Branch Trestle, Ala,
May 13th, 1864

My dear mother,

I have received but one letter from you since coming to this place now more than a month since the one received to was dated April 16th. You had not than received my last.

The order relieving me from this post and returning to my regiment. I am informed had sent me by mail some two weeks since. I have not as yet got it and accordingly much to my disgust have to remain at this stupid point. My regiment is in the front with Sherman, the last I heard from them they were near Dalton. Probably there has been a battle there before this. I hope to be with them in a few days. Letters have been sent to me from the regiment since I came here but have not reached me. I probably should not have got yours had not an Officer brought it to me.

So, after much tribulation New London has now the Navy Yard. I congratulate the inhabitants of that quiet bay, the respect and trust it will inspire my new life then here—certain suggest existence. it is to be hoped also that the value of real estate will be increased at least a thousand per cent—probably in Connecticut. You think it is like summer down here in Alabama, but if you could have been transported here.

Yesterday you would have supposed judging from the weather that you were in Maine or still farther north, about a week since there was quite a heavy frost, destroying what cotton there was up and severely ruining the early vegetation. A fire is necessary to one's comfort now. The other night a rather unpleasant incident occurred to me-somewhat serious I thought at the time but to a distinguished spectator, no doubt it would appeared very laughable.

A little after midnight in the midst of a furious wind and rain I was awakened by the rattling of my pail canister. It had stood so many such onslaught of the elements that I thought I was pretty safe, but I had only two minutes to indulge in only such dressing forth need instant with a low deport it split into and was pole stand into a neighboring rifle pit. - while the rain was pouring on me in torrents. I trot a hasty retrial in so belly by footed through the mud to a log house that was near where I was forced.

I should be protected from the storm-but had barely got inside. When another small hurricane divided the building of the grandeur portion of its roof. I was nearly as bad off as before but finally succeeded in rounding up some of the servants and having had a few men sent out a party to recoup. My clothes were found scattered around in the mud indiscriminative. Some having been blown quite a distance from my original camp. After hours were finally got together in a very limp state. The next day I had a large group out with a party of men who took now a small unoccupied house to now had it put up and now occupy now safe quarters there.

With the exception of having a few chills I have been very well and only determined to be with my regiment where there our action operating in Georgia. If I get there I shall probably have an opportunity of seeing Gen. Newton. Give my love to Anna and the children

Your affectionate Son   Pierre

You had best direct your letters to the 39th as before.

Pierre

Head Quarters 39th Reg. Ohio Inf.
Near Chattahoochee River Geo. July 6th, 1864

My Dear Mother,

Very probably you are concerned since receiving my last informing you of my intentions of going to the front, of learning of my health and safety. I should have written before, but the times are few and now I don't know of whole moment. I shall be unable by orders to move for the last two weeks we have been continually on the move. Since marching here have hardly for a moment been out of hearing of artillery and musketry.

On my way to the regiment I was detained at Ringgold Geo. For a couple of days by the fact the Rebels having burnt some bridges in a path of us. Traveling in this country of guerillas in dirty box cars cannot be regarded as pleasure and my trip to Nashville to Big Shanty was no an exception to the general rule. However, I was abundantly satisfied with having got through at all. First it is a way by no means safe to travel.

We were continually passing the charred remains of bridges or cars pitched off the track and shattered to pieces by a torpedo or burnt remnants of long trains burnt perhaps the day before by guerillas. We passed also all two places made historic by Rosecrans and Grant and Sherman- Chattanooga-Chickamauga, Dalton, Tunnel Hill, Buzzards Roost, Resaca Geo. And finally, around midnight at Big Shanty. The endless of the Union end of the war and within a few miles of the Regiment.

Until daylight I slept on some sacks of corn in company with some Officers with whom I had made the journey and then procured a horse and started for the 39th I found them on the extreme front at the base of Kennesaw Mt. within a few hundred yards of the enemy and rather unpleasantly exposed to the musket balls which were continually flying into camp. The pickets were plainly in view within talking distance of ours.

I suppose you have heard all about Kennesaw, and the unusually strong position the Rebel Army had there. Too strong for any frontal assault and not rendered valueless by Sherman's Maneuvers. We were before Kennesaw Mt. 18 days during which there was an almost continuous boom of artillery and roar of musketry day and night. On the night of the 2nd July the 16th Corps (in which is the 39th) was ordered to take up the line of march towards the right, to gather with some other corps for executing a flank movement and so force the enemy to abandon his position. We were to leave at midnight and of course there was the greatest necessity for screening.

A little before dusk to confuse them we were still in our original position. All our artillery opened upon them and a most terrific shower of shot and shell was poured into them as it became a little dark, the sight of the bursting shell was most grave. The artillery wheels were muffed, and every precaution taken from the works and the Rebels were running at full speed for the rear. They were in line of battle behind breastworks but could not stand the impetuous charge of our ten regiments.

But now the sad part of the affair—the dead and wounded are being brought in. Almost the first one carried from the field was our Col. His ankle shattered by a musket ball, during the evening his leg was amputated. In a few moments the road was full of wounded, dead, and dying. All that could be done there was to ones their wounds temporarily and send them to the hospital about a mile in the rear. All were in fine spirits even those terribly wounded. My regiment lost in killed and wounded 36 – the 27th lost 41. It was found that the enemy had retreated about two miles to a second line of works. Our troops remained on the field the night of the fourth, and expected another fight the next day, but did not meet the enemy.
We are about three miles from the Chattahoochee River. The Rebel army is making the best of its way across, harassed all the time by our

troops. It is not generally believed that they will make another stand this side of Atlanta.

South Bank of the Chattahoochee River – this picture taken after retreating Confederates had burned the bridge and Sherman's engineers rebuilt it (Bernard Library of Congress)

Our troops are in the best of spirits and all have unbounded confidence in Gen. Sherman. He certainly has conducted affairs with great ability thus far, and I have no doubt he will continue to do so. Lt. Col. McDowell - whom you will remember-acted in the charge with the greatest bravery unimaginable. The Col. Fell in the very beginning of the affair, the command of course fell to McDowell and everybody speaks of him in the highest terms.

It is terribly hot here it would seem impossible for men to march and fight, yet they do both, though a number fall under the effects of the sun. We are living in a very rough style at headquarters, we have one tent fly, there is not a tent in the regiment. The men bivouac at night. I have not had the pleasure of taking off my pants at night for about ten weeks. - we have been in such proximity to the enemy that we always had to be on the alert. Beans and salt pork with hardtack constitute all we have to live on. We have not seen any such thing as green vegetables since coming into Geo. It would be the greatest luxury if I could have a potato, but the country is stripped of everything eatable by the retreating army.

I had intended to go around to see Gen. Newton, but have not had an opportunity- moving as we have been all the time. The surgeon is detailed now, and I am in charge of the Regiment. We have lost so far in this campaign about 70 men and the Col. And 3 Officers. I have lost my mare again, this time she has been gone a couple of months and I have given up ever finding her. Col. McDowell got me another horse, she is rather young but promises to be a fine animal. I sent you by express from Nashville about the 16th of last month $110.00 and also wrote you. I have been expecting every day to hear from you in regard to it.

Cannonading is heard quite plainly at the river about 2 miles distance - an Officer who has just come from there says the Rebels have fortifications on the opposite side and considerable artillery, we expect to move down there tomorrow or next day to affect a crossing- we have pontoons along and hope to be in Atlanta in the course of a month. I send Jed by this mail an Atlanta-paper which I picked up on the battlefield of the fourth. Please give my love to Anna and the Children. I am expecting to hear from you every day, as I have not recd. A letter since leaving Sulphur Trestle.

> Your affectionate Son,
> Pierre

(also with the July 6 letter)

Fourth of July and one which I shall long remember. We started again. We advanced about three miles-our Brigade was in front when the enemy was found to be in the neighborhood. We were halted and a Company of the sent out as skirmishers to ascertain the state of affairs. The Rebels were found, and the order given to the reg. to advance on the double quick, the bullets whistle unpleasantly close around me. Their pickets were driven to their main force which was in their rifle pits, and there we came to a halt to ascertain their position and throw up breastworks and form the line of the Division. Our brigade was all the time in front, about two hundred yards from the breastworks, shoots were continually being exchanged but we lost only a few men.

Late in the afternoon the order came for my regiment and the 27th Ohio to charge their works. Immediately in our advance was an open field, about 200 yds. In width on the opposite side of which were the breastworks the regiments were about to charge.

At half past six the bugle sounded "forward" and instantly the two regiments, with a cheer, dashed out for their work determined to take the Rebel breastworks or die trying. The excitement was intense, the cheer was taken up by the rest of our troops and as our men rushed forward across the field toe Rebels opened with a fire of musketry that was terrific., it seemed to a listener as if it were impossible for anything human to live under it. Our men did not fire a gun but went at them with the bayonet and in about five minutes from the time the bugle was sounded, the regimental colors of the 39th were floating that they might not hear the movements of the trains. We were all ready to start when the order countermanding the previous one was recd.

The enemy being supposed to be massing on our right for an attack, accordingly not move that night. Before daylight on the 3rd July our pickets discerned that the Rebs had run and when I got up after sunrise the Stars and stripes were floating from their works, and soldiers in blue were lining the crest of the mountain. Immediately after an early breakfast the Col. And I started for the summit. The mountains 1800 feet high divided really into two by a gorge- and the side are step and rocky in places. It was as much as I wanted to do to get to the top under the most favorable circumstances. A number of bodies of Union and Rebel we passed on our way up, bodies of those whose lives were lost a few days before in an attempt to advance our skirmish line.

The view from the top was splendid. The little town of Marietta seems right under us and through it the rear guard of Johnston's army could be seen winding away. Skirmishing with our cavalry, sent out to reconnoiter. It was very interesting to see the arrangements they had made for annihilating us in case we attacked. Their departure from the mountain was by no means anticipated. Various summaries on the subject had been made, and certain movements of Sherman the day before rendered them too uneasy to remain in their strong hold. A few hours after we had learned of Johnston's departure, we started in pursuit and marched about ten miles.

Hosp. 4th Div. 16th Army Corps

Dear Jack,

The reason for the delay is because of the change in the commanders in the Rebel army. Hood has decided to fight, and this pleases Sherman. A prisoner was taken, and while being marched past piles of dead was asked how many men Hood had under his command. The prisoner replied, "enough for two more killings"

On the 4th of July we were in pursuit of the enemy and on that morning, we bumped against them again and that historic day was celebrated by a display of fireworks more exciting than amusing. Bullets were thrown about very carelessly and not the slightest respect seemed to be shown the medical. In the afternoon a charge was ordered on the enemy rifle pits. It was here that the colonel lost his leg.

Pierre

Confederate artillery emplacements overlooking Peachtree Street
(Library of Congress)

Confederate palisades, on north side of Atlanta, Georgia, 1864
(Library of Congress)

Near what today is the Georgia Tech Campus (Courtesy National Archives)

Series of 3 abatis placed in front of Confederate earthworks - Ponder House)
(Courtesy National Archives)

Hosp. 4th Div. 16th Army Corps
(Near Atlanta)

Dear Jack,

On the morning of the 19th (July) we started again for Atlanta. Our first
point Decatur on the Augusta and Atlanta R.R. Here we anticipated a
fight, but nothing was seen of the enemy and we entered the town
with flags flying and bands playing in glorious style, when suddenly a
half dozen or more shells came crashing through the trees killing and
wounding a few of my brigade, among them our division surgeon,
breaking his thigh. Our batteries quickly came up on the gallop and
opened. After a few rounds the Rebs hushed up. We bivouacked and
the few women who remained looked cross. Especially when they saw
their potatoes and chickens appropriated by the horrible Yanks.

On the 21st we were within 2 miles of the fated city in line of battle, the enemy about a mile off, suicidal disposed, the skirmishers keeping up a continuous rattle of musketry and about every five minutes the would fire. The morning of the 22nd presented a marked contrast. The enemy had left our front and there was Atlanta in front with nobody to defend it. We advanced to the outskirts and then awaited orders to capture the city.

After dinner musketry was heard about a mile and a half to the rear where an army of 1500 to 2000 were parked and there the enemy were rushing down in tremendous force to capture it. Instantly a line of battle was joined. I cannot pretend to describe it, bullets flew around too thick to admit of calmly watching it, bullets flew around too thick to admit of calmly watching. The lines at times were touching one another as charge followed charge. Our regiment lost 122 men and 3 Officers. Our soldiers acted like heroes.

The enemy fought like the devil. They didn't have the slightest regard for their lives. Artillery battery mowing them down by the score as they advanced. You could see men and Officers falling every instant. As standard bearers fell others took their places and, so it went for two hours. They gave up the field leaving about 8,000 dead and wounded and we about half that. Our greatest loss was General McPherson who was killed. I was about a hundred feet from him. The Rebels got possession of his body and riffled it of his papers, money and watch.

After words their line was pushed back, and his body was recovered. I thought that I was gone too, several times as the balls whistled past, but I got off without a scratch. Some of the wounded had to lie on the ground throughout the night without blankets, theirs being lost during the fight. Twice we had to move the hospital out of range of the enemy guns ...(*rest of letter missing*)

In the field Near Atlanta Geo.   (Library of Congress)

August 2nd, 1864
My dear mother,

I believe I wrote you last from the South bank of the Chattahoochee on
which we bivouacked a few days. On the morning of the 17th July the
army recd. Orders to march and we were early on the road for Atlanta!
During the advance of that day and there succeeding, we were
constantly skirmishing with the Rebel Cavalry. On the 18th we crossed
the much spoke about Peachtree creek and the evening of the Sunday
we entered Decatur on the line of the Rail road from Atlanta to
Augusta. The 23rd Corps stopped about a mile from town while our
Corps - the 16th was ordered to advance and occupy the place.

Union soldiers photographed shortly before the Battle of Atlanta.   *(Library of Congress)*

Our Regiment was in the advance and with flags flying and everybody in good spirits we entered the town and had just got into its center by the court house, when some Rebel guns opened on us most unexpectedly. The shells burst around us quite lively for a time. In a short in which our batteries got into position and the Rebs were soon silenced. Our division Surgeon was unfortunately struck with a piece of shell and his thigh fractured.

We remained in Decatur that night and in the 19th again started late in the afternoon and advanced about 3 miles. On the 20th we remained quit above 2 ½ miles from Atlanta. On the 21st we advanced again and got into position in line of battle on the extreme left with the 17th Corps on our right. The 17th had a severe fight in the morning driving the Rebels from their breastworks which we occupied during the day. On the 22nd we had the seventh engagement our Regiment has been in as yet.

On the morning of the 22nd we found that the Rebels had left our front. No large bodies could be seen but there and here and there a few visible near the city, carelessly walking away, everything else was quiet, not even the rift of constant views of Atlanta and watching the advance of our skirmishers, some of which had entered the city. We had just got through dinner and were lying about on the grass, making ourselves as comfortable as possible, when some sharp firing was heard about a mile in the rear and a little to the left.

In about five minutes an order came for our Regiment to go back on the road in the double quick. Immediately the Regiment was under arms and started on the run. We soon reached a larger open space about a mile and a half to the rear and then we met the enemy coming in on our left flank. Our whole division was soon in line of battle and a most fine musketry fight began. We had the whole of Hoods Corps opposed to our two divisions.

It was the most grand and exciting scene I have yet witnessed as our men advanced to the battle field with flags flying and men cheering while the bullets were whistling about like hail, and then our cannon opened with grape and canister on the Rebel ranks, actually mowing them down as they advanced not more than a hundred yards from our lines. I stood about fifty yards in the rear of my regiment. Balls came most unpleasantly near, whistling through the leaves and cutting through the dirt in a most savage style.

Maj. Gen. McPherson was killed early in the fight. It was about 100 feet from here when he was killed. The Rebels were just in line on our right when he was killed. The Rebels were coming on our right when he was killed, and it was with great difficulty that his body was secured. The Rebels had at one time had possession of him and riffled his body of his watch, valuable papers and money, our ambulances and ourselves came very near being capture our hospital. I forgot now what Corps it belonged to fell into the enemy hands. It seemed for a time doubtful whether the enemy would succeed in their plans or not of taking the left of our army.

All of our trains were in imminent danger of capture, within easy musket range of the enemy, and driver were killed as they were trying to get them off to a place of safety. It was a grand sight, the Rebels advancing, not a quarter of a mile from when I saw, a solid column

238

with their banners flying, pouring the shot at us, then our forces would charge them, and our cannons poured the grape into their ranks.

You could see their men and Officers falling by the scores. At one instant their colors would be on the ground, their bearers killed or wounded, the next another would seize them and still advance. Our soldiers acted nobly and when the battle was over it lasted about an hour and a half, we still held the field and saved the army. My regiment lost 123 men- 19 killed dead on the field. You can understand by our loss that we were in the hardest of the battle, other regiments of my brigade lost in the same proportions.

We were exposed to fire from the front, the right and the Rebels were also putting shells into our ranks. Anywhere around us, one would be in a decidedly hot place. Our battery belonging to our brigade was captured and two if its Officers either killed or captured. Nothing certain is known of their fate. The battery as always been with us and we had become much attached to the Officers, they were west Point men and fine artillerymen. The morning of the battle however it had been ordered to report for duty to the 15th Corps, so our Brigade was not responsible for it loss, however much we deplored it.

The surgeons of the brigade had a busy time. Those of us had all the duty to performed and by night we had nearly 400 wounded men to take care of and with very insufficient means at our command. You would think it very hard that men terribly wounded, and with their limbs just amputated should lie all night on the ground and many without- a blanket to cover them or a meal to eat. Yet such was the condition our men were in. Their knapsacks and haversacks having most all been lost during the battle, and our trains were in such confusion that they could not be got at that night.

-----Since we were obliged to move the hospitals in order to get the wounded out of range of the enemy shells. Every day since we have been as busy as possible. We have now in our division hospital about

300 men wounded- have sent off 130 and have received a few -------------
---.

My regiment has lost the last month, in battle, 162 men and five Officers, nearly every day we have been under the enemy's guns. I can't tell you anything new in regard to operations here. You must learn from the newspapers more than I can inform you of and sooner. I had letters from Jack a few days since. He told me about your great fire in the old lumber yard on the 4th of July, the same day that my regiment was having a severe fight. I am glad that you escaped so fortunately, and that Jack was with you. I have not recd. a letter from in a long time. I had been expecting one from you but have no doubt now but mine to him with $25.00 enclosed failed to reach him. I will like however to know for certain if you can inform me please do so. I have hardly had a moment to spare since I have been on the campaign and have not had an opportunity to see Gen. Newton. His division has done a great deal of fighting and lost more men than any other in the army. Our hospital is a few miles from the regiment, we are expecting to get our wounded off north in a day or live and then I shall return to it at present there is no Medical Officer with the command. The wounded requiring all our attention.

I hope by the time I write again that we shall be in Atlanta, we are now in sight of it and are pitching shells into the city. If Johnston had remained in command we should have been there some days ago, but Hood sure determined to have his army slaughtered here and nothing suits us better, though our advance is somewhat delayed by the new regime. I have been writing in a great hurry with interruptions every minute-so excuse appearances. Col McDowell is commanding the brigade. Give my love to Anna and the Children

> Your Affectionate Son,
> Pierre

Hospital 4th Division, 16th Army Corps,
2 miles from Atlanta August 8th, 1864

Dear Jack,

Yours was recd. a few days since together with one from mother. You see by the heading that we have got pretty near the seed of our journey, two miles from Atlanta, and it has been two miles for the last ten days. The charge of command in the Rebel army has been the cause of our delay. I have no doubt that Johnston would have long before this respectfully retired beyond Atlanta as we advanced and probably he would have acceded a wider part.

Hood had determined to fight the thing out here and doubtless Sherman is well prepared with his resistance. If he succeeds no better than he did in the fights of the 22nd, 28th he will soon have no Rebel Army to within this quarter. A prisoner was taken the other day and while being conducted across the field where dead Rebels were piled was asked how many men Hood had assembled? "About enough for two more killings handsomely"

My last was dated at Kennesaw Mt. which after bumping against for about two weeks, the enemy was obliged to evacuate by reason of one of Sherman's successful "flanking Movements" The pickets informed us in the morning of the 2nd July that the birds had flown, everything certainty was remarkably quiet and on getting out of our blankets and looking to the top of the Mt. which had been throwing lead balls at us so long there we saw the Stars and Stripes which some enterprising picket had carried to the top.

I couldn't resist my curiosity and clambered up 1800 ft. and had a magnificent view a little after sunrise. The Rebel column was then slowly winding its way farther southward through Marietta, skirmishing as it went with our advance cavalry. Any number of interesting points were in sight, but the whole thing is stale now.

In two or three hours we are in pursuit and on the morning of the 4th July we bumped against them again, at which time that hastened any was celebrated by a display of fire-works decidedly more exciting then amusing. Bullets were thrown around very carefully and not the slightest respect seemed to be paid the medical fraternity,

In the afternoon a charge was ordered to be made upon the enemy rifle pits, it was done, and we lost 35 killed and wounded and the Rebs was routed. It was here the Col. Lost his leg. Next day we were again on the march, fighting more or less as we advanced now and then we would be saturated by a shell or a volley of musketry, but no determined opposition was made—arriving on the South side of the Chattahoochee, we remained there several days resting and getting supplies.

On the morning of the 19th we started again for Atlanta-our first point was Decatur of the Atlanta and Augusta R.R. Here we anticipated a fight but nothing was seen of the enemy and entering the town with flags flying and bands playing in glorious style when suddenly about half a dozen more shell came crashing through the ranks, killing and wounding a few in my Brigade, among others our brigade surgeon, breaking his thigh & our batteries quickly came up on the gallop and opened after a few rounds the Rebs hushed up and we quickly bivouacked in the town. Fav, besides women remained and they looked terribly cross. Especially when they saw their beans, potatoes and chickens appropriated by the horrid Yanks.

Decatur is about five miles from Atlanta - on the 21st we were within two miles of the fated city in line of battle-the enemy about ¼ mile off summarily disposed- the skirmisher keeping up a continuous rattle of musketry and about every five minutes artillery would roll out. The night was very noisy while the morning of the 22nd presented a marked contrast which was soon explained by our learning that the enemy had left our front and there was Atlanta plain in view with apparently no one to defend it, our skirmishers advanced to the outskirts of the city without any opposition.

(Library of Congress)

All the morning we laid around on the grass, impatient to be ordered to advance and take possession. Just after dinner however sharp musketry five was heard to our rear about a mile. We were on the left of the line a part of the 16th Corps being between us and the extreme left immediately, we were ordered out and started back on the road on the double quick- after a run of about a mile and a half we reached a large open space when the line of 1500 or 2000 were packed and there the enemy were in sight rushing down in tremendous force to capture them-instantly line of battle was formed by our division and the battle was begun - I can't pretend to describe it, bullets from about one almost too thick to admit of calmly sightseeing - of yet I had a splendid view of the whole affair though I would hardly be willing to risk my head for another one even as grand a sight as it was.

The two lines at times were touching one another as charge followed charge. My regiment was in the hottest of the affair - and lost 123 men, and 3 Officers. Or soldiers acted like heroes and the enemy fought like the devil, they seem to have the slightest regard for their lives. Our battery mowing them down by the score as they advanced against us-you could see their men and Officers falling every instant. As their Standard Bearers fell others took their places and so it went for two hours. But with their greatest efforts and against a lesser force, yet they couldn't break our lines and finally had to give up the field leaving their dead wounded in our hands. They all though lost on that afternoon about 8,000 - we scarcely lost half that. - just before the line of our regiment 400 hd. were killed outright and buried by our men.

Confederate dead after the Battle of Atlanta, July 23, 1864. Sketch by Henry Dwight. (Courtesy Ohio Historical Society)

Our greatest loss was in McPherson. I was about 100 feet from him when he was killed. The Rebels got possession of his body lifted it of his papers money and watch, after that their lines were pushed back and his body recovered. I thought I was going up several times as ball whistled so wickedly around, but I got off without a scratch. At night we had two Medical Officers besides myself- nearly 400 wounded men to take care of- and with very insignificant means at our command, men there. Half the poor fellows are lying on the ground through the night without a blanket to cover them as having lost them during the fight. Twice our hospitals had to be moved out of rage of the enemy guns.

The next day we got them blankets and made them somewhat more comfortable. We now have them all under canvas and are getting them North as soon as possible- by this morning report we still had 226 sick and wounded remaining. Since the 22nd there has been more or less fighting every day. I am about five miles   the Reg. though not over a mile from the front. Yesterday I rode over to the 4th Corps too see Gen. Newton, he is commanding the 2nd Division in that corps. I like him very much.

We are getting hard up here for clothing. Transportation is so limited that I left one of my valises full of clothing behind and there is no opportunity here for getting anything more-consequently I have to call upon you help again. I want you to get me a shirt. Do you remember what I worn when I was home? You will know I want what—A woolen traveling shirt. The size about the neck should be 16 inches in other respects I want as large as you can get it. The larger the better. You can send it by mail without any trouble. By doing it up as compactly as possible and putting some extra stamps. I leave color Etc. to your taste and judgment. The last one I got was a very poor one at Stewarts. I was sorry to learn the fate of the red stone. I am glad you will be at home and that the affair was no worse. You speak of extremely hot weather in N.L. What would you think of campaigning and fighting in Geo. With such weather greatly intensified. It is a perfect torrid zone here. During the present July my regiment has lost in action 168 men. Sickness don't trouble us much. I wrote another yesterday.

Your affectionate son
Pierre

Hospital 4th Div. 16th A.C.
Marietta Geo. Aug. 26th, 1864

My Dear Mother,

As you will see I have changed my base again. About two days since I as ordered here, and was not at all unwilling to come, having become thoroughly tired of the noise of Artillery and musketry. I am living in one of the stylish houses of this pretty little town- appropriated for the use of the surgeons of the Hospital. Dr. Follette, surgeon of my Reg. is in charge of the Hospital, which makes it very pleasant for me.

We have about 600 sick and wounded men here. Many of the wounded or killed on the picket line every day. I suppose something very important will happen here in a few days, as the whole army with the exception of the 4th Corps started on the march with 15 days. Rations. I hope before you receive this you will learn by telegraph that Atlanta is ours. We have now been before it over a month. On the 22nd of last month our big fight occurred and there we expected to be in the city within a day or two. But Hood has acted very stubbornly in the matter.

I wish I could enjoy your sea breeze for a time, the air here is some time stifling, and SO hot. I have never received any letters from Dr. Green, if he ever wrote which I very much doubt, it was miscarried. I recd. a letter from Jed a few days ago since acknowledging the receipt of money I sent. A few days before I left the front I called upon Gen. Newton, had a very pleasant ca; and was surprised to meet than a number of the Generals Staff name Carrington. He was in Yale at the same time with myself and all thought I was not in the same class and not very well acquainted with him thou. I sure like meeting with an old mate to find him so unexpectedly out here. The Gen'l was very polite and kind and I shall take great pleasure seeing him again whenever I get a chance. I am very pleasantly located here shall probably remain some time, though there is something which is very fascinating at the front which makes me continually wish I was back there again.

One old cow which we procured in Miss. About two years ago, which has trans versed with us hundreds of miles, and always ready to refresh us with an abundance of milk was while standing in camp a short distance from Headquarters shot dead by one of the enemy's bullets. She was considered a great loss. I hardly know what I shall do when I get back to the reg. without her, but such is fate of war. And there is no exception to cows. I have been writing such a long letter lately that I suppose I may be pardoned for a short one now, especially as there is nothing to write about. You can direct your letters to me at, 4th Division, 16th Army Corps- Marietta Geo.

> Love to Anna and the children
> Your Affectionate Son,
> Pierre

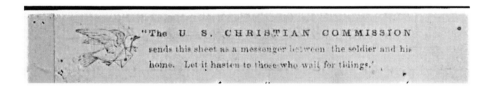

No. 9 ward, 4th Division Hospital, 16th A.C. Marietta, Ga.
Sept. 2nd 1864,

My Dear wife,

Not having any breeches to wear (having sent mine to the washer woman) and consequently having to stop today I think I cannot improve my time better than by writing to you, I have yet just made a contract with a woman to wash my pants for about one third of a pound of coffee, which I fortunately had by me when I left the regt. Not being in possession of any money makes it rather awkward sometimes if a fellow wants anything done for him.

I suppose you would like to know what sort of place this is. Well it is a right snug pleasant, place and before the war must have been a thriving handsome town. There are a great many fine buildings in it, and streets are well planted and protected from the rays of the sun, by rows of white walnut trees mostly. There is a large public square planted, but that is in a ruinous condition now. To many troops of both armies have made it a camping place. The principal stores & warehouses in the place are arranged on the side of this square and are of good size for so small a place. A present however they are all occupied by the Sanitary Society, Quartermasters, and others connected with the army.

There are some 5 or 6 good sized church's all of which are at present used for hospitals. In one of these St. James Episcopal Church, I am at present staying. It is about the size or a little larger than Globe Road Chapel and capable of seating some 360 persons, there are now in it 107 sick and I assure you we have none too much room. You recollect the last pew on the right side of the gallery where Old Mr. Spillman used to sit at Globe Road Chapel, well I occupy the corresponding pew here. I have got a board level with level with the seat & it makes it a first-rate bunk. True it is not very soft, but then it is better than the trenches.

There must be some thousands of sick and wounded to our division alone. Then there are the sick belonging to tow other divisions of our corps, and the sick belonging to other corps here. You who stay at home can form no idea of a large army. One blessing this is a healthy place, and full of wells of excellent water. Every house has its well, for 30 to 60 feet in depth and the water comes up cold as ice and clear as crystal.

One misfortune is the impossibility of procuring vegetables or fresh fruit. The Sanitary Society furnished considerable of dried apples $ peaches with canned fruit, but what is it among so many. Of course, the wounded are thought of first as they ought to be, but by the time they and the worst of the sick cases are attended to there are not many luxuries left for the balance. Fortunately, I do not require many nice thing, I am like I was at home if I can only get enough bread & meat anyone can have the fancy fixings for me.

I often think though that I should like a mess of green corn or beans or tomatoes, but it doesn't trouble me to do without them. I crave an apple more than anything, but they are four dollars per bushel and no account at that. I am sorry to say that Miller has been compelled to lose his arm, it was amputated last Monday, just eight weeks from the time he was wounded. I saw him the night it was taken off and did not think he would survive it. But he is much better now, and I think in a fair way of doing well. Bill Cook whom you have heard me speak of more than once left for home last Wednesday. I would be glad when you write you will let me know how Sam Griffin is getting along. He is at Rome 30 miles from here and I have no means of course pondering with him but suppose he will soon be strong enough to leave for home now.

I do not know when I shall see or hear of my Regt. again, for the 16th and 15th Army Corps are out on a raid and communications with them are closed. They started 3 days back with 15 days rations of more & more to follow. I am glad to say that I am considerably better than I have been though whether I shall ever get the full use of my limbs again I don't know. However, if I don't, I suppose when I get home again I will have to give up farming and do something else.

Please give my love to the children and believe me your affectionate husband George H. Cadman. You must not send any more paper as I can get plenty now from the C.(Christian) Commission.

Atlanta Geo. Sun. Sept. 4th, 1864

Dear Jed,

Atlanta was taken by very bold move. There our army has been in front of the place for over a month in front of this place for over a month in front of this place close to their main works not over 300 yards distance the artillery and skirmishing of each side continuously firing at one another and gaining nothing as neither dare to assault the other's works. As there was no chance of getting into Atlanta on this side, Sherman tires another plan. Having got 15 days rations on hand. He suddenly on night starts, leaving one corps of the 20th to take the place of the whole army, while he leaves his communications and quickly gets 40 miles south of the city, cutting their railroad and shutting off all their supplies.

In the meantime, Hood thoroughly deceived, thinks that our army is on the retreat that the 20th Corps, which of course had to fall back as the whole Rebel army advanced is our rear guard, he was thus tolled on nearly to some 12 miles north of it, before he found out his mistake, then of course he turned around and made for Sherman to keep his communications intact, but we have got a day and night march and Sherman is 40 miles away and has already destroyed the railroads.

Hood met Sherman's co. 40 miles south of Atlanta. We have as of yet very unreliable information on the fight except Hood was badly whipped. Atlanta was left in a great hurry.

The 20th Corps made reconnaissance on the 2nd and found it evacuated. They did not even stop long enough to destroy their commissary stores and the machinery in the manufactories, which had been brought back to the place after Hood had determined to hold it was untouched and still in good running order. It is said that enough tobacco was found to supply the army most of the war. The cellars and garrets of most of the houses were reported to have been filled with Georgia militia in a great state of trepidation but you will get all the information that I can give and a great deal more from the papers. I certainly hope that we have taken thousands of prisoners and killed the rest of the army. The news of the capture of Atlanta was here by a placard at Gen. McArthur's headquarters as follows

"Atlanta is ours, Glory to God Bully for Sherman!!"

I am sorry I happened to be away from the regt. On their present trip, but since the Battle of the 22nd I have been away in the general Hospital. When the battle occurred, there were but two medical Officers besides myself with the brigade and as we had some 300 wounded men of course we all had to be at the hospital to take care of them and this we couldn't half do, working night and day. Our surgeon had been detailed sometime before and I had been alone with the regiment since the fight of 4th July. So that where I was detailed there was no medical Officers with the reg. We had the hospital at the front for some time and when it was ordered here I still had to remain with it.

We have here a hospital for the whole division with nearly 900 sick and wounded men. They occupy 3 churches, 8 or 10 houses and a larger number of tents and have 7 medical Officers to attach to them. We occupy a fine brick house of some ones (probably) Rebel of this pretty little town and live in a great deal of comfort, but I am never satisfied away from the Regiment and had rather a great deal been bivouacking with it, then to be left here in the rear. We are about 20 miles from Atlanta. I am going down there in a day or two to as the place the cars are already running there.

You ask me if I have seen much fighting - I have certainly seen enough to satisfy all my curiosity on that point. When I rejoined the 39th they were lying under Kennesaw Mts. In the extreme advance, but a few hundred yards from the Rebel army and our picket lines were not 100 yards apart.

Federal rifle pits in front of Kennesaw Mountain (Library of Congress)

The Rebs had their batteries posted on the top, and took great delight in pouring the shells into us while their skirmishers who were within easy musket range of us and dropped a Minnie ball into camp whenever they could see a head. We slept in holes in the ground and had, every opportunity of becoming familiar with the shriek of the shell and the wiz of a musket ball. Remained there about 10 days. When the enemy were made to evacuate the place - on the 4th of July we met them again. You said you read about that affair in the paper-we lost 35 men killed and wounded with the Col. Who had his leg amputated!

Thure de Thulstrup (April 5, 1848 – June 9, 1930, Kennesaw Mountain,

On the 22nd we were 2 1/2 miles from Atlanta on the left of the line. We were suddenly attacked by Hardee's Corps, again the 39th suffered losing 123 men. I was in the middle of the affair and can testify to the fact that the bullets came terribly thick and sounded very wickedly as they whistled be one's ear. The McPherson was killed, but Hardee was terribly whipped, his dead were found filling the graves. Ever since then till I came to Marietta about ten weeks since we heard nothing but artillery and musketry in almost one continuous now all the time. Shells fly lower when through camp- one came through the tent, hurting no one however.

Our old cow which has followed us everywhere for the last two years traveling hundreds of miles was shot dead. We had many men wounded there. I hope the fighting is now over for a time at least. I have had another misfortune in the horse line. You remember I lost my mare at Decatur Ala. About 3 months ago. Col. McDowell made me a present of another very fine animal of which I thought a great deal— about ten days ago the orderly took her and a valuable horse belonging to Col. Noyes out of town a little ways to graze, carelessness of the orderly they both got away and ran outside the picket line. They were followed as far as the guard would let the orderly go. I gave him orders to find them if it were at all possible. Since which time neither the orderly nor horses have been heard of. He no doubt was captured.

Pierre Starr

Marietta Geo.
Sept. 11th, 1864

My Dear Mother,

I have not yet received an answer to my last-perhaps the reason why is that we have not received a mail for the last week and more. Think of not seeing a newspaper for over a week in these momentous times the fate of the southern confederacy might be decided in a life time. Certainly, our magnificent Army has done its part towards settling the thing very advantageous for us.

Of course, you know all about Atlanta's Capture. Our army took possession on the 2nd, One Corps - the 20th did. The rest of the army being some 30 miles 'south of the city' Hood seeing that all his communications were destroyed, and that Sherman was in his rear where least expected. Hurriedly abandoned the city to save his army. He lost, it is said. Some 300 or 400 prisoners and about 30 to 40 cannons. Those ominous guns which had been shelling us with so long from his fortifications all fell into our hands, and it is said that we retook the Battery which belonged to my Brigade and was captured in the battle of the 22nd July - this however is

Upon evacuation of Atlanta on September 1, 1864, Confederate general John B. Hood destroyed an ammunition train of 81 cars. Wrote one witness:. "As the flames reached each car, it exploded with a terrific din. Five hours were occupied in this work of demolition... Flames shot to a tremendous height and the exploding missiles scattered their red-hot fragments right and left. The earth trembled. Nearby houses rocked like cradles, while on every hand was heard the shattering of window glass and the fall of plastering and loose bricks. Thousands of people flocked to high places and watched with breathless excitement the volcanic scene" (Library of Congress)

I cannot give you my personal notions of Atlanta - not having been there yet. Probably going shortly, it is only 20 miles from here by rail. My division is six miles south of the city at a place called Eastpoint. Sherman in his congratulatory order, says that the army is now to rest for four weeks-be paid off- clothes to get and then at them again.

The enemy are now supposed to be at Macon. Every family in Atlanta whose head is away is ordered from the city - south, and every northern man who is not connected with the army and not in the employ of the government is ordered North to Chattanooga. Sutlers-hangers ons to the great army all have to leave, and the army proper alone occupied the place-and surroundings. And now I suppose Sherman will push on important supplies and be ready for the face Campaign next month. I only hope it will be successful as the summer one has been. I trust that before it begins I shall be out of General Hospital and with my Regiment again.

Perhaps you remember that 3 months ago, I lost my horse, I got another and a like misfortune has again occurred, I am very unlucky in the Horse Flesh certainly. About two weeks ago forage being rather scarce here. One of our orderlies took Col. Noyes horse (our Col. Who had his leg amputated and went home) which he valued very highly, having brought him from Cincinnati with him three years ago – and mine, a little way out sides the country to graze.

Through some great carelessness on the orderly's part, both horses got away and ran through the lines. The guard would not allow the orderly to go past, so he returned to town for a pass to go outside the lines. The following morning, he started with orders to go anywhere after them. From that day he has not been heard from. Doubtless he was taken prisoner and is now an inmate of a Rebel prison, as a reward for his negligence in losing the horses. To add to my loss, he rode my new saddle. Which is now probably the property of some secesh cavalry man.

I have passed about a month now, very quietly and comfortably in this pretty town of Marietta. We have between 500 and 600 sick and wounded here, it is expected that in the course of a month the hospital will be cleared out and removed to Atlanta. The last that we heard from Nashville, General Wheeler and Forrest were fighting our forces at Murfreesboro, this comes about ten days since from that time we haven't received a mail or a northern newspaper, and of course very desirous in hearing of Grants operations-the draft-the democratic nomination and Mobile.

We would like to know whether the Rebs are in Pennsylvania or we in Richmond, whether the copperheads are in the a send ever and played "Swash" with the draft (as for merely N.Y.) or that the news of the capture of Atlanta - made them too sad for a demonstration of the kind, and the union people too exultant to permit it- we would also like to know whether our own "Feed" is to gain out and we feed on half rations" I hope 500,000 men tough and hearty, will now be added to our armies. I don't want Jed or Jack included in that number- Grant can take 300,000 and Sherman 200,000 additional, can sweep this part of county of every Rebel and possess every city. Please give my love to Anna and the Children

> Your affectionate Son,
> Pierre

Marietta Geo.
Sunday Sept. 18, 64

Dear Jack,

The desired shirt arrived some three weeks since, your accompanying letter about two weeks late with stamps enclosed. The shirt was exactly what I wanted and did credit to your taste. I haven't had a better shirt for two years. These colored shirts one negro can wash, and you need not be particular about anything. Consequently, very convenient in this country. I've enclosed six dollars ($6.00) You do not state what the postage was on the bundle, if the enclosed will not cover it let me know.

Our battles and siege have at last cumulated in the capture of Atlanta. We were all perfectly confident that such would be culmination, but it is not the less pleasant to be able to say that it has been. I was very sorry not to be with the command during the last great movement of Sherman. Yet I am confident my time has been used to much greater advantage t myself here in the hospital, In the last two or three months

I have gained a good deal of useful practical knowledge with none to me thare are my pay. As far as the on along goings of the place are concerned,

Atlanta is dying rapidly depopulated. A long train of cars and to wagon trains daily leave the city crowed with its former inhabitants and what little household goods they are allowed under a flag of truce. They are taken miles South and delivered over to the Rebels- they are permitted one day's ration and they must live off their own government instead of eating our supplies. Atlanta will here forth belong entirely to the army.

Everyone not belonging to the army or in the employ of the government been ordered away. Even including sutlers. I am allowed to leave if you were drafted from accounts we hear volunteering has been going very briskly- and I am in hopes, but a small number will have to be drafted, yet I hope the whole 500,000 will be forth coming. We have had a great deal of Newspapers here. I have seen but one or two the last two weeks and our perfectly green about everything that has happened. I would like much to hear that Grant has brought his campaign to as successful a conclusion as Sherman thus we might have hopes of closing this little fracas up within a number of years.

Last train leaving Atlanta. With overloaded cars, it will not have enough room for civilians to bring all of their belongings which can be seen littered beside the wagons left behind (National Archives)

I have lost horse N0. 2- a handsome mare that everyone told me was a very valuable animal at all events she suited me quite nicely and I took considerable pride in her, but alas! She didn't appreciate her respectable position-ran away and doubtless is now the pet of some gay guerrilla the orderly is to blame-while grazing Col. Noyes horse and mine a little ways out he let them both escape him. They ran thought the lines and that was the last seen of them. This occurred more than three weeks ago.

No trains came through from the north for about a week. Sherman however has a sufficiency of supplies. Since Atlanta was taken, Marietta has become a secondary importance, almost deserted. It's used as one of the army depots quite a lively town. Nearly all the corps have their hospitals here yet, though they are being removed as fast as possible. Within the last two days we have sent from our division Hospital 300 or 400 men to the front. We have yet a number of wounded who cannot be moved. I hope my next will be from Atlanta in the Regiment.

> Your Aff. Bro.
> Pierre

Head Quarters 39th Ret. Ohio Inf.
Atlanta Geo. Oct. 2nd ,1864
My dear mother,

Your last, which was rec'd some days since, would have been
answered before but no mail has left here lately and I thought it not
worthwhile to write—I have no idea when you will receive this. The
trains have been used exclusively in caring troops town. We have
received no papers North of Chattanooga for a week. A couple of days
ago I was relived from duty at Marietta and rejoined my regiment in
Atlanta. Today I have been riding about and around the city.

Surrounded with fortification of the strongest description- and which
doubtless Hood would have been delighted to have seen us try to take.
Circle after Circle of works about the city- beginning on its edge and
extending two or three miles out. In fact, you might say they extend all
the way to Chattanooga. As they have always had this place mainly in
view and it preservation to the Confederacy this great endeavor. But
after all it is not so very much of a city - nothing like as fine a place as

Memphis, it compares very well with Nashville, and probably when its inhabitants were here, its population numbered 20,000.

It don't seem to be laid out with any particular regularity and its business blocks are not at all impressive in appearance. A great many of the private residences are pretty- a few handsome. Its most important feature is its Railroad and manufactories. They had an ammunition arsenal here and made great numbers of cannons and supplied a good share of shot, shells and musketry ammunition used by the Confederacy. The arsenal and the works were all blown up when they left. Nothing connected with the R.R. seems to have been destroyed except the engines and cars. The large fine depot with its warehouses all intact, also the immense "Round House" for making and repairing Machines.

Roundhouse following its destruction during the Atlanta Campaign
(Library of Congress)

The city was pretty well battered up by our artillery-riding down the principle street Whitehall - I saw hardly a single building that was not struck by our shells. Great jagged holes were made in the brick walls - in a wooded house nearly the whole side would be knocked to pieces - of course general havic was made with the inside. In the parlor of the house in which we have head-quarters (which by the way is a pretty little cottage with a handsome lawn and fine shade tree) a shell exploded. A large hole is made in the side of the building and the shell evidently burst just as it entered. There must be 40 or 50 holes in the sides-cutting and floor, making a perfect shell of the place. The windows were sheared to pieces not a whole pain left - the Negroes tell us that some half a dozen shells exploded within 10 yards of the house.

From this you can imagine to what the city was subjected, nearly every other house had the same experience. That the inhabitants were in great terror is evident from the "Gopher Holes" they dug to protect themselves from the shells and shot. Hardly a house but what is provided with one.

You may not be learned as to "Gopher Holes"- a hole is dug in the ground about six feet square and about the same depth- logs are then laid across the top and four or five feet of dirt thrown on top them. There is an opening in the side and steps leading to the bottom of the hole. In there the frightened Rebels took refuge when we opened up on the city. The time passed in there must have been anything but pleasant. I have been down in a number of them- some are nicely floored- with niches in the side as if a family in them all the time.

A shell exploded in a church one night in which many women and children had taken refuge - a number were injured- one or two killed. I don't suppose there are more than five hundred of the original inhabitants now remaining. Sherman's order sending all unconnected with the army either North or South has been Ridgely enforced, and the city is possessed and occupied by the military.

Generals Sherman and Thomas occupy fine residences in the city. A day or two ago some 150 of our Officers who had been captured this campaign returned from Rebel prisons having been exchanged. They had been in the hands of the enemy but two or three months, yet they showed in their appearances their harsh treatment. All were poor and haggard, and many had to use canes to get along. Many were barefooted and all very dirty- with clothes of varied wear and very ragged. The only Officer with whom I was immediately acquainted of those taken prisoner on the 22nd July. I ascertained had died in Macon of Surg. Fever, shortly after his capture. He was a young West Pointer, about my age commanding a battery in my brigade.

"The left wing 16th Corps" to which we have been attached has been broken up. It consisted of two divisions under the Command of Maj. Gen. Dodge- our division now belongs to the 17th Army Corps Maj. Gen. Frank P. Blair commanding. So you can hence forth direct to the "1st Division- 17th Army Corps, Army of the Tenn. Atlanta Geo." I wish you would send me some handkerchiefs - I would like half a dozen white ones and cant get them here. I think you can send them in a letter or paper - the former perhaps would be the safe mode. You can enclose them by "detachments" one or two at a time. Jack sent me a woolen shirt the other day in the mail. Lt. Col. McDowell goes North in a day or two. He probably will get to Conn. He intends going to New Haven for some rifles for the regiment. He was very desirous for me to make an application for a leave and accompany him. I think I could have got a furlough- but considering all things I concluded I had better not at present, though I would like to see home very much. That you may not think we are all entirely destitute of rational amusement down here I enclosed you a program of a concert we had here last evening. The idea of a Mass Band giving a concert here would have been regarded a few months ago by the Georgians as beyond the range of possibility, but Sherman with his army can do anything.

I believe I wrote you that I had lost my horse. She has not been heard from, neither has the man who was sent after her. I take pleasure of sending you by Adams express $400.00. Invest it as you think proper. I know nothing about it. I shall be satisfied- whatever you do with it. We have just received orders to move tomorrow morning. The whole army of the Tenn. Goes- where I don't know. The campaign has once again. Hood is said to be on the move. Threatening our communication & probably we are after him in that direction. I would like to know as soon as the money reaches you-as the R.R. is cut and guerrillas are pretty numerous. Rendering transportation unsafe- give my love to Anna and the Children.

Yours, Pierre

Occupied Atlanta – Whitehall Street (Library of Congress)

Head Quarters 39th Ohio Reg. Ohio Vol. Inf.
Galesville Ala. Oct. 22nd, 1864

My dear mother,

This is the first opportunity since leaving Atlanta on the 5th that I have had to write you, except the few lines I sent by Col. McDowell.

We are having a long hard campaign. The time which was to have been devoted to resting and recruiting our army has by Hoods Endeavors been broken upon. He got into our rear with his army, destroyed our Railroad and necessitated our moving out of Atlanta.

We have been marching every day since we left, and more than half the time we marched all night. Started from Atlanta on the afternoon of the 5th of this month and did not reach camp until 8 O'clock the following morning. On the afternoon of the same day received orders and marched until 4 O'clock the next morning in the rain, the remainder of that day and the next we rested near Kennesaw Mountain. At eleven at night we again started and arrived at Ackworth at 4 a.m.: at 8 A.M. started again and reached camp in the evening. The following morning went on to Kingston Geo. And in afternoon 8 mile farther toward Rome getting into camp about Midnight. The next evening, we were again on the road.

Marching all night to Adairsville and laid in a barn yard a couple of hours until day light where we took the cars to Resaca-arrived there at noon. There had been a fight here the preceding day and the Rebels were, when we marched there, but a few miles out. During the evening the 39th Ohio and another Regiment were sent out on a reconnaissance to what called Snake Gap - in the mountain range near.

We went out, had a skirmish with the Rebels lost eight men (one Killed - seven Wounded) returned to the town by daylight and at seven O'clock the same morning were again ordered to march-we skirmished with the enemy all day and marched about twelve miles. We marched again through the whole of the next night and, so it has been until the present time. I give you the preceding as an example of the way it has been through all this campaign.

I have slept under a tent hardly a single night. But laid on the ground on the blanket and never failed to sleep soundly, except when it rained. In the matter of eating we have been at times very hear up. For two days we had nothing but fresh pork without salt, bread or anything else. We have come to a stop here for how long I don't know- probably but for a day or two; very many of the men were barefooted and it became necessary to stop and refit them. We have had a long chase after the Rebels, but could neither catch them or make them fight. They destroyed the R.R. for some 20 or 30 miles more or less- completely- probably it is all repaired by this time.

I suppose you have not heard much of our movements by the papers. We have been so entirely cut off from communicating with the North. We received orders this morning to send to Rome Geo. All of our sick and those unable to stand a long march, So I suppose we will soon be off again. It is believed that the enemy have gone southward from Here. The day before I left Atlanta I wrote you and put into the express $400.00. I hope it has reached you by this time. I wish in whatever way you see fit. I also wrote you to send me some white handkerchiefs. We got an old mail yesterday- but no letters for me. Col. McDowell has gone North for 30 days. I envy his being in the north, and wish I could enjoy some of the comforts that ought to be obtained there. You mentioned home having served his three years. He entered the service after I did, and I was not aware of having been in three years by some months yet.

Won't you ask Anna to send me a photograph of herself, should like much to have one. I am well in spite of rather rough living. Don't worry if you don't hear from me very regularly.

Love to Anna and the Children   Your affectionate Son
                    Pierre

Head Quarters 39th Ohio Vol. Inf.
Galesville Ala. Oct.28th 1864

Dear Jack,

Yours of the 9th reached me yesterday. My last to you was I believe
written from Marietta. I was relieved from there a short time
afterwards and went to Atlanta after remaining there a few days we
started on the present campaign. Atlanta did not strike me very
favorably. It has had a population of about 20,000 but does not equal
in style and evidence of wealth any of our northern cities of that size.
It's railroad facilities are very Complex and from its main
infrastructure was doubtless very important to the Confederacy. Our
shells played the ------with this place.

I doubt if there is a single building in the principal parts of the city
without one or more ragged holes in it- a number of blocks have also
been burnt and the city has the appearance give the country is very
rich. Government has furnished us only hard tack, salt, sugar, coffee,
we procured an abundance of Pork and potatoes and feed for the
animals as we went along. We usually bivouacked in one of the
numerous cornfields, which are so plenty, so that our stock could be
easy to spend the night, but we could only put up a tent, build a bed in
a soft firm with a big fire a bountiful as on a spring mattress at home.

Col. McDowell went north about a week since for 30 days, doubtless is
now enjoying the comfort and luxuries to be obtained nowhere else. I
envy him. This morning our Division was reviewed by Major Gen.
Mower, now commanding the 17th Corps to which we now belong
having been transferred from the 16th. We have all heard of rumors
about our going to Montgomery, Savannah, or Memphis. I think more
than likely our corps will go down to Atlanta again.
A day or two since I rode over to the 4th Corps to call on Gen. Newton,
but sometime since he was ordered to Key West Florida. For some
reason other he is in disfavor with the powers to be and is now
probably shelved for the remainder of the war. I am glad you speak so

emphatically and encouraging about the election though I never had any idea that the north was going to replicate the war at this stage of the game. I never cast a vote yet but intended my maiden on to go for Lincoln.

The N. Y. paper you sent I recd. At Kingston, while on the march we stopped a few hours and the mail was distributed the first in ten days. It was actually new and gave me a good deal of pleasure. Should like to receive them often. I have not heard from mother for at least a . month though I have written her two or three times during that period. While home last, Jed promised a box of his fine pears to me. I have thought often about them this fall but thought it useless to try and get them here, though I would willingly pay a good big expressage for a box full. We don't get any decent fruit. When at Marietta I had a few grapes, which were pretty good- and Apples and peaches are hard and worthless. Pears, I have never seen here. Persimmons grow in abundance they are regarded by some as a great delicacy. I don't like them. Figs grow he also and if you like sweet potatoes you can have in abundance, the biggest you ever saw. Irish (potatoes) are poor and scarce.

I most sincerely congratulate you on your increase in pay and hope it may continue steady to magnify till you made a fortune. I was enabled to put in the express for home on the 4th of the month- the day we left Atlanta- $400.00 having been paid up to August 1st. I have now two ninety more due me. I shall be much better satisfied were I confident it had eve reached home.   I don't think there has been any R.R. communications North since I left Atlanta- we have now been about 25 days out.

If Jed's farm produces in any sort of abundance such fruit as you his prospects speak of he surely ought to make some money. Something I am afraid he has done yet. If you go in there I shall be interested on learning of his prospects. It will not be very long now before congress meets and then I hope to hear good news about the navy yard and have our futures made- in a honor.

We have just had orders to move- going to or near Rome, there to remain until paid off. It is a shame that our western soldiers have not been paid before- and yet I don't know that could be helped for since last May we have been continually on the move to admit pay masters coming to us. The soldiers have now all of name. Their fair cities, without aid from the patriotic stay at home must I think have suffered. The soldiers don't need any money-except a little to purchase tobacco with and I have heard men grumbling when the sutlers have been out of it. There from any other cause. You would be surprised to see immense quantities of it come in by mail. But I must close as tents are about to be struck.

I learn that on the raid by Forrest on the Nashville R.R. that Sulpher Trestle Tenn. When you remember I was doing a couple of several months-was attacked. 75 men were lost together with the Col. And Asst. Surgeon Killed I think I got out about the right time. The col. Was formally Major in the 39th . Shall be glad to hear from you soon,

Yours Truly,
Pierre

Head Quarters 39th Ohio Inf.
Near Savannah Geo.
Dec. 22nd, 1864

Dear Mother,

It is over a month since I last wrote you, but such a long delay has been unavoidable, and I hope you have had no uneasiness on that account. I told you in my last that we as about to start on a campaign for some distant and to us unknown point. We have almost at our destination- been successful in all our undertakings -have had a delightful trip. We have lost but few men. I will endeavor to give you in brief what we did, and how we faired.

On Saturday the 12ᵗʰ Nov. we rec'd marching orders. Sometime previously our baggage had been reduced-cut down to the smallest possible limit. The men had been supplied with everything needed in the any of clothing and equipment and we were in splendid condition for long and severe march. We had been expecting to order for some time and eager to start.

We were in camp at the time near Marietta Geo. We had returned but a few days previously from our march north after Hood. We were anticipated going in an opposite direction, but to our surprise our front was turned northward again, only however for a distance of eight miles- the campaign may then be said to have before as we proceeded to tear up R.R. our only connecting link with the north and our supplies. Until Midnight the troops were at work destroying the road as far as eye could see in either direction the fires of burning Rail road ties could be seen and by morning more than 75 miles of track was destroyed never I think never to be Rebuilt during the war. Every tie was burnt and ever rail bent.

At daylight on Sunday we started south again! that day my regiment marched 29 miles and Monday morning we were in Atlanta. We remained there during the day. The city looked decordly decapitated. The public buildings had been burnt or were then burning. The fire depot was a mass of ruins. Everything of value had been removed from the city and in a day, it would literally be a deserted city.

 Tuesday, we pulled out of Atlanta and reached Jackson-50 miles from Atlanta, on Tuesday afternoon we found what had been a foundry town town-quite pretty. The inhabitants have hastily departed leaving most of their effects behind them including many of their negros; the last were very anxious to join us. They were not however encouraged to do so- they were not wanted to eat up our supplies.

Friday, we crossed the Ocmulgee River. The enemy had burnt the bridge, but we were freely provided with the means of overcoming all such little obstacles as heavy pontoon bridges in which we crossed. It was expected that the Rebels would attack us while getting over the river, but they failed to do so. For the next two days we passed through the towns of Hillsboro and Blountsville. Here we came within 20 miles of Macon about 15 miles of Milledgeville the capital. Our cavalry went to the latter place and burnt the depot ad some public building.

On Tuesday the 22nd we started out of camp at daylight with vertical snowflakes flying around and are air keen enough to do ample Justice to one of New England's November days and by now marched to Gordon, here we first struck the Geo. Central Rail-road which connects Macon and Savannah and to destroy which was one of the objectives of the campaign. We rested for a day and the only day from the tome we left Atlanta until we marched Savannah. For the next few days we made short marches - spending much of the time in burning R.R. in fact all the way to Savannah the road was most thoroughly destroyed ether by our men or other corps

Our march was continued through many towns and a most beautiful country-rich in corn, potatoes, hogs and beef-which with salt, coffee and hard bread- with which we were supplied offered good substance for our troops and animals. Each day a mounted man was sent out who at night returned loaded with chickens, turkeys, ducks, honey, flour Etc., etc. for our tables. The army lived off the country.

From Battles and Leaders of the Civil War, vol 4., edited by R. U. Johnson and C. C. Clough Buel

Coffee Salk and a limited supply of hard bread was all that our men were furnished with. Yet we lived finely. Our stock also was greatly improved we captured a great number of mules and horses to take the place of our worn-out animals. The weather fortunately was very fine, and so mild that it could be considered no hardship to sleep out of doors. At hardly any time after the first two or three days march was an overcoat coffee and usually it was as warm as a June day at home. We crossed successfully the Oconee and the Ogeechee rivers and by Saturday the 10th of December we were within of Savannah and here for the first time we met anything like serious opposition from the enemy. We continued to advance through until we were within 5 miles of the city where we came upon the Rebel fortification.

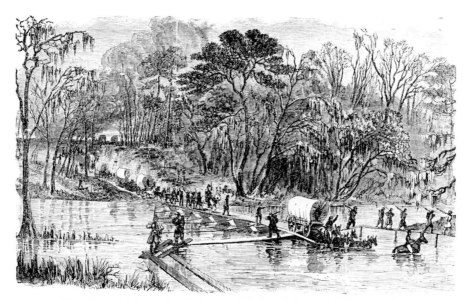

Crossing the Ogeechee (Harpers Weekly, Library of Congress)

My division was in advance of the corps and was under fire all of Sunday the 11th- lost but a few men. Sunday night my regiment to throw up works on the extreme front. We were so close to the Rebels that we could hear them conversing. The rattle of their muskets was plainly heard. By midnight our works were completed and until morning I had the pleasure of sleeping (soundly to) in an open cornfield-during a heavy rain storm, with but a blanket for shelter. With morning came shells and bullets shrieking over us. The enemy forts were very close we could see the smoke of their cannon just in time to duck our heads before the ball would go over, and we were in easy range of there sharp shooters.

Our breastworks of the previous night have protected us. Towards night our Corps (17th) was relieved the 14th and we were marched around to the right which has been our position since in reserve. Six days ago, our division was ordered on an expedition to the Gulf R.R. which involved a march of 100 miles. Last night we returned and were meet with rumors that Savannah had fallen into our hands and such turned out to be fact. The enemy evacuated the city in the night of 20th. Yesterday our troops took possession. Tomorrow I am in the city. The first mail since we left Marietta reached two or three days since- I got five letters from you- one carton, pocket handkerchief- I recd two others while near Marietta. Was glad to learn the $400.00 have arrived safely. What are you going to do with it? Some papers came to hand from Jed. I will write his in a few days. I am well, and everybody is in good spirits including myself-it is late and I am tired-being busy all day-have moved camp this morning.

Your Aff. Son Pierre

Please send me by letter a pair of sister thread gloves equivalent in size to 71/2/ ladies size P.

Head Quarters 39th Ohio Inf.
Near Savannah Geo. Dec. 27, 1864

Dear Jack,

After returning from a ride this morning to Ft Jackson, Benefaction - the pride of the Savanah people- and other interesting spots. I am happy to find your letter awaiting me. Your patriotic wishes as to the success of this "glorious army" have all been fulfilled and we all now are quite possible of Savannah. After a rest of three or four days from all march after Hood, sufficient to fit our now for another campaign, we broke up camp near Marietta Geo. and started for salt water on the 12th Nov.

On the 21st Dec. Savannah came into our possession. We had a really delightful trip. Of course, we had some rainy days and long night marches, but as a general thing the weather was lovely sufficiently warm to make overcoats needless - the country was rich in fine plantations abundant with corn, sweet potatoes chickens, beef, hogs etc. from which we draw a most liberally supply and the was abundantly in vegetation wholly strange to us in the North. We completely destroyed before leaving Atlanta the R.R. up as far as Dalton, burnt or blew up all the Sutler buildings in the city together with some of the extensive business blocks. I don't think it will be a desirable place to live in for some years to come.

Our communications we had now voluntarily cut off, our nearest base of supplies was distance a march of 150 miles, our destination was to us a matter of speculation for Sherman did not dare to enlighten anybody to his future design, but everybody was confident and in the best of spirits. The army was in splendid condition. The baggage had been cut down so that not a superfluous provision was haled supply train carried only coffee, sugar, salt, and a small quality of hard bread and the men had been furnished with all necessary clothing. Men and animals was fed off the country and lived finely too.

The objects of the campaign were to thoroughly destroy the Geo. Central R.R. from Macon to Savannah & capture the latter city and in our transit through the state as to destroy as much as possible of the supplies necessary to the maintenance of the Rebel army. These objects were completely accomplished. The Geo. Central R.R. will never be Rebuilt in this war. Sherman estimated that we used 40,000 bushels of corn per day-we destroyed immense quantities of cotton and there was a line of blazing Rebel mansions-cotton-guns and rail fences from Atlanta to Savannah a large number of mules and horses were captured, and valuable animals were substituted for our worn-out stock so that our trains came out of the campaign a much better condition then they started.

On the 10 Dec. (the date of your letter) we had arrived within miles of the city- previous to that time the opposition to our advanced had been insignificant. My regiment was in the line of battle but once since leaving Atlanta. Now they came out in rather stronger force but were quickly thrown back to their main line of works about five miles from the city. At night the 39th was ordered out to throw up works which was done in very close proximity to the enemy, so close that we could readily hear the movements, conversations and the fact of having but a blanket for shelter and the wet ground was no obstacle.

The next morning the Rebs. opened their batteries on us and shot and shell came shrieking over in no very musical style. Our works were in place round of the Rebs and rec'd their particular situation of their artilleries and sharpshooters. The nearest I came to being hit was to have the dirt thrown over me while eating lunch. Sunday the 11th the 17th Corps was relieved and moved around to the right of our line and held in reserve. My division however was not allowed to not, but was started off to the Altamaha near almost down to Florida to destroy a portion of the Gulf R.R. We returned on the 21st the day the aristocratic City of Savannah fell into the hands of the Ruthless Invaders.

The next day we came in and the regiment is now encamped a pleasant ride from the city. I don't wonder the F.F.Gs. were unwilling that their city should fall into the hands of the Yankees. It is really a very pretty place of about 30,000 inhabitants. I think most of the people remain. They look, as yet rather glume, and don't come out much., but we have had just such the deal with before and know every feature of their disposition.

The Rebs raised the depth of the river by placing obstacles in the channels when our fleet showed signs of coming up the Savannah a long time ago. These have not yet been removed and our supplies come in very slowly. The only way of getting to the city by water is up the Wilmington River or by Warsaw sound through one of its inlets into the Savannah River. Our horses are suffering a good deal for want of forage, and the men are in ----ration. This occurrence will probably last but a short time.

I paid a visit to Ft. Jackson today. It has been our obstacle to our gun boats for long time and a few days since I would have made it very unhealthy for the monitors and other vessels which now lie securely just below the spikes and other obstruction which you see stretched across the river. A vessel is now busy exploring for torpedoes, a number which they had put down.

Speaking of torpedoes, they make them subsume their hellish purpose on land as well. We had about a dozen men in our brigade killed or wounded by the infernal machines which they had planted in the road about ten miles from the city. The adjutant of the 1st Alabama Cavalry lost a leg by his horse stepping on the connecting with the thing, for his horse was killed instantly and his own leg was so shattered that amputation was required. We had about 50 prisoners along at that time these Sherman ordered to go in front and dig up the torpedoes it was a rather delicate operation as a step in any direction might cause an explosion which would send them to eternity very quickly. They protested and begged profoundly but Sherman was inconsolable and very settled they groped about until they had dug up seven, which were laying alongside the road.

When I passed a few miles afterwards every house about that spot was burnt. The Rebels burnt all of Ft. Jackson that was combustible, In the Fort and the earthworks near it they left about fifteen guns. We have taken in all during the campaign about 100 guns. There are very heavy works all about the city in which the cannon are still remaining. Their coast defenses were most formable -the fleet never could have taken this place, neither I think any force coming from the coast, but Sherman did not fulfill their wishes, but came a mostly the back door.

There are already indications   and rumors of another campaign against Augusta or Charleston. I don't imagine we will remain inactive long, though I shouldn't object to it as a change. From the 1st Oct. until the 20th Dec. with the exception of one week we have been continually on the move. Every and nothing would have day I have been in the saddle from day light tell dark, but the time has passed quietly and pleasantly and nothing would have enticed me to miss this campaign which will live forever in history. I would have liked very much to have been with you on Thanksgiving Day and t have exchanged my cold lunch for Mast Turkey and plum pudding instead however we were destroying Geo. Central R.R. and marching about ten miles that day.

You considering it too hard to be endured to be on duty as patrol guard for one hour and a half each two days is rather amusing. Let me tell

you how we faired (39th) the two or days is out from Atlanta- I copy
from a diary- Tuesday- Nov. 15th at noon started out as rear guard to
the train marched the remainder of the day and all night until 6 A.M.
of Wednesday. We rested until A.M. this contained the march all day
until 3 A.M. of Thursday. Started at 7 A.M. of Friday and reached
Jackson Geo. About 5 P.M. Friday. Pierre

Headquarters 39th Ohio Inf.
Near Savannah Geo. Jan. 3rd 65

My dear Mother,

I have been expecting to hear from you for some time, but suppose the
irregularity of the mails is the cause of my disappointment, the last
letter I rec'd was dated the 14th Nov. and with it came a handkerchief,
by the same mail also came on the 2nd both of these I acknowledged
about the 22nd of Dec.

A few days after, the regiment was moved to within a short distance of
the city and here we have been for the last two days. We are expecting
to move a day tent are struck and everything in readiness to embark on
transports probably for Port Royal South Carolina. Whether we are to
remain there any time or immediately start on another campaign. We
do not know. I am or did rec'd the other day from Gen. Howard, he
informed us that we would soon start in "another short and decisive
campaign." Perhaps we are to regret the move. But we have been
soldiers long enough to learn not to trouble ourselves about the
ultimate destination. As I might not have another opportunity to write
soon. I thought to make the most of the present, if marching or duties
do not interrupt me

I have had ample opportunity to get acquainted with the city of
Savannah and surrounding point of interest. It is the prettiest city I
have yet seen in the south. The people have very quietly summited to
Yankee rule, and in a meeting called by the Mayor expressly their
desire to receive the benefits of the Presidents Amnesty Parole.
Promising hereafter to be good children. Business had of course been

entirely suspended if is known gradually moving- and the stores one after another, being reopened as supplies come from the North. Navigation in the Savannah river is as yet rather, on account of the torpedoes and obstructions that remain. The Rebels use them on land as well as on the water. Several men in our brigade were killed and wounded by stepping on and so exploding those infernal Machines, they have been planted in the road for the purpose of blowing us up. I saw seven that were dug up and lying by the roadside as we marched by. This may be all proper in war, but it seems to me must more refined to shoot a man.

It gave me great pleasure to smell salt water again-there was something in it much like home. We have been indulged in fresh oyster too, something to us before we were in the army. Some of our Officers went on slugging a few days since and returned with about a load of thirty bushels. So, we had a suffice of beloved. We don't yet succeed in getting Northern papers, and kavain in a good deal imagination in regard to affairs in which we have a good instinct.

Did you ever receive a linen coat by mail from me? I sent one just before we started on the campaign as you make no mention of it. I take it for granted that it was lost. My valise was overflowing with articles, and I could disperse with that for the present, and yet there have been many days this winter down here where I would have been much acceptable.

Probably now you are having pretty cold weather in the U.S. Here in Savannah the sun is warm and the air so mild that I am writing in the open air without fire and am perfectly comfortable. Good sea and this, we have a day very much like our March days north which are very uncomfortable. The green pines and live oak woods with now and then a patch which now and then a patch of new grass look likes the winters I have been accustomed too. James desires of learning what action, if any, the progress in regard to our Navy Yard. I have a letter from Jack the other day in which he tells of his trip to Newport on Thanksgiving Day. I would have like to have been a participant in the roast turkey, Plum pudding and other good things. But about that time was in a very different business. In my last I asked you to send me a pair of sister Thomas gloves- please don't forget them.

> With much love
> Your affectionate son
> Pierre

CAMPAIGN OF THE CAROLINAS.

Beaufort South Carolina
Jan. 7 (1865)

The preceding you will see I wrote some days since but have had no opportunity to mail it. As I anticipated on the afternoon of the 3rd we embarked on Steamers and came to this point. We now treat the sacred soil of South Carolina and the distance roaring of Artillery as we are not far from the seat of war.

Beaufort is quite a town. I was very pleasantly disappointed in finding a good hotel as which a many other to us delicacies we had Butter the first I had tasted for over six months and together with Buckwheat cakes and molasses was a great luxury. This has been a very good waiting place for 5 days. For almost two years past it has been almost wholly garrisoned by Negro Soldiers. Our white men in their dirty and tattered campaigning clothes did not improve by comparison with these lucky soldiers in their clean suits and white gloves. The "Arago" arrived yesterday from N. Y. with a large mail. As it has not yet been distributed I do not know whether I am among the fortunate ones.

I am expecting every minute that my tent stakes break loose and make for the summit is blowing a perfect sate and the canvas is shaking and the tent is swaying nu a very threating style. Last night our lumber was distributed by the Saw men. More than once we roused our Darkey servants to fasten down tie piles and tighten up ropes or we would be houseless. The route from Savannah to this place is pleasant for us for the reason that have our supplies in abound for men and forage for our horses. In S. both men and animals eat fine. My horse during ten days had but three feeds and the rations for the men were very small. I shouldn't wonder if you herd from us next in the vicinity of Charleston. We are only 44 miles distance.

> Your Afft.
> Pierre

Pocotaligo, S.C. Jan. 19, 1965

Mrs. Cadman;

Dear Madam; your letter of Nov. 7 was received by me upon reaching Savannah about one month since. I should have answered it before, but my time has been much occupied. I do not know that I can communicate much more information to you concerning young husbands death. The Surgeon's name who attended him was Davis. He belongs to the 17th New York, in on the 14th Corps. George is buried decently in the burial spot occupied decently in the burial spot occupied by the 4th, Division, 16th Corps. A neat headboard marks his grave. A fence surrounds the burial spot. It is on the outer edge of Marietta, on the left hand side of the Railroad as you come in from the north. Again, expecting my sympathy for you in your double sore bereavement. I remain.

Respectfully Yours,
George R. Gear

Fayetteville, North Carolina,
March 12th, 1865

My Dear Mother,

At last I have an opportunity of sending you a few lines. The first time we have had communication with the North since starting on the Campaign, Likely you have heard in your papers all sorts of summaries and speculating in regard to this army; and extracts from Southern Papers that ----- informed you pretty accurately of our course through South Carolina and thus far into the "Old North State" The last to you was dated from Pocatalico S.C. On the 30th Jan. we started from that place on our new campaign and cut loose from our base without an uneasy foreboding in spite of the trouble fate that awaited us, (according to the Rebel Papers) if ever Sherman attempted to invade the sacred soil of South Carolina. Every creek was to be disputed, every plain was to be a battlefield.

Yankee corpses were to strew the highways and their blood would be drawn the whole land - and yet our splendid army has marched steadily on to its present point in fine spirits and ready for anything. The campaign has been much longer than we anticipated and in consequence the soldiers are in a rather deplorable state as regards to clothing etc. many of our men have walked long miles barefooted. We have lived pretty well- the country furnished everything bet coffee & salt which our Uncle Sam kindly donated in view of the "Big Things" we were doing for him. Along the whole course of our march we have been moor or less opposed by the enemy. We have been obliged to cross many forms of streams which of course gave excellent opportunities to the enemy.

Of course you heard that Columbia the Capital was taken. I entered the city but an hour tow after our skirmisher first got in, and a more indescribable scene I ever witnessed. The principle streets were full of burning cotton bales, stores had been broken and valuable furniture strewn the sidewalks. Fine wines and liquors were in the greatest profusion. Tobacco which had been selling in camp for two or three dollars per plug was thrown out of the ware houses by the box for everyone to help themselves. In fact the town was sacked and as night came on fires sprung up in every direction and by the next morning the beautiful city of Columbia where the first act of secession was passed lay in ashes.

At least 50 % of the city was burned as I rode over it the next day instead of the fine residences which adorned its streets the day before now they were lined with chimney stacks and smoldering ruins. It is impossible to concern of the amount of destruction. You could ride for a mile along any of the streets and not find a house remaining. It was really a sad scene, thousands were made homeless and destitute and South Carolina has at last reaped a small portion of her sowing. I haven't time to write a hundredth part of what I might as the mail leaves in a few minutes.

A dispatch boat has come up the river to Gen Sherman and by it we can send a mail. I have never felt better than as this trip though we have often had hard times for the last two weeks it has rained almost constantly. The fall of "Charleston" must have been pleasing news to the North for which you can also thank Sherman's Army we first heard of that just after crossing the Santee River. We arrived here yesterday driving out the Rebels who were in the city. It is expected that we will soon from a junction with Schofield's Corps which left Wilmington some days since. I suppose we will go farther into the state, perhaps visit Raleigh- as we are paying complements to South Carolina. I must close or I shan't get what letter I have off in the mail.

> Your affectionate son,
> Pierre

Hdqtrs. 39th Reg Ohio Inf. Goldsboro N. C.
March 26th, 1865

My dear Mother,

I have seen many of our soldiers killed and wounded. I have seen many of our returned prisoners worn out with Rebel cruelty and have heard them detail their sufferings and inhumanity of our enemies until. I have every little sympathy for anything connected with the Rebellion. On the fires of the month we had quite a spirited battle in which my regiment lost 23 the night of the same day. General Johnston's army retreated toward Raleigh. We now have 2 railroad lines running from New Berne to Wilmington for supplies. Our men were destitute of shoes and clothing when we arrived here. 200 men in my regiment were barefoot.

> Your affectionate son Pierre

Headquarters 39th Reg. Ohio Inf.
Goldsboro N.C. March 27th, 1865

My dear mother,

I wrote you briefly from Fayetteville North Carolina- where the army rested a couple of days. We are now at Goldsboro and at the end of our campaign. The army left Poclaligo S.C. on the 30th I am and arrived at this point on the 24th March-very nearly two months of continued marching. The roads were almost impassable at times. We floundered along through mud and swamps and rain until thoroughly disgusted with everything related to the Carolinas. If you have read the papers- and of course you have-you know the course of our march and long before this have got all the details of the campaign. Yesterday we received all unreceived mail- nearly all the letter that have accumulated during the last two months.

I am sorry to say however that I was the recipient of but one from you dated Jan. 7th containing the parts of a letter from Mrs. Smith in regard to Harriet. I have no doubt she is suffering in common with the rest of the Southern people with whom she has chosen to identify herself. If I have an opportunity to assist her as you desire I will do so. I have seen to many of our soldiers killed and wounded, have seen to many of our returned prisoners worn out with Rebel cruelty, and have heard them detail their suffering and inhumanity of our enemies, until I have very little sympathy left for anything connected with the Rebellion. Yet I would do anything in my power to assist my sister and if an opportunity occurs I will most assuredly do so.

On the 21st of the month we had quite a spirited battle in which my Regiment lost 23 men. The night of the Sunday Gen. Johnston's Army left their works and retreated toward Raleigh and we came out towards Goldsboro. We have two lines of R.R. in running order- one from Newton the other from Wilmington, and both all worked to the quoted compactly in bringing supplies. Our men were very destitute of Clothing and shoes, when we arrived here over 200 of the men in my regiment were bare-footed. They are now getting re-clothed and by the 10th of the next month we expect to be again on the move.

For about six weeks we heard nothing at all from the north except through Rebel papers- and I saw but few copies of them—The campaign on the whole has not been by any means as easy as the Georgia Trip-it has been nearly living-as-long- the weather has not been as pleasant- the men were not as well filled out- we have had a good deal more fighting to do and rations have not been as plenty. But we have been splendidly successful in all we have, and the County has

285

received immense benefit from and I shall always be glad that I was fortunate enough to be one of this army. I will write again in a few days.   Please send no more postage stamps

Your Aff. Son   Pierre

Head Quarters 39th O.V.I.
Goldsboro N.C. April 6th, 1865

Dear Jack,

Ever since we came again to light here in North Carolina, I ever been intending to write you, yet, since being relieved from the necessity of being in the saddle fourteen or fifteen hours each day. I have been perfectly dormant more asleep then awake. So not having sufficient energy to detail the many incidents of our trip from the salt water to our present base. I have sufficiently long delayed until a narrative of what you have already read in the papers. Mine would only be a bore. Suffice to say that when you read of the fight at the Sallthocee River at the Ederle at Cheraw- where my brigade captured 27 pieces of artillery and my regiment the first one behind the skirmishers driving the Rebels through the town and across the Peedee River. The affairs at Columbia and the subsequence burning of the city and the last fight at Bentonville—you can consider me there.

I have been instantly acquainted with the Carolina swamps and can appreciate the rainy season. I experienced a good deal satisfaction in the hackability that Chivalrous Yankee hating Rebel hole. It received but little mercy from the hand soldiers who took as much satisfaction in tearing up R.R. running off the horses and mules - appropriating to their own as the neatly cared houses, molasses - flour-chickens-& some weatly platers and then burning the house - as the latter would have experienced the aforesaid Yankees dangling from the highest branches of his patriarchal Oaks. After all it was a pretty hard campaign-the weather was often impossible - the creeks were constant immense swamps and the bottom would fill out the roads.

The wagons would go down to their beds and the mules to their bridles- consequently though starting at daylight, we rarely reached camp until long after dark. Before we had got half through the trip the mules shoes began to give out, and when we reached Goldsboro we had in my regiment over 200 men who had marched bare footed two weeks-feet blistered and torn by traveling over corduroy roads and through the woods.

Our appearance to one experience to the same, when we entered this town must have been very grotesque. Uncle Sam's been had long since worn out and in lieu thereof the men wore clothes of every conceivable shape and color, a swallow tailed broad cloth coat of an aristocratic planter-with perhaps gray pants or drawers-soles no boots with a plug hat to worn out would adorn a figure covered with mud and with Lennard hands blackened with the smoke of many a pine tree fire. In the rear of every regiment were from 75 to 100 sore backs, skit rear of mules and horses campy as many sore- footed soldiers, ragged and dirty.

The good purpose of the north, judging from our outward appearance would I think have been loathed to place the interest of the country in our hands. Where we met Scholfield's men here the tobacco clothes and varied costumes of our men excited the moment to a great degree and we certainly presented a woeful appearance. Such tattered soldiers gain nothing in looks by comparison with their new clothes, paper collars and blackened boots, however we are perfectly satisfied with the gloomy without the style.

This morning we ride the news of the capture of Richmond and Petersburg, it gave us the greatest delight. The telegraph wire read to the brigade when out on line, and the cheering that followed the constant chant of was immediate. The band struck up and there was alternate cheering and music throughout the day. It is surmised that we will give us a rest night. This army would like to have an opportunity of hoisting the demise of that doughty ledger. We have been expecting to move on Monday next. We moved down towards

Danville, which may alter our plans.

We are already now to move and for my post I am tired of lying still.
Do you remember our Officer of the regular army named Mower who
used to be in N.L. Maj. Gen, Joseph A. Mower has been commanding
our division since we left Atlanta While conversing with him I
ascertained that we were acquainted in N.L. He asked after you and
father and seemed were acquainted with the Plugins, Bill Dikeman
and everybody near there. His wife is now staying in N.L.

Since we came to Goldsboro he has been put in the 20th Corps. I have
received one letter from home since January. To be sure the mail since
we reached communications have been very irregular bus. I think I am
entitled to a few more entries. Perhaps we are so long in the dark that
we are forgotten. Now that Richmond is taken I hope that Harriet will
have the sense to say where she is and get --------

The loss of my regiment in the campaign is about 30 killed wounded.
We lost a few prisoners besides. Just before starting we received nearly
200 recruits. The had a -------and gave me a good deal of trouble—I am
in charge of the regiment (Medical) have been for the last six months.
I hope by this next summer I shall have an opportunity of a venture
home. Don't think I shall leave the army now until the Rebellion is
dead. Quarter Master stores marched with last marching guard. It
reminded me of you very often. I imagine you beginning with the
army here has been pretty brisk of late. I wrote mother from
Fayetteville and again from here- but have received but one letter and
that dated six weeks since. Several papers have come to hand from
you. Write soon

Yours   Pierre
Head Quarters 39th Ohio
Goldsboro April 19th, 1865

My dear mother,

I have just time to write you a few lines, as we have received notice that the mail leaves in fifteen minutes. We break camp tomorrow morning for another campaign where we are going Gen. Sherman alone can tell and he does not usually divulge his plans. So, you will remain in the dark until you hear of us at some unexpected point. We have all got tired of the grind of camp life and are anxious to be on the move again. I should have written you before but have been expecting to hear from you. I have received but one letter and that dated a month or more ago.   I am well as possible. We hope to put a finishing touch to our glorious work and help finish up their Rebellious business in short nature. Everybody is in excellent spirits and anxious to move.

> With much love,
> Your Aff. Son
> Pierre

I will write you again as soon as we have mail to send.

Head Quarters 39th Ohio Inf.
Near Raleigh N.C. April 26th 65

Dear Jack,

Yours came to hand yesterday together with a N.Y. Paper containing some of the particulars of the Presidents assassination – that terrible calamity had a much demising effect on here. Johnston had just expressed his wiliness to surrender and all were in excellent spirits at the prospects of a speedy termination to hostilities. On the reception of the tragic news, the termination of the war summed are which all wished for. Officers and men unanimously express their desire to wreck the remains up what was left of the Southern Army, and in fighting the thing out, that is enter there cannot be a southern left. The government however does not appear to have been satisfied with the terms which can naturally get when believe Sherman and Johnston and accordingly we pulled out of camp yesterday morning at Raleigh- and came eight miles up the R.R. to settle the affair in a less friendly manner way.

We left Goldsboro N.C. when my last to you was dated, on the 11th of the present month arriving in Raleigh on the 14th. On the morning of the 15th we broke camp as usual to continue our march after Johnston who was then about fifteen miles in advance of us. The rain was coming down in perfect deluge. The roads were in horrible condition and a trying day for both man and mules was in frustration. The advance had got out several miles. My regiment was more fortunate and had a hardly left camp when a cheer upon us came rolling back to us. - the column was halted and present it was announced that Johnston had offered to surrender. A most tremendous seen followed-most gave vent to their feelings by lowly caring line regards of rain and mud-we were immediately ordered back to camp and negotiations were started.

For several days subsequently, Sherman passed our camp in the cars for Johnston's line moving in the evening. Finally, terms were agreed upon and an Officer of Gen. S. Staff went to Washington with them. A day or two since he returned and yesterday we got marching orders. The armistice provision agreed upon was not up till now-to day. We are now within five miles of the Rebel lines. Generals Sherman and Howard went the morning to consult with Johnston. I think he will accord to all that is demanded of him. It is generally understood that the point of objection at Washington was the stipulation that the Rebels were to take their arms to the Capital   of their respective stores and then turn them over to such Officers as might be appointed to receive them.

Johnston can't give us fight- The city of Raleigh swarms with his soldiers and they were passing our camp continually- their Officers according to their deserters- make no effort to detain them-apparently regarding their cause defunct. J. offered to surrender on this side of the Rio Grande. In anticipation of the surrender it was expected that this army before many weeks be mustered out of service. Such an event may possibly be delayed some by the existing circumstances. It is thought that we march to Washington when that thing occurs. The day previous to our leaving Raleigh this corps-17th- was reviewed by Lt. Gen. Grant-Sec. Stanton and Sherman was present. The 23rd and 20th Corps have been reviewed on the two days previous by Sherman. On Sunday Grant and Stanton arrived.

It is getting very warm here for campaigning- we had a comparatively easy march yesterday and yet three men fell out dead in the division, supposed from the effects of the sun is a great danger. One of my regiment a recruit- fell in the ranks as we were marching along and died within two or three minutes. Yesterday we received from Ohio 150 recruits- our aggregated is now 900, about the largest regiment in the division. I suppose I shall have the usual number of measles cases and other ills to which recruits are subject on my hands. Our mails are very singular, the latest paper I have seen was on the 18th, when the news from the north am so anonymously locked. This is rather trying.

The other day I wrote to my brother in Cincinnati- the only one north who has my measure to make me a pair of boots, and directed him to send them by express to you-give him your 20th Canal St. If there is a probability of getting North in a couple of months. I don't wish you to send them to me. Please take care of them for present- until you hear from me in regard to them. I hope you anticipated in regard to taking the surrender yarn will be full filled. I shall look to you to keep up the old place- no other one of the family seems interest about U.C. It would be stern though if Harriet and her husband showed having given up the idolized Confederacy settle army to the horrible Yankees. You will probably learn in a few days of Johnston's surrender or that we have started on a stern chase into Georgia. I surly hope that the former event may occur. I don't wish the idea of a campaign just now.

> Your aff. Bro
> Pierre

Head Quarters 39th Ohio Inf.
Raleigh North Carolina April 29th 65

My dear mother,

I wrote you since arriving at this city but as there is a probability of writing for some time. I will take this most of the present. My next letter will very likely be written at Richmond in two weeks. On the

24th the news arrived that the terms of surrender received by Sherman for had not been satisfactory to the authorities' in Washington and in consequence's that we would move on the in the morning. Accordingly, on Tuesday the 25th we pulled of camp towards our old foe. Johnston however did not appear to relish the proceedings and in consequence a meeting was had between him and Sherman- and Johnston finally agreed to accord to such terms as were desired. As there were no opportunity to fight the next morning we started back to our old camp and here we are in the same position as when I wrote you last.

As I have written before we expect to start for Richmond Va. Very soon at least & said order recvd. last night from Maj. Gen. Howard. Our ammunition is being turned over, we expect to have no further use for such implements. Gen. Schofield with his troops is to remain here to see that the terms of the surrender are complicated with our march to Richmond will probably take about three weeks. Somewhere near there we will be mustered out to service. In a month or two I expect to be out of the service. What my future will be is rather troublesome-beginning is not pleasant. It is getting decidedly warm here. I dread our leg march into VA. On that account. Our mail is very irregular, but I think though receive a letter from home by express mail. I look forward with pleasure to the Idea of spending the summer in Connecticut quietly- near salt water. Since getting to North Carolina – considered a quietly loyal state.

Foraging has been strictly prohibited in fact that is but little forage for miles around here- and therefore we are and have been living miserably for some time past. Fried salt pork and dry bread have been the only articles of diet for the past two weeks. I am in a state where I can appreciate anything good in the culinary department and when I get North for I don't expect to get anything before then. I hope to make up for past difficulties, and yet don't imagine that I have been getting leave-this sort of a life eventually agrees with me and I believe I write this ever before. You may not get a letter from me again for some time & perhaps not until I am in a loyal state.

Your affectionate Son,   Pierre

Head Quarters 39th Ohio Inf.
Near Alexandria Va. May 24th, 1865

My dear mother,

Probably from the newspapers you have a knowledge of the were
about of the 17th Corps and of course my regiment. After a march of
about 350 miles from Raleigh N.C. we arrived at this point.- 3 miles
from Alexandria last evening. We left the first mentioned city 30th
April reached Petersburg Va. About the 9th May and Richmond a
couple of days later. At both of the most interesting points in the
whole Confederacy.

I had the opportunity of spending a day in the contested lines about
Petersburg were of course an object of interest as there the battle of
Richmond was fought and in fact for the Confederacy. The city is
really a fine one, the business portion had quite a metropolitan
appearance and to us who for the past eighteen months had seen
nothing of "dry goods and groceries" it presented an attractive and
novel appearance.

As usual the Yankees have filled the stores and the people were once
near reviling in good things from the North. I expect however the
advent of Sherman's army- being its first appearance on the boards in
the East was as much an object of interest to the inhabitants as their
city was to us, at least so I judged from their curiosity in not case to the
Yankees- and the questions asked.

Richmond is 22 miles North. We are camped at Manchester, a town on
the opposite side of the James River. A pontoon Bridge connects the
two places as the Rebels had destroyed the old bridge. About the first
object of interest on arriving on the Richmond side is "Castle
Thunder", by no means the style of building that its prominent name

would lead one to suppose-but a common 3 story building in a most common street, as water streets always are.

Deserters, negroes, Rebels now occupy the dirty building with their legs dangling from the windows between the bars. Two or three hundred yards farther on the opposite of the street is "Libby Prison"-renowned for the "Notorious as the pen selected by the Rebel authorities for the imprisonment and holding of Captured Union Officers.

So, may descriptions of the place have been given that I suppose you are well acquainted with its lines. Men approached and entered it now with a very different emotion from what they did a few months back. I should think that about 75 % Richmond, almost all the business portion had been destroyed by fire. The capital building is a decapitated common the like of which I suppose only the innocent-shiftless Virginians could have been satisfied with. The ground about it are rather pretty-with some fine status- like Washington and others.

The glorious residence borders on side- Jeff Davis home at some little distance from here in a house presented him by the citizens I believe, If it was paid for in Rebel currency, I think it ought to return to its former owner. The streets were filled- a mixture of Union and Rebel Officers, each with their respective Uniforms, and the latter however did not appear particular fitting and their clothes evidently left their tailors hands some time since.

The bona fide inhabitants were numerous Male, and Female-all looked as if they were out of employment and funds too. I feel now as if I were pretty near home- we are expecting first to be "bored" with a grand Review and then be mustered out of the service, for the later purpose I suppose the different regiments will be sent to their respective states which will necessitate my going to Ohio again. In the course of ten days or two weeks probably we will leave here. All this in regard to our being mustered out of service is hearing. We have received no official notification that any such thing was about to occur.

I am going to Alexandria this afternoon if it doesn't rain, perhaps I shall meet someone of my very distance relatives. I take it for granted that Harriet is with you. A mail reached us last night- the first in sometime, but as usual I didn't get anything. It is so long since I have received a letter from home that I have forgotten when or where I was at the time, though I suppose there was a last one received at some time or another. I anticipated spending a quite summer in Connecticut and outside the military. I hope I shall not be disappointed. For the last 12 months I have had anything, but an easy life and I intend to make it up before sitting down at anything.

Your affectionate Son,   Pierre

Head Quarters 39th Ohio Inf.
Sunday June 4th, 1865

My dear, Mother,

We are under moving orders bound for Louisville Ky. We were ordered to be ready at 7 A.M. It is now after two and there is as of yet no sign of our leaving, except that our baggage is packed, and everything feels and looks unsettled. We are to leave here (Washington) on the cars for Parkersburg on the Ohio river where we will take boats to Louisville - it is supposed that we go there for the purpose of shortly being mustered out of the service. I hope it will be consummated before many weeks.   I had much rather be campaigning in Georgia or South Carolina than to remain in camp about some city with nothing to do. It is to be presumed that we will have a tedious trip to the west of about four days. I have had some experience in moving with troops on cars and steamboats and I have never found it pleasant.

You ask if I have any preference as to room when I get home again. The third story I think- shall be proper- if all the same to you. I received your letter of the 20th containing an obituary of Lieut. Carrington and also one of the 24th (Ohio) The last two or three days since after I had left Alexandria. It is much of your desire information I cannot give. I can tell you however that the place is much improved at least as far as business is concerned, of course by far the greater portion of it is dependent on the army- with it departed business will decline- and in a year I expect Alexandria will have resumed its former Status. Billy told me that the house would now sell for $500.00 per Anuran. I think you made a mistake in selling the place, though partake then was some sick in holding and some trouble.

Suppose Harriet is with you by this time. I wrote you about seeing Billy, and that I had hoped to take Harriet to N. L. (New London) I could not accomplish it though our movements were too undecided that I proposed to stay until getting some official information. While here I have had ample opportunity of visiting all places of interest in Washington. It has a more bustling aspect than where I was here some years since. The city swarms with Officers- Majors and Brigadier Generals are as common as street corners. I was fortunate yesterday in meeting some of my Yale Class mates and unfortunate in not having found them until the day previous to our leaving.

Now that there is not a Rebel army even in Texas there seems to be no reason for keeping any of the volunteer forces staying in the service. We don't think they will- if however, such ever to be determination I shall resign before the summer is over. To muster out a large army to make out the necessary rolls is no trifling job and takes some time in its accomplishment. By the time we reach the Ohio River this regiment will have made quite an exhaustive circuit of states. A pretty long walk to say the least, Through Tenn., Alabama, through Georgia nearly to Florida- up the coast of North and South Carolina and Virginia and with the exception of a few hours sail from Savannah to New Bern- have marched every mile to this point. After such a tramp it is no wonder the men are tough and hardened, and in consequence united envisioned comment by those who witnessed the nerve of Sherman's Army.

The weather was previously hot and when in the city inconveniences we much more than where down South last summer, very likely the great reason is the necessity as being well dressed, while than we count the steady comfort at the expected appearance.

From Jacks last letter I presume he is by this time with you. You will soon have a full house. I hope Jack won't find it necessary to leave home, he fits naturally in N. L. and as that is a virtue that runs of the rest of us seem to possess of great decree. It is a pity if he cannot indulge in it. I was pleased to receive a letter from Jed a few days since. You will probably hear next from me at Louisville.

You affectionate Son,
Pierre

13

all the sick in the field again and for myself I was glad enough to get out of a house and into my tent on the field again.

I came on the cars with a surgeon of the regular army, who is to take charge of the hospital, he wanted to stay with him as an assistant, but I preferred remaining with the 39th. I have however to attend to their men everyday tell relieved by others who are to be regularly approved there. There are I said to be many pretty rides about here, as would very likely be the case in such a watering place, but the secsh are altogether too inviting to be pleasant and if is not at all safe to go more than a mile or two from the cams in any direction.

We had a supply train captured a day or two since several men shot by guerrillas and other news incidents which bring forcibly to our minds the conviction that we are in an enemy's country, and the propinquity of the Rebels. Speaking of rides, I have got a fine horse of my own now, and my riding experience in here fore comes very nicely into play, as I ride more or less every day, as of course one never thinks of getting about the country in any other way than on horseback. I have written you a letter and some papers from Jed and also a letter from Jack. Please tell them that I will answer them as soon as I get time. This is considered an important point in a military point of view, and it is thought will play a part before the war is over.

I am glad people north are waking up to the idea that this is a real live war and no play work and that if the country is to be saved they have got to fight. My direction is the same as here to fore, and always will be whatever may go. I like this life first rate for a change. Everything is very high- Milk per Qt. 25 cts. -eggs per doz. About 50 cts. -Butter per pound, little chickens 75 cts. etc.

As all are secesh about here of course they get as much as they can out of us. Saw an order from the Provost Marshall, however this morning regulating the prices, so now they can't check us more, That the law allows-which is certainly enough to satisfy any rascal. By later order we can now send out parties who take corn, potatoes, Etc. from the Rebels when they meet them which is certainly no more then proper.

In haste,
Your affectionate son, Pierre

Report forms of hospital goods on site and returned to supply Quartermaster. These four original documents of Pierre Starr's Civil War Medical records are in possession of Robert Starr 3rd

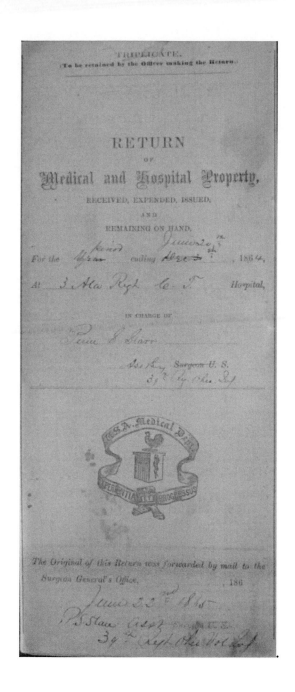

RETURN

OF

Medical and Hospital Property,

RECEIVED, EXPENDED, ISSUED,

AND

REMAINING ON HAND,

For the *period* ending *Dec.* 1864,

At *3 Ala Regt C. T.* Hospital,

IN CHARGE OF

Wm S. Starr

Ass Surgeon U. S.

The Original of this Return was forwarded by mail to the Surgeon General's Office, 186

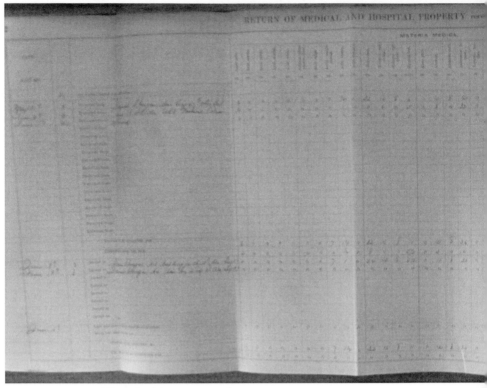

Hospital inventory sheet

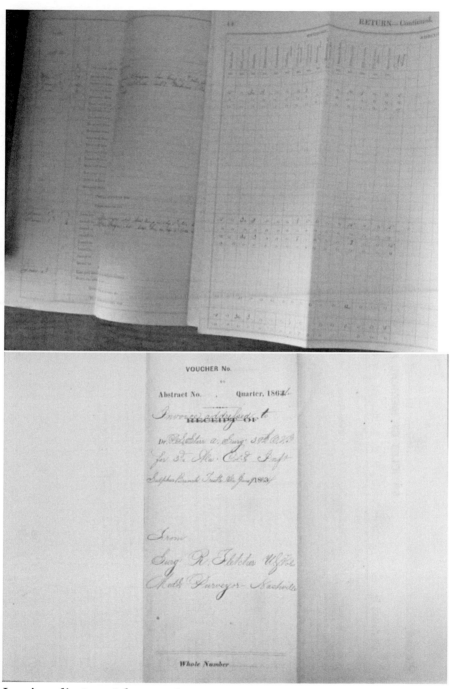

Invoice adjustment document

Received,

ARTICLES OF MEDICAL AND HOSPITAL SUPPLIES, &C.

Contained in ___ Packages, marked U. S. A. Hospital Department ___

ARTICLES	Quantity	ARTICLES	Quantity	ARTICLES	Quantity	ARTICLES	Quantity	ARTICLES	Quantity	ARTICLES	Quantity
Materia Medica.				**Hospital Stores.**		**Dressings, etc.**		**Books and Stationery, &c.**		**Bedding**	

invoice

COL. EDWARD F. NOYES, 39TH O. V. V. I.
Brevet Brigadier General.
Governor of Ohio.

BREVET BRIGADIER GENERAL EDWARD F. NOYES.

Thirty-ninth Ohio Veteran Volunteer Infantry.

FROM "OHIO IN THE WAR," REVISED BY CAPTAIN W. H. H. MINTURN.

Edward Follensbee Noyes was born at Haverhill, Massachusetts, October 3, 1832. His parents died in his infancy and at the age of thirteen years, he was apprenticed as a printer boy. In this position he remained four and one-half years. He entered Dartmouth College in 1853, and graduated four years afterward. He immediately removed to Cincinnati and studied law, graduating in the Cincinnati Law School in 1858. He practiced law successfully until the breaking out of the rebellion. On July 8th, 1861, his law office was changed to recruiting headquarters, and in less than a month a full regiment was raised and ready for the field. Of

13

In the Field foo of [...]
Monday June 2[?] 186[?]

My Dear Wife

With a heavy heart I commence this [...] In the letter I sent you yesterday I told you that our company was then on the skirmish line, but as none of our boys had been brought in, I supposed they were all safe. Alas it was not so. Of the best one of our best men [...] He had moved from the rifle pit his [...] and defending, and was not missed particularly till the company was relieved last night, when he did not answer to his name. Search was made for him & his body was discovered this morning not more than five paces from his fort. We could not get him then as the rebel rifles covered the place but tonight we shall try and get his body and give it a soldiers [...] We had one again wounded in our company besides [...] a young fellow about 18 being in the California [...] the little [...] he was single, but poor Mc[...] leaves a wife and [...] & children to lament his loss [...]

George H. Cadman was a farmer and an older man as Civil War soldier's enlistment ages were. George was 46 years old at his enlistment. But he was a stout and strong man. George did all that was asked of him.

George enlisted in the 39th Ohio Infantry. The same regiment that Pierre Starr was the Surgeon. When the 39th was camped near Atlanta Georgia George took sick and was placed on a rail car and sent to the 16th Army Corps, 4th Division Hospitals in Marietta Georgia. The 16th Army Corps hospitals were in three churches in Marietta, The Saint James, First Presbyterian and the First Baptist. These churches were just north of the town square of Marietta. These three Churches had nearly 1000 beds with sick and wounded.

Pierre and George were in the Saint James Church. Pierre had been in Marietta for nearly three weeks when George arrived at the church sick. George died late in September and was taken 150 yards north of the church and buried on the east side of the Western and Atlantic railroad tracks. The cemetery had a picket fence around it.

In January of 1866 Georges brother traveled down from Ohio by rail and gathered Georges remains and brought them home to Ohio. On the same day George died in Marietta his oldest son George Jr. was killed in a farming accident.

Georges letters are used to add more evidence of the writing of Pierre and his 1912 Journal. Georges letters and photos are at the University of North Carolina.   10

George H. Cadman

Co. B 39th O.V.I.
Prospect Tennessee
Dec. 20th /63

My dear wife,

After a longer silence than usual, I again sit down to write you a few
lines to let you know that I am blessed with excellent health and am in
good spirits. The reason I have not written to you for some days is, that
I have not had time during the past week to write, with the exception
of one letter I wrote to my brother William. I received the other day a
letter from Sarah with the letter from my brother, all the I enclose to
you, so I need not comment on them as they speak too plain for
themselves. I am very much obliged to you my dear for the
promptitude with which you, but little forwarded my letter to Sarah
and hope it did not put you to any inconvenience.

Last Sunday I was on Camp Guard we had a very cold time of it, the
wind was very boisterous and rough all day, and at night blew a
perfect hurricane while the rain fell in torrents, the fly we had for a
shelter was overturned by the wind and there was nothing to do but
stand and take the weather the best we could. On Tuesday, I was on
picket and you can scarcely imagine the difference in the weather. The
day was intolerably hot, and the sun seemed sufficient to scorch a
fellow but toward night it got cloudy.

On Wednesday morning we were relieved and returned to camp just
in time to escape the rain which came poring down again. Toward
night we had a most terrific storm of wind accompanied by thunder &
Lighting which lasted with little interruption the whole night. It was
one of the most furious storms it has we were being fortunate to
behold. Fortunately, it was not the turn of our company to be opposite
to it.

On the next day Co. B was detailed to go out in the woods to make
Gabions for the Fort, we are building on the Elk River, by the way, I
forgot to tell you the storm of Wednesday night carried away a great

portion of the Railroad Bridge we were building over the Elk River, which will cause some delay in opening our direct Railway communications with Nashville, but I have not told you what Gabions are, they are large woven baskets made very strong to line the inside of an earthwork, they are placed on end close together and then filled up with sand or earth, when they are fixed and filled, bundles of fascines are laid lengthwise across the tops of them and staked to keep them from slipping and the earth thrown up against them, so as to make a solid wall.

Gabion Wicker baskets

Thursday & Friday I spent in the woods making the baskets or Gabions and yesterday (Saturday) I was detailed to superintend hauling them to the fort. We had two wagons and two men to each wagon. All I had to do was to stay at the Fort and receive them of the men. For three days it has been freezing hard and the weather very cold, with no sign of it moderating and I found it pretty keen to stand up on the hill all day doing nothing. During the day an incident occurred which shows how many things hard to fear occur during war time. The top of the hill where we are building the Fort has been used by the inhabitants as a grave yard, and the course the ditch takes necessarily disturbs many of the graves.

Last August a year ago a man was buried there by the name of Allen, close on the right of our sally port, and where the grave would be crossed by the extreme left of the Breast Work. While waiting there yesterday morning his widow came to beg us to allow her to have her husband's body recovered, so that she could have it buried in some place when it would not likely be disturbed for she could not bear the thought of a flight taking place over husband's grave. It seems that when Allen died, she herself was sick, and had not seen him either during his illness or after death. The colonel very kindly detailed 4 men to take the body up and then seized one of my wagons to haul it off.

I went over with the detail and helped Rebury the poor fellow and shall never forget the gratitude of the poor woman. She said she did not think the Yankees could be so kind, she took down all the names of the squad who helped her, that she might pray for them and promised me she would pray for me and my wife and children. So, if a Rebels Prayers are any account I suppose I shall gain something by it. But best of all she got us good dinner. We had fried sausage, Roast & boiled beef& Pork, Head cheese, Peach Pies and Sweet Milk and an invitation to go and see here whenever we could get leave. As I commanded the squad of course I came in for a double share of thanks and invitation, but as she is 60 years old you need not get jealous without you like

Tomorrow we commence making the Fascines & I wish they would keep our company at work all winter as it is more comfortable at work than standing guard. I guess I have about going you all the news, and don't know what else to write except that Christmas is close onto us and I should like to be able to step in and spend the evening with you and have some fun with the Children. Will old girl there's only one more Christmas after this before my time will be out anyhow, and then will keep up another Wedding Day. In the meantime, love, keeping stiff upper lip. And don't be scared at Trifles. I hope Santa Claus won't forget to visit the Children because I am away, should he come you must send me word what he left them.

I am very pleased that Willie gets on so well with his book. Why don't he write me another letter? I am glad George is satisfied with his place and would be glad if he remained there at any rate till I come home again. Tell him to be a good boy and not be afraid of killing himself with hard work, for it is very seldom work kills any one. Give my love to him, and I shall be happy to hear from him, as often as he can find time to write. And so, Phil can say DADA how I long to see him. It seems hard that, I can't come and see you all, but country first and home afterward. I am not so homesick as to fret because I cannot get to see those I love for though you may not think it, I have some love for Wife and Children yet. In my last letter that I sent you I enclosed 10 dollars which I hope you got safe, but I shall not send any more this time as the mail is very uncertain. I have lent the balance of my money to some of our boys till next payday when there may be a better chance of sending it home. What on earth made you think I was mad, because I sent you a detail of my expenses, but I guess you was only joking. Esther there's one question I want you to answer- how as Phil's tongue. You do not mention it for some time and I would like you to let me know exactly how it is. Please let me know in your next letter. Give my love and best wishes to all my friends. Kiss the children for me and believe me you affectionate Husband

G.H. Cadman

Prospect Tennessee
Dec. 8th, 1863

My Dear Wife,

On a miserable wet afternoon. I sit down to write you a few lines hoping they will find you quite well, as you will be glad to hear they have me at this time. My health was never better than it has been since I left Memphis. I was weighed a few nights back and my weight was then 152 pounds, in fact I am getting too fat and need some hard work to get it off my bones again. There is some prospect of having some hard work for a time as our regt. Has been ordered to build a fort on Elk River about a mile from our Camp.

Last Friday I took a walk with our second Lieutenant to see the Bridge for the Railroad that our boys are building over the Elk River. It seemed the most delightful walk I had taken for a long time as the country had not been ravaged by, the fences were all standing, and the situation of the country was beautiful in the extreme. I can't think how the Rebels were driven out of this country for it is one of the most strongly fortified places by nature that I ever saw. Sometimes for miles as abrupt and precipitous as any one can imagine, while the soil is rich and the climate capable of producing anything, while we have been living off the country all the while we have been here, and it will sustain a long time yet. All we need from the war department is clothing and ammunition, salt, pepper and a few little odds & ends.

On the banks of Elk River was a spot I would have liked you and the Children to have seen, the Rocks of Limestone rise perpendicular from the to the Height of a hundred feet. Just as the river takes a sharp bend in the elbow lies an island of about 12 acres, over grown with trees, and in some places you cans see for miles, the rock itself clothed with cedar, in every crevice you see a cedar sprouting out of the rocks and between them are some of the most delightful forms you ever saw, and plenty of catnip to make tea, I chewed some of the catnip and thought of Ohio. And all the friends there as I sat, and I thought of home and all it delightful association. When shall I be able to sit up with Willie at my side, Phil on my knee and George and yourself sitting open mouthed listening to all I shall have to tell you when I get back. We are having a great time out here now dispensing the veteran Volunteer question. The Regt. Seems divided on the subject. Many of the boys will go and if Sam Cufpin joins I shall go too. I am not certain whether us who joined last year are eligible, but the Colonel has written Washington for positive information and I suppose will soon get a decided answer. I am for going, but Sam holds back, whatever we do we shall do together as we will not leave each other. Should we be able to go, I shall see you all the sooner, as those who volunteer will be sent back into their own states to be reorganized, and I do not think any how that I should have any longer period to serve than if I stopped the balance of the three years. We have been busy putting up houses the last few days.

Last Saturday I went down in the woods with my squad and got out the timber for our house. On Sunday we built it and Monday fixed the fire place and can now live at home and laugh at the weather. What would you give to see our house? And how do you think we can build a house with-out a nail or any other tool than an axe, crosscut saw, and an auger. I have seen some housed fixed up a litter better in my time, but I tell you I. We have expected to sleep in it as sound as if it was a palace. The dimensions of the interior are, length 8 feet-six inches width 7 feet and it holds 5 men very comfortable, and I expect we shall soon have a sixth who was left behind in Corinth with the small-pox.

Abandoned Winter Camp. Mathew Brady (Library of Congress)

The paymaster arrived here on Sunday and I expect we shall get-paid to the 31st of October (two Months) in a day or two, If I get the money u paid me that I lent, I want to send you thirty dollars for a Christmas box. Be sure you recollect to hang the stocking for Santa Claus, could you not get the old fellow to give the young one something from their Father? How I would like to spend Christmas with you. Our church gets on first rate, there is service there on Sunday, Monday,

Wednesday, & Friday and on the other nights we are going to have a literary and debating society.

I see by the papers Boyette Langdon is mortally wounded, how fortunate our Brigade has been, have strained every nerve, and marched hundreds of miles, and yet can't get the enemy to stand in front of us. It has long been a standing joke with us, that it is no good taking us out to find the Rebs for they won't stay till we get to them. I recd your letter of the 18th and was glad to find you were well. You must excuse Phil for putting the ink in the plate. Poor fellow he wanted to write to Gaddi and didn't know how to go about it. It is as you say, the marching has taken the dullness out of me. You need not laugh at my shirt. I was glad the rain had taken the starch out, for you know starch and I never agree. You seem to think we must have suffered much with the cold lying out at nights, no so we get used to it, and if it is too cold we sleep, one can always stand by the fire. There is one habit I can't break myself of, that of going to bed late and getting up soon. My bunkmate curses me every night and morning we are in camp, he says I go to bed and wake him out of his first sleep and get up so soon that I cheat him out of his last. When I get home, I will make you laugh for hours about him. He is an original and we quarrel every day, his name is William H. Cook, we have bunked together nearly a year, I think I gave you his description in my notice of our square some time ago, by the by Esther what do you do with the rubbish I send you, do you tear it up or do you save it, I do not care what you destroy so as you save Willis letter that I sent.

I think I see you these cold nights piling on the bed clothes and shivering under them. I expect when I get back to have to sleep on the porch for I shall cut up some shines, the house will be too hot to hold me. We are out with general Sherman our duty is to guard his rear. General Hurlburt commands us. You are about right when you suppose the women could not see much of my face, and it is mighty handy now. I am in a civilized country again for you know I am naturally of a bashful disposition.

I am glad the persimmons seeds came safe, they are a different kind then those I sent you from Holly Springs. They are much larger and ripen earlier, I wish they may come up safe, as I would like them to remind me of a day when I was really in more danger the at any time since. I have been in the army for if the Rebs had attacked us then, our force was so small nothing could have saved us. Give my respects to Mr. Hale & Family. I am much obliged to Mr. Griffin for the trouble he has taken for me give my love to him and all the folks on the hill and to all my friends, Kiss the children for me and believe me.

Your affectionate Husband   G. H. Cadman

Ira Cosgrove 39th Ohio Infantry Company Enlisted Cincinnati Ohio August 23 1862. Reenlisted as a Veteran Volunteer December 27, 1863. Wounded in Action July 22, 1864 near Atlanta Georgia. Died in Regimental Hospital August 12, 1864.This letter from his mothers pension in Washington D.C. Archives

March the 26th 1864,
Athens Alabama

Dear mother, I seat myself to pen you a fiew lines in answer to yours of the 12th. Is come to hand the other night and found me in good health. This wrighting found me the same kindly hoping the same. You stated that William had enlisted. I think he had very little to do to leave you without any help. There was enuff of the family alredy in the service for the present & think he mite of stayed at home till I served my time out. If the war should of last so long then I would have no objections to him enlisting, however there is no danger of you coming to sufferance. yet a while there was a powerful scare at Decater the other day and the order came to us to be redy to march in one hous of this being 9 oclock at night. We took up the line of march at 10 and landed at decater a little before daylight crost the river next morning and found nothing to fite. So we returned to this place a distance of 18 miles. We have had some very cold weather here for this part of the country. There fell two inches of a snow on the 23rd and we marched to decater and found it some six inches deep in that short distance.

The citizens says they never seen such cold weather at this time a year. There is a heep of sickness here. There is more sickness in our Regt. then have ever been in Regt. Though not but one death so far as I no.Tell me what Regt. William is in. Some says he enet in the 33rd and some says he went in a new Regt. Give me his address also give Pelegs address. I don't know the war he is in. Today is a very nice sunny day, how long it will stay so is hard to tell for wether here changed every fifteen minutes. This it is a kind of a world of change. We don't know one hour what next will bring forth. There is no move so far as I no with this part of the army. We are likely to stay here some time so far as I no. I shall close for the present hoping to hear from you soon, no more, but remain you son till death. . Remember me when this you see the many miles apart we be interest in your prayers crave that we may meet beyond the grave.

Ira Cosgrove to Lory Cosgrove

June 29th (64)

Gen. Sherman rode along our lines this morning. Gen. Dodge seems to think the campaign cannot last much long. I have been busy all the morning with company accounts, but it is not very pleasant work, for about thirty yards in our rear is a battery containing two Rodman guns and two twenty-pound Parrott. Some of the shells are not perfect and burst over our heads as soon as they leave the cannon.

It would amuse you to notice the sounds of the different shells. The rodman gives a sharp snap like a thunderbolt striking when it is fired, and the shell whizzes through the air like the sound of a locomotive at full speed. Some of them growl, some make a spluttering noise like a flock of birds. There is one gun the boys call "the old hound" because it howls like a bloodhound, and there is another casemated battery the boys call "The old hound" because you can't hear the report of the gun when it is fired till the shell flies over you. Yesterday the Rebels had the impudence to open a battery on us and fired two guns, but before they could fire a third, at least twenty or thirty grounds were brought to bear on the gunners did not stop long. It was the prettiest artillery practice I have seen yet.

We could not lift our heads above the works without the almost certainty of being shot, and as there was no chance to return fire, it was no use to rick it. After the spat was over it was amusing to hear our men ridiculing the Rebs, and they back again. The night was so cold and clear that voices could be heard for a considerable distance. The jokes were all in good humor, but it did seem strange for men who only five minutes before were trying to take each other lives, to be laughing and joking with each other.

The Rebel sharpshooters have some very good rifles of English make, Whitworth's, that beat anything we have in our army. It is said they will killed a thousand yards. It is a great advantage to them, as fellow can dig a hole, get into it, and fire away with impunity.

If you do not send word that you are tired of these rambling letters, I shall send you one every few days, but if they should cease for a week or two, do not be uneasy, as circumstances may turn up to hinder me from writing, wishing you, my love, all health and happiness, I remain my dear wife,

George C.

The U.S. Christian Commission
Sends this sheet as a Soldier's messenger to his home
　　Let it hasten to those who wait for tidings

4th Div. 16th A.C. Hospital, Marietta Georgia, Aug. 20/64

My Dear Wife,

I once more try to pen a few lines to you, hoping they will find you
and the Dear Children in good health. No doubt it seems a long time
to you since I last wrote, but I have been so low spirited and dull. I
have had no inclination to do anything. In y last I wrote you word that
I was clerking at the Hospital near Atlanta, and while I was there, the
time passed away very comfortably but Genl. Sherman suddenly gave
notice for the Hospital to be broken up, and that the 14th and 16th Army
Corps should make a rapid movement to the right and endeavor to
outflank Hoods army and destroy the only line of Railroad he had left
to him. Of course, there was nothing to do but obey orders and the
sick and some of the wounded were brought- here while the balance,
among whom was Sam Griffin were sent to Rome. But we might as
well have remained where we were for when our Corps were in the
very act to be abandoned at that time and I believe our Corps still
remains in the same place as when I left the Regiment.

The siege of Atlanta still goes along, and it is hard to say when it will
be ours, although judging by what the prisoners who were brought in
this morning say, it can't hold out much longer. There were 150
deserters brought in to Marietta this morning of all ranks from private
to Major. They reported that all the most valuable Machinery and most
of the heavy guns had been removed, and there was no chance of
getting any more supplies by Railroad, that the Rebel Army could only
get its substance now by Wagons and there were not more than three
days rations ahead. They further stated that in consequence of the
disaffection in Johnsons or Hoods Arm there could not trust their new
guards on the skirmish ling any more. That as soon as the dark nights

came on again there would be plenty of men desert.

From the people are more civilized than in any Southern State I have been in yet. There is not the rabid feelings against the federal soldiers here that I have witnessed in other states and the men are manly enough to acknowledge they have bought their punishment on themselves. They own that they are whipped.

I was rather surprised at the Rebel account you sent me of the battle of the 22nd July, with the exception of them having been in a fight on that day there was not a particle of truth in the whole account True at Decatur our men got it back the same evening and hold it yet. They run out our 2nd Brigade, but instead of capturing 300 wagons they only got one wagon and that the teamster shot the mules belonging to it, so they could not move it off and as for the victory they claim, some of their wounded lay outside our lines a day and a half. Then we fetched them in and tended them. We also buried their dead for them. Does that look like a victory for them? It was a very well laid plan and had we all been asleep it would have been most disastrous to our cause, for had our men faltered or given ground, the whole wagon train of the 15th,16th Army Corps with the Hospitals would have been captured. We lay on the same ground till the 25th at midnight and then moved off to take our position on their extreme left which we succeeded in doing most effectually.

I was sorry to hear the General Dodge was wounded yesterday but whether badly or not I do not know. I am getting along well Esther I am sorry to say that I am not doing any better and I see no chance of going back to my Regt. Yet. I have the full use of my arms and hands buy my hips and knees are as weak as ever. Nothing but time will do me any good unless I could get home awhile and there is no chance for that. I expect you will see Sam home in a couple of weeks and he will be able to give you all the news of the war better than I can. I had a curious dream of you the other day. I thought that in one of our marches we had camped near home, and I walked all night to get to see you. When I found you, it was at a picnic or some other fool thing, and the folks were all dressed up in their best, and there was I in my ragged soldier clothes that I had bought and laid in the trenches with. I thought I looked so different to the stop at home folks, that I wished myself anywhere else, and when I found you-you liked so cold as if you wished me away too.

I asked you where Phil was, and you took me into a strange room where he was lying asleep. I spoke to him and he woke up and holding up his little arms shouted Dats Pa. I felt so bad at the Childs recognition of me and your coldness that I thought I turned right around and went back to my regiment. You will be glad to hear that it has been decided that the 1862 men are not Veterans consequently I am now in my last year of service and hoping the time will soon come when I shall be a free man once more.

> I remain my dear wife,
> Your affectionate Husband,
> G.H. Cadman

Direct to the Regt. As usual, you must excuse this letter being so dull, but I am so low spirited, I can't help it.

Hospital 9th Ward, 4th Division, 16th A.C.
Marietta Georgia August 27/64

My Dear Wife,

It was with much pleasure that I yesterday received your ever-welcome letters of the 11th & 16th instant and was glad to find by them that you were all well. You complain very much of the heat in Ohio, but I expect we could beat you at it hear. It is now several days since I have venture out in the sun or if I did I should measure my length on the ground sure. I am very sorry to hear so bad an account of the crops. I was in hopes there might be a good field this season that, so the distresses of the people might be in some degree alleviated. By the by while I think of it let me thank Willie for his letter. I forgot to mention it when I received it, tell him to write as often as he can. I shall always be glad to have one from him.

I think your Idea of George digging potatoes on shares a very good one, and he might by that means furnish you with enough to last you all the winter, and I have no doubt some good neighbor would let you store them in their cellar or you could have them buried near home and only open the hole when the weather was favorable. You complain my dear that you have not had a mess of sweet corn yet, I assure you that I have not had any either, there was plenty of corn planted when we first came into Georgia, but it has all been consumed for forage, at least anywhere near our lines. Water-melons the size of a quart bowl are 1 dollar each and other fruit in proportion. Potatoes are very rarely to be seen. Most of the inhabitants of Marietta draw their rations from the quartermaster Department or they would starve. I would like to see Phil eating a water melon. I fancy I can see the water running down his fat chin now. I am much obliged to Mr. Stricker for letting you have the apples. I wish I could l get a few they would do me good I know.

Atlanta still holds out and may for a month longer yet as we can not take it by force and have not more than half men enough to invest it thoroughly. As for Sherman or Thomas saying they could take it in a week, that's all moon shine, some newspapers correspondent 20 miles back in the rear said that for them. I suppose they could take it, but it would be at such an awful waste of life that it would not pay. I am glad to hear that Jim Myers is likely to get home, but you must not think because he could have detailed on such a job that I could, there's a great difference in the eye of the commanders between the man who carries the Gun and the man who is only armed with a drumstick, one protects the rations in a time like this while the other only consumes them. As Jim says however the Veteran business is played out, and you may begin to count the months now till I come home.

On August 16th of next year, I shall be a free man again if I am alive, you may depend I shall never reenlist again, the government has fooled me three times and I will never give it another chance. I wish the paymaster would come around so that I could sand you some money to Philadelphia but knowing the time that is coming on for you

I can't help feeling uneasy. I think with you that Henry Schnerings employment does not promise much happiness for Lizzie, nor will it I fear be very good for him, unless he gives up some of his old feelings. However, I hope they will be happy and prosperous. I am sure I wish them every success. If you see them remember me to them and give them my best wishes. I am sorry I cannot send a cross for Mattie, but the one I did send was on I got Sam purposely for Mrs. Hall. I thought it would please her better than anything else. I could send her, I forgot we had any more Catholic neighbors at the time or I would get more of them.

I am very sorry that our neighbors have had such an accident with their fences as labor is so scarce they must have enough to do without extra work that won't pay. I guess it would not have hurt the clover if it had all burnt off most likely it would have shot up again the first rains. The neighbors feel bad no doubt there being so little water to use. I often think how foolish of Alfred to be always being bothered so with want of water when he has wasted more time and money over that old Astern and the spring, than would have fixed them both up properly so as to last his lifetime. Its no use trying to do things too cheap, they generally turn out bad in the end. I often think of Bob Norton's "Cheap Furniture Song" and there is a great deal of truth in it.

I am glad to hear your chickens are so fine, I suppose that is the brood Mrs. Williams promised Phil, but if he fills them with bread and butter, I don't think they will be very cheap. They serve to amuse him however and that is something. I must say you are turning quite a farmer, 2 hills of sugar corn, and one of water melons, why Esther how on earth do you manage to tend them, or do you hire a man for a day now and then to plough and hoe them, and then your corn beans too I am afraid Esther you are trying too much and want to get rich too fast.

Don't think I am laughing at you immersing crops. I am only wondering how you will dry the corn and what you will do with the money you get for the melons. Never mind old girl one year and I shall be home again, and I bet if I recover the use of my limbs you shall not want for vegetables them, or even if I get no stronger than I am now. I think our piece of ground will furnish u all we need, and a little over.

Now don't you worry yourself any more about my getting a furlough, it can't be doing no how, when you see a stream run up hill or a tree growing roots upwards then a sick soldier of the 39th Ohio may have a chance of coming home. We have had several men die of disease in our Regiment, who if they had been sent home might have been sound now. I have no doubt a trip home would do me good and that I should get well in half the time I shall here. But then on the other hand it would cost me some 20 dollars for transportation, and you would have to feed me for a month or perhaps two, and altogether it would tell up right smart. Besides you know what a cross grained fellow I am when I can't get out of the house, and so perhaps it is as well as it is I do not intend to go back to the Regt. again till I am sent back, I am not in any pain, do not take any kind of Medicine and can manage to walk about now pretty will. I am waiting for time to cure me, and the Doctor says that is the only thing that will do me any good.

If I could some writing to do to pass my time away. I should be happier, but the days are so dreadful long, and then the nights, I can't sleep, and I turn from might till morning. I have had no sleep of any consequence since I was Sun struck. It seems to have injured my brain some so that it won't keep still.

I have been unlucky since I came here, the second day I was here I applied at Head Qtrs. For a clerk's place, and was just 5 minutes too late, for two. Then I had a ward masters place offered me in the hospital, but was not strong enough to attempt it and now this morning since I commenced this letter I have had an order to report to Head Qtrs. I went, and they wanted me to guard the house of a lady living on the outskirts of town. I should have nothing in the world to do but help her clear out the pantry and might have stopped there perhaps for months, but could not go, because I left my gun and traps at the regiment. But perhaps you'll be glad I did in this case. Never mind something will turn up for me to do yet till I can get back to the front, which from my present feelings will not be, I think, much

324

before Christmas I am very much obliged to Mrs. Hurd for thinking of the boys and bringing them books, you must give my respects to her and thank her for me when you see her again.

I wonder what Osborne is doing now. Do you know whether he is in Alabama in the Sutler business yet, and so you have heard of Sam's Wound? Tell Sarah I think Sam pretty lucky for he has got off six months hard soldiering and very likely saved his life for it is doubtful if he will be able to wear a cartridge box till next summer and by that time his term of service will be nearly over. Then again, he is made Corporal just in time to give him 2 dollars a month extra all the time he is sick, and he will be at home most likely all though the worst of the winter and be able to save her a heap of cold work in the hard weather. I would like to change places with him. A hole in my side wouldn't save me. After seeing the awful sights, I have witnessed the last three months a simple shot hole seems nothing.

I saw Wes Miller of Fulton Yesterday, it is quite uncertain yet whether he will save his arm, or no. It is now over 7 weeks since he was wounded, and he may lose his arm yet. He was in pretty good spirits however. You wouldn't believe the difference there is in a sick and wounded Hospital. In a sick ward everything is quiet and the men out of spirits, but as soon as you get in among the wounded there is nothing but fun and merriment except in extreme cases. I am sorry that you have sent those things by Ben Griffin for it is not likely that I shall ever see him, our line of duty is so different the best and safest messenger is the post office. I did get the tobacco you sent for me and am much obliged to you for sending it to me. If you have it made you can send me one of my new shirts by mail in about six weeks. I think my old one will last that time and I don't want to carry more than two and when I want the other I will let you know.

I have not sent anything home by any of the boys for I was not with the regiment when they left but I expect some of our wounded boys will soon be leaving here for home, and I will then send the watch and Willies Knife if I can. I have directed them to the care of Mr. Weston who I have no doubt will oblige me by delivering them to you. Ask

Willie if he thinks he can carry the knife as many hundred miles as I have. Tell Mrs. Stucker I congratulate her on her good luck and only wish I was back home to drink the Childs Health in a glass of bitters. You seem quite in raptures over Mrs. Weston's Baby and I wish it was so that you had a daughter but as you have not, and this is sure to be a boy (Samuel) why we have got to try our luck again. Give my respects to Mrs. Weston and family. But I must conclude as I get stronger, so I get in better spirits, and thinking I can promise that I won't send you any more such dull letters as the last.

I remain my Dear Wife
Your Affectionate Husband
(letters as usual) Love to the Children

No. 9 ward, 4th Division Hospital, 16th A.C. Marietta, Ga.

Sept. 2nd, 1864,

My Dear wife,

Not having any breeches to wear (having sent mine to the washerwoman) and consequently having to stop in today. I think I cannot improve my time better than by writing to you, I have just made a contract with a woman to wash my pants for about one third of a pound of coffee, which I fortunately had by me when I left the Regt. Not being in possession of any money makes it rather awkward sometimes if a fellow wants anything done for him.

I suppose you would like to know what sort of a place this is. Well it is a right, snug, pleasant, place, and before the war must have been a thriving handsome town. There are a great many fine buildings in it, and the streets are well planted and protected from the rays of the sun, by rows of white walnut trees mostly. There is a large public square well planted, but that is in ruinous condition now, so many troops of both armies have made it a company place

The principal stores & warehouses in the place ranged on the sides of this square and are of good size for so small a place. At present however, they are all occupied by the Sanitary Society, Quartermasters, and others connected with the Army. There are some 5 or 6 good sized Churches all of which are at present used for Hospitals. In one of these St. James Episcopal Church I am at present staying. It is about the size or a little larger than Globe Road Chapel and capable of seating 350 persons, there are now in it 107 sick and I assure you we have none too much room. You recollect the last pew on the right-hand side of the Gallery where Old Mr. Spillman used to sit at Globe Road Chapel, well, I occupy the corresponding pew here. I have got a board level with the seat & it makes it a first-rate bunk. True it is not very soft, but then its better then the trenches.

There must be some thousands of sick and wounded men in Marietta, there are 800 belonging to our Division alone. Then there are the sick belonging to two other Division of our Corps, and the sick belonging to other corps here. You who stay at home can form no idea of the sickness and suffering that exists in the rear of a large army. One blessing this is a healthy place, and full of wells of excellent water. Every house has its well, from 30 to 60 feet in depth and the water comes up cold as ice and clear as crystal.

One misfortune is the impossibility of procuring vegetables or fresh fruit. The Sanitary Society furnishes considerable of dried Apples & Peaches with canned fruit, but what is it among so many of course the wounded are thought of first as they ought to be, but by the time they and the worst of the sick cases are attended to there are not many luxuries left for the balance. Fortunately, I do not require many nice things, I am like I was at home if I can only get enough bread & meat anyone can have the fancy fixings for me.

I often think through that I should like a mess of green corn or beans or tomatoes, but it doesn't trouble me to do without them. I crave an apple more than anything, but they are four dollars per bushel and no account at that. I am sorry to say that Miller has been compelled to lose his arm, it was amputated last Monday, just eight weeks from the time he was wounded. I saw him the night it was taken off and did not think he would survive it, but he is much better now, and I think in a fair way of doing well. Bill Cook whom you have heard me speak of more than once left for home last Wednesday.

I would be glad if when you write you will let me know how Sam Griffin is getting along. He is at Rome 30 miles from here and I have no means of corresponding with him, but I suppose he will be strong enough to leave for home now. I do not know when I shall see or hear of my Regt. again, for the 16th and 15th Army Corps are out on a raid and communications with them are closed. They started 3 days back with 15 days ration & more to follow. I am glad to say that I am considerably better than I have been though whether I shall ever get the full use of my limbs again. I don't know however if I don't. I suppose when I get home again I will have to give up farming and do something else.

Please give my love to the Children and believe me your affectionate Husband

George H. Cadman

Death of George H. Cadman

East Point Georgia
Sept. 21st /64

Dear Wife and Children the dearest on earth to me it is with sorrow that I sit down to let you know of the death of George Cadman. He died last Friday at the hospital in Marietta from the effects of the sun stroke he received at Roswell after we crossed the river. I did not hear of his death till last night, so I went over to the Regiment and asked the doctor if it was so and he said it was so that he died on Friday the doctor - the doctor said he did not know anything for a few days before he died. Poor fellow I am so sorry for him and his family.

Well Martha Co. B lost a gentle and a soldier when they lost Cadman. I want you to go and tell his wife or get father to go for I know she will take it very hard. Poor George suffered a grat deal. I would like to have been with him, but I could not as you know that I must stay where I am ordered.

Well Martha I suppose his pay will be sent to his wife and I don't know whether his knapsack and things will be sent home or not. It is about 25 miles from here to Marietta, so you see I can't go there to see to his things or I would go very willingly. For I know it is a hard stroke for his family to hear. I suppose Mrs. Cadman will have him brought home for burial as she can do it now for it is getting cool weather. Well Martha I suppose Sam Griffin has got home by this time and it will surprise Sam to hear of Georges death. I think his Capt. Wrote Mrs. Cadman a letter yesterday and directed it to Columbus, so you can tell her where to look for the letter or you can get it out for her yourself.

George Gear

Pocotaligo S.C. Jan 19, 1865

Mrs. Cadman,

Dear Madam; your letter of Nov. 7th was received by me upon reaching Savannah about one month since. I should have answered it before, but my time has been much occupied.

I do not know that I can communicate much more information to you concerning your husband's death. The Surgeon's name who attended him was Davis. He belongs to the 17th New York, in the 14th Corps. George was buried decently in the burials spot occupied by the 4th Division 16th Corps. A neat headboard marks his grave. A fence surrounds the burial spot. It is on the outer edge of Marietta, on the left-hand side of the Railroad as you come from the north.

Again, expressing my sympathy for you in your double sore bereavement.

I remain Respectfully yours,   George R. Gear

SURVIVORS OF THE BRIGADE AT NATIONAL G. A. R. ENCAMPMENT, TOLEDO, O., 1908.
Gen. Fuller's Monument in Background.

EXCERPT: CORRESPONDENCE PERTAINING TO SHERMANS FORCED EVACUATION OF ATLANTA

HDQRS. MILITARY DIVISION OF THE MISSISSIPPI,
Atlanta, Ga., September 20, 1864.

Maj. Gen. H. W. HALLECK, *Chief of Staff, Washington, D.C.:*

GENERAL: I have the honor herewith to submit copies of a correspondence between General Hood, of the Confederate army, the mayor of Atlanta, and myself touching the removal of the inhabitants of Atlanta. In explanation of the tone which marks some of these letters I will only call your attention to the fact that after I had announced my determination General Hood took upon himself to question my motive. I could not tamely submit to such impertinence, and I have seen that in violation of all official usage he has published in the Macon newspapers such parts of the correspondence as suited his purpose. This could have had no other object than to create a feeling on the part of the people, but if he expects to resort to such artifices I think I can meet him there too. It is sufficient for my Government to know that the removal of the inhabitants has been made with liberality and fairness; that it has been attended by no force, and that no women or children have suffered, unless for want of provisions by their natural protectors and friends.

My real reasons for this step were, we want all the houses of Atlanta for military storage and occupation. We want to contract the lines of defenses so as to diminish the garrison to the limit necessary to defend its narrow and vital parts instead of embracing, as the lines now do, the vast suburbs. This contraction of the lines, with the necessary citadels and redoubts, will make it necessary to destroy the very houses used by families as residences. Atlanta is a fortified town, was stubbornly defended and fairly captured. As captors we have a right to it. The residence here of a poor population would compel us sooner or later to feed them or see them starve under our eyes. The residence here of the families of our enemies would be a temptation and a means to keep up a correspondence dangerous and hurtful to our cause, and a civil population calls for provost guards, and absorbs the attention of officers in listening to everlasting complaints and special grievances that are not military. These are my reasons, and if satisfactory to the Government of the United States it makes no difference whether it pleases General Hood and his people or not.

I am, with respect, your obedient servant,
W. T. SHERMAN,
Major-General, Commanding

HDQRS. MILITARY DIVISION OF THE MISSISSIPPI,
In the Field, Atlanta, Ga., September 7, 1864.

General HOOD, *Commanding Confederate Army:*

GENERAL: I have deemed it to the interest of the United States that the citizens now residing in Atlanta should remove, those who prefer it to go south and the rest north. For the latter I can provide food and transportation to points of their election in Tennessee, Kentucky, or farther north. For the former I can provide transportation by cars as far as Rough and Ready, and also wagons; but that their removal may be made with as little discomfort as possible it will be necessary for you to help the families from Rough and Ready to the cars at Lovejoy's.

If you consent I will undertake to remove all families in Atlanta who prefer to go South to Rough and Ready, with all their movable effects, viz, clothing, trunks, reasonable furniture, bedding, &c., with their servants, white and black, with the proviso that no force shall be used toward the blacks one way or the other. If they want to go with their masters or mistresses they may do so, otherwise they will be sent away, unless they be men, when they may be employed by our quartermaster. Atlanta is no place for families or non-combatants, and I have no desire to send them North if you will assist in conveying them South. If this proposition meets your views I will consent to a truce in the neighborhood of Rough and Ready, stipulating that any wagons, horses, or animals, or persons sent there for the purposes herein stated shall in no manner be harmed or molested, you in your turn agreeing that any cars, wagons, carriages, persons, or animals sent to the same point shall not be interfered with. Each of us might send a guard of, say, 100 men, to maintain order and limit the truce to, say, two days after a certain time appointed. I have authorized the mayor to choose two citizens to convey to you this letter and such documents as the mayor may forward in explanation, and shall await your reply.

I have the honor to be, your obedient servant,
W. T. SHERMAN,

HDQRS. ARMY OF TENNESSEE, *OFFICE CHIEF OF STAFF,*
September 9, 1864.

Maj. Gen. W. T. SHERMAN.
Commanding U.S. Forces in Georgia:

GENERAL: Your letter of yesterday's date [7th] borne by James M. Ball and James R. Crew, citizens of Atlanta, is received. You say therein "I deem it to be to the interest of the United States that the citizens now residing in Atlanta should remove," &c. I do not consider that I have any alternative in this matter. I therefore accept your proposition to declare a truce of two days, or such time as may be necessary to accomplish the purpose mentioned, and shall render all assistance in my power to expedite the transportation of citizens in this direction. I suggest that a staff officer be appointed by you to superintend the removal from the city to Rough and Ready, while I appoint a like Officer to control their removal farther south; that a guard of 100 men be sent by either party, as you propose, to maintain order at that place, and that the removal begin on Monday next. And now, sir, permit me to say that the unprecedented measure you propose transcends, in studied and ingenious cruelty, all acts ever before brought to my attention in the dark history of war. In the name of God and humanity I protest, believing that you will find that you are expelling from their homes and firesides the wives and children of a brave people.

I am, general, very respectfully, your obedient servant,
J. B. HOOD,
General

HDQRS. MILITARY DIVISION OF THE MISSISSIPPI,
In the Field, Atlanta, Ga., September 10, 1864.

General J. B. HOOD, *C. S. Army, Comdg. Army of Tennessee:*

GENERAL: I have the honor to acknowledge the receipt of your letter of this date [9th], at the hands of Messrs. Ball and Crew, consenting to the arrangements I had proposed to facilitate the removal south of the people of Atlanta who prefer to go in that direction. I enclose you a copy of my orders, which will, I am satisfied, accomplish my purpose perfectly.

You style the measure proposed "unprecedented," and appeal to the dark history of war for a parallel as an act of "studied and ingenious cruelty." It is not unprecedented, for General Johnston himself, very wisely and properly, removed the families all the way from Dalton down, and I see no reason why Atlanta should be excepted. Nor is it necessary to appeal to the dark history of war when recent and modern examples are so handy. You, yourself, burned dwelling-houses along your parapet, and I have seen to-day fifty houses that you have rendered uninhabitable because they stood in the way of your forts and men. You defended Atlanta on a line so close to town that every cannon shot and many musket shots from our line of investment that overshot their mark went into the habitations of women and children. General Hardee did the same at Jonesborough, and General Johnston did the same last summer at Jackson, Miss.

I have not accused you of heartless cruelty, but merely instance these cases of very recent occurrence, and could go on and enumerate hundreds of others and challenge any fair man to judge which of us has the heart of pity for the families of a "brave people." I say that it is kindness to these families of Atlanta to remove them now at once from scenes that women and children should not be exposed to, and the "brave people" should scorn to commit their wives and children to the rude barbarians who thus, as you say, violate the laws of war, as illustrated in the pages of its dark history.

In the name of common sense I ask you not to appeal to a just God in such a sacrilegious manner; you who, in the midst of peace and prosperity, have plunged a nation into war, dark and cruel war; who dared and badgered us to battle, insulted our flag, seized our arsenals and forts that were left in the honorable custody of peaceful ordnance sergeants; seized and made "prisoners of war" the very garrisons sent to protect your people against negroes and Indians long before any overt act was committed by the, to you, hated Lincoln Government; tried to force Kentucky and Missouri into rebellion, spite of themselves; falsified the vote of Louisiana, turned loose your privateers to plunder unarmed ships; expelled Union families by the thousands; burned their houses and declared by an act of your Congress the confiscation of all debts due Northern men for goods had and received.

Talk thus to the Marines, but not to me, who have seen these things, and who will this day make as much sacrifice for the peace and honor of the South as the best born Southerner among you. If we must be enemies, let us be men and fight it out, as we propose to do, and not deal in such hypocritical appeals to God and humanity. God will judge us in due time, and He will pronounce whether it be more humane to fight with a town full of women, and the families of "a brave people" at our back, or to remove them in time to places of safety among their own friends and people.

W. T. SHERMAN,
Major-General, Commanding

ATLANTA, *GA., September* 11, 1864.

Maj. Gen. W. T. SHERMAN:

SIR: We, the undersigned, mayor and two of the council for the city of Atlanta, for the time being the only legal organ of the people of the said city to express their wants and wishes, ask leave most earnestly, but respectfully, to petition you to reconsider the order requiring them to leave Atlanta. At first view it struck us that the measure would involve extraordinary hardship and loss, but since we have seen the practical execution of it so far as it has progressed, and the individual condition of the people, and heard their statements as to the inconveniences, loss, and suffering attending it, we are satisfied that the amount of it will involve in the aggregate consequences appalling and heart-rending.

Many poor women are in advanced state of pregnancy; others now having young children, and whose husbands, for the greater part, are either in the army, prisoners, or dead. Some say, "I have such an one sick at my house; who will wait on them when I am gone?" Others say, "what are we to do? We have no house to go to, and no means to buy, build, or rent any; no parents, relatives, or friends to go to." Another says, "I will try and take this or that article of property, but such and such things I must leave behind, though I need them much." We reply to them, "General Sherman will carry your property to Rough and Ready, and General Hood will take it thence on," and they will reply to that, "but I want to leave the railroad at such place and cannot get conveyance from there on."

We only refer to a few facts to try to illustrate in part how this measure will operate in practice. As you advanced the people north of this fell back, and before your arrival here a large portion of the people had retired south, so that the country south of this is already crowded and without houses enough to accommodate the people, and we are informed that many are now staying in churches and other outbuildings. This being so, how is it possible for the people still here (mostly women and children) to find any shelter? And how can they live through the winter in the woods? No shelter or subsistence, in the midst of strangers who know them not, and without the power to assist them much, if they were willing to do so. This is but a feeble picture of the consequences of this measure. You know the woe, the horrors and the suffering cannot be described by words; imagination can only conceive of it, and we ask you to take these things into consideration.

We know your mind and time are constantly occupied with the duties of your command, which almost deters us from asking your attention to this matter, but thought it might be that you had not considered this subject in all of its awful consequences, and that on more reflection you, we hope, would not make this people an exception to all mankind, for we know of no such instance ever having occurred; surely none such in the United States, and what has this helpless people done, that they should be driven from their homes to wander strangers and outcasts and exiles, and to subsist on charity? We do not know as yet the number of people still here; of those who are here, we are satisfied a respectable number, if allowed to remain at home, could subsist for several months without assistance, and a respectable number for a much longer time, and who might not need assistance at any time. In conclusion, we most earnestly and solemnly petition you to reconsider this order, or modify it, and suffer this unfortunate people to remain at home and enjoy what little means they have.

Respectfully submitted.
JAMES M. CALHOUN,
Mayor

HDQRS. MILITARY DIVISION OF THE MISSISSIPPI,
In the Field, Atlanta, Ga., September 12, 1864.

JAMES M. CALHOUN, *Mayor, E. E. RAWSON, and S. C. WELLS,*
Representing City Council of Atlanta:

GENTLEMEN: I have your letter of the 11th, in the nature of a petition to revoke my orders removing all the inhabitants from Atlanta. I have read it carefully, and give full credit to your statements of the distress that will be occasioned by it, and yet shall not revoke my orders, simply because my orders are not designed to meet the humanities of the case, but to prepare for the future struggles in which millions of good people outside of Atlanta have a deep interest. We must have peace, not only at Atlanta but in all America. To secure this we must stop the war that now desolates our once happy and favored country. To stop war we must defeat the rebel armies that are arrayed against the laws and Constitution, which all must respect and obey. To defeat these armies we must prepare the way to reach them in their recesses provided with the arms and instruments which enable us to accomplish our purpose.

Now, I know the vindictive nature of our enemy, and that we may have many years of military operations from this quarter, and therefore deem it wise and prudent to prepare in time. The use of Atlanta for warlike purposes is inconsistent with its character as a home for families. There will be no manufactures, commerce, or agriculture here for the maintenance of families, and sooner or later want will compel the inhabitants to go. Why not go now, when all the arrangements are completed for the transfer, instead of waiting till the plunging shot of contending armies will renew the scenes of the past month? Of course, I do not apprehend any such thing at this moment, but you do not suppose this army will be here until the war is over. I cannot discuss this subject with you fairly, because I cannot impart to you what I propose to do, but I assert that my military plans make it necessary for the inhabitants to go away, and I can only renew my offer of services to make their exodus in any direction as easy and comfortable as possible.

You cannot qualify war in harsher terms than I will. **War is cruelty and you cannot refine it, and those who brought war into our country deserve all the curses and maledictions a people can pour out**. I know I had no hand in making this war, and I know I will make more sacrifices to-day than any of you to secure peace. But you cannot have peace and a division of our country. If the United States submits to a division now it will not stop, but will go on until we reap the fate of Mexico, which is eternal war. The United States does and must assert its authority wherever it once had power. If it relaxes one bit to pressure it is gone, and I know that such is the national feeling. This feeling assumes various shapes, but always comes back to that of Union.

Once admit the Union, once more acknowledge the authority of the National Government, and instead of devoting your houses and streets and roads to the dread uses of war, and this army become at once your protectors and supporters, shielding you from danger, let it come from what quarter it may. I know that a few individuals cannot resist a torrent of error and passion such as swept the South into rebellion, but you can part out so that we may know those who desire a government and those who insist on war and its desolation. You might as well appeal against the thunder-storm as against these terrible hardships of war. They are inevitable, and the only way the people of Atlanta can hope once more to live in peace and quiet at home is to stop the war, which can alone be done by admitting that it began in error and is perpetuated in pride.

We don't want your negroes or your horses or your houses or your lands or anything you have, but we do want, and will have, a just obedience to the laws of the United States. That we will have, and if it involves the destruction of your improvements we cannot help it. You have heretofore read public sentiment in your newspapers that live by falsehood and excitement, and the quicker you seek for truth in other quarters the better for you. I repeat then that by the original compact of government the United States had certain rights in Georgia, which have never been relinquished and never will be; that the South began war by seizing forts, arsenals, mints, custom-houses, &c., long before Mr. Lincoln was installed and before the South had one jot or tittle of provocation. I myself have seen in Missouri, Kentucky, Tennessee, and Mississippi hundreds and thousands of women and children fleeing from your armies and desperadoes, hungry and with bleeding feet. In Memphis, Vicksburg, and Mississippi we fed thousands upon thousands of the families of rebel soldiers left on our hands and whom we could not see starve.

Now that war comes home to you, you feel very different. You deprecate its horrors, but did not feel them when you sent car-loads of soldiers and ammunition and molded shells and shot to carry war into Kentucky and Tennessee, and desolate the homes of hundreds and thousands of good people who only asked to live in peace at their old homes and under the Government of their inheritance. But these comparisons are idle. I want peace, and believe it can now only be reached through union and war, and I will ever conduct war with a view to perfect an early success. But, my dear sirs, when that peace does come, you may call on me for anything. Then will I share with you the last cracker, and watch with you to shield your homes and families against danger from every quarter.

Now you must go, and take with you the old and feeble, feed and nurse them and build for them in more quiet places proper habitations to shield them against the weather until the mad passions of men cool down and allow the Union and peace once more to settle over your old homes at Atlanta.

Yours, in haste,
W. T. SHERMAN,
Major-General, Commanding

September 12, 1864.

Maj. Gen. W. T. SHERMAN,
Commanding Military Division of the Mississippi:

GENERAL; I have the honor to acknowledge the receipt of your letter of the 9th [10th] instant, with its enclosure, in reference to the women, children, and others whom you have thought proper to expel from their homes in the city of Atlanta. Had you seen proper to let the matter rest there, I would gladly have allowed your letter to close this correspondence, and without your expressing it in words would have been willing to believe that whilst "the interests of the United States," in your opinion, compelled you to an act of barbarous cruelty, you regretted the necessity, and we would have dropped the subject. But you have chosen to indulge in statements which I feel compelled to notice, at least so far as to signify my dissent and not allow silence in regard to them to be construed as acquiescence. I see nothing in your communication which induces me to modify the language of condemnation with which I characterized your order. It but strengthens me in the opinion that it stands" pre-eminent in the dark history of war, for studied and ingenious cruelty."

Your original order was stripped of all pretenses; you announced the edict for the sole reason that it was "to the interest of the United States." This alone you offered to us and the civilized world as an all-sufficient reason for disregarding the laws of God and man. You say that "General Johnston himself, very wisely and properly, removed the families all the way from Dalton down," It is due to that gallant soldier and gentleman to say that no act of his distinguished career gives the least color to your unfounded aspersions upon his conduct. He depopulated no villages nor towns nor cities, either friendly or hostile. He offered and extended friendly aid to his unfortunate fellow-citizens who desired to flee from your fraternal embraces.

You are equally unfortunate in your attempt to find a justification for this act of cruelty either in the defense of Jonesborough, by General Hardee, or of Atlanta by myself. General Hardee defended his position in front of Jonesborough at the expense of injury to the houses, an ordinary, proper, and justifiable act of war. I defended Atlanta at the same risk and cost. If there was any fault in either case, it was your own, in not giving notice, especially in the case of Atlanta, of your purpose to shell the town, which is usual in war among civilized nations.

No inhabitant was expelled from his home and fireside by the orders of General Hardee or myself, and therefore your recent order can find no support from the conduct of either of us. I feel no other emotion than pain in reading that portion of your letter which attempts to justify your shelling Atlanta without notice under pretense that I defended Atlanta upon a line so close to town that every cannon shot, and many musket balls from your line of investment, that over-shot their mark went into the habitations of women and children. I made no complaint of your firing into Atlanta in any way you thought proper. I make none now, but there are a hundred thousand witnesses that you fired into the habitations of women and children for weeks, firing far above and miles beyond my line of defense. I have too good an opinion, founded both upon observation and experience, of the skill of your artillerists to credit the insinuation that they for several weeks unintentionally fired too high for my modest field-works, and slaughtered women and children by accident and want of skill.

The residue of your letter is rather discussion. It opens a wide field for the discussion of questions which I do not feel are committed to me. I am only a general of one of the armies of the Confederate States, charged with military operations in the field, under the direction of my superior officers, and I am not called upon to discuss with you the causes of the present war, or the political questions which led to or resulted from it. These grave and important questions have been committed to far abler hands than mine, and I shall only refer to them so far as to repel any unjust conclusion which might be drawn from my silence.

You charge my country with "daring and badgering you to battle." The truth is, we sent commissioners to you respectfully offering a peaceful separation before the first gun was fired on either side.

You say we insulted your flag. The truth is we fired upon it and those who fought under it when you came to our doors upon the mission of subjugation.

You say we seized upon your forts and arsenals and made prisoners of the garrisons sent to protect us against Negroes and Indians. The truth is, we, by force of arms, drove out insolent intruders, and took possession of our own forts and arsenals to resist your claims to dominion over masters, slaves, and Indians, all of whom are to this day, with a unanimity unexampled in the history of the world, warring against your attempts to become their masters.

You say that we tried to force Missouri and Kentucky into rebellion in spite of themselves. The truth is my Government, from the beginning of this struggle to this hour, has again and again offered, before the whole world to leave it to the unbiased will of these States and all others to determine for themselves whether they will cast their destiny with your Government or ours? and your Government has resisted this fundamental principle of free institutions with the bayonet, and labors daily by force and fraud to fasten its hateful tyranny upon the unfortunate freemen of these States.

You say we falsified the vote of Louisiana. The truth is, Louisiana not only separated herself from your Government by nearly a unanimous vote of her people, but has vindicated the act upon every battle-field from Gettysburg to the Sabine, and has exhibited an heroic devotion to her decision which challenges the admiration and respect of every man capable of feeling sympathy for the oppressed or admiration for heroic valor.

You say that we turned loose pirates to plunder your unarmed ships. The truth is, when you robbed us of our part of the navy, we built and bought a few vessels, hoisted the flag of our country, and swept the seas, in defiance of your navy, around the whole circumference of the globe.

You say we have expelled Union families by thousands. The truth is not a single family has been expelled from the Confederate States, that I am aware of, but, on the contrary, the moderation of our Government toward traitors has been a fruitful theme of denunciation by its enemies and many well-meaning friends of our cause.

You say my Government, by acts of Congress, has "confiscated all debts due Northern men for goods sold and delivered." The truth is our

Congress gave due and ample time to your merchants and traders to depart from our shores with their ships, goods, and effects, and only sequestrated the property of our enemies in retaliation for their acts, declaring us traitors and confiscating our property wherever their power extended, either in their country or our own. Such are your accusations, and such are the facts known of all men to be true.

You order into exile the whole population of a city, drive men, women, and children from their homes at the point of the bayonet, under the plea that it is to the interest of your Government, and on the claim that it is an act of "kindness to these families of Atlanta." Butler only banished from New Orleans the registered enemies of his Government, and acknowledged that he did it as a punishment.

You issue a sweeping edict covering all the inhabitants of a city and add insult to the injury heaped upon the defenseless by assuming that you have done them a kindness. This you follow by the assertion that you will "make as much sacrifice for the peace and honor of the South as the best born Southerner." And because I characterized what you call a kindness as being real cruelty you presume to sit in judgment between me and my God and you decide that my earnest prayer to the Almighty Father to save our women and children from what you call kindness is a "sacrilegious, hypocritical appeal."

You came into our country with your army avowedly for the purpose of subjugating free white men, women, and children, and not only intend to rule over them, but you make negroes your allies and desire to place over us an inferior race, which we have raised from barbarism to its present position, which is the highest ever attained by that race in any country in all time. I must, therefore, decline to accept your statements in reference to your kindness toward the people of Atlanta, and your willingness to sacrifice everything for the peace and honor of the South, and refuse to be governed by your decision in regard to matters between myself, my country, and my God.

You say, "let us fight it out like men." To this my reply is, for myself, and, I believe, for all the true men, aye, and women and children, in my country, we will fight you to the death. Better die a thousand deaths than submit to live under you or your Government and your negro allies.

343

Having answered the points forced upon me by your letter of the 9th of September, I close this correspondence with you, and notwithstanding your comments upon my appeal to God in the cause of humanity, I again humbly and reverently invoke His Almighty aid in defense of justice and right.

Respectfully, your obedient servant,
J. B. HOOD,
General

$$\star\star\star\star$$

HDQRS. MILITARY DIVISION OF THE MISSISSIPPI,
In the Field, Atlanta, Ga., September 14, 1864.

General J. B. HOOD, *C. S. Army,*
Commanding Army of Tennessee:

GENERAL: Yours of September 12 is received and has been carefully perused. I agree with you that this discussion by two soldiers is out of place and profitless, but you must admit that you began the controversy by characterizing an official act of mine in unfair and improper terms. I reiterate my former answer, and to the only new matter contained in your rejoinder I add, we have no negro allies" in this army; not a single negro soldier left Chattanooga with this army or is with it now. There are a few guarding Chattanooga, which General Steedman sent to drive Wheeler out of Dalton. I was not bound by the laws of war to give notice of the shelling of Atlanta, a "fortified town" with magazines, arsenals, foundries, and public stores. You were bound to take notice. See the books. This is the conclusion of our correspondence, which I did not begin, and terminate with satisfaction.

I am, with respect, your obedient servant,
W. T. SHERMAN,
Major-General, Commanding

Halleck's Response to Sherman's Report

WASHINGTON, *September* 28, 1864.

Major-General SHERMAN, *Atlanta, Ga.:*

GENERAL: Your communications of the 20th in regard to the removal of families from Atlanta and the exchange of prisoners, and also the official report of your campaign, are just received. I have not had time as yet to examine your report. The course which you have pursued in removing rebel families from Atlanta and in the exchange of prisoners is fully approved by the War Department. Not only are you justified by the laws and usages of war in removing these people, but I think it was your duty to your own army to do so. Moreover, I am fully of opinion that the nature of your position, the character of the war, the conduct of the enemy, and especially of non-combatants and women of the territory which we have heretofore conquered and occupied, will justify you in gathering up all the forage and provisions which your army may require both for a siege of Atlanta and for your supply in your march farther into the enemy's country.

Let the disloyal families of the country thus stripped go to their husbands, fathers, and natural protectors in the rebel ranks. We have tried three years of conciliation and kindness without any reciprocation. On the contrary, those thus treated have acted as spies and guerrillas in our rear and within our lines. The safety of our armies and a proper regard for the lives of our soldiers require that we apply to our inexorable foes the severe rules of war. We certainly are not required to treat the so-called non-combatants and rebels better than they themselves treat each other.

Even here in Virginia, within fifty miles of Washington, they strip their own families of provisions, leaving them as our army advances to be fed by us or to starve within our lines. We have fed this class of people long enough. Let them go with their husbands and fathers in the rebel ranks, and if they won't go we must send them to their friends and natural protectors. I would destroy every mill and factory within my reach which I did not want for my own use. This the rebels have done, not only in Maryland and Pennsylvania, but also in Virginia and other rebel States, when compelled to fall back before our armies.

In many sections of the country they have not left a mill to grind grain for their own suffering families, lest we might use them to supply our armies. We must do the same. I have endeavored to impress these views upon our Commanders for the last two years. You are almost the only one who has properly applied them. I do not approve of General Hunter's course in burning private, houses, or uselessly destroying private property--that is barbarous; but I approve of taking or destroying whatever may serve as supplies to us or to the enemy's armies.

Very respectfully, your obedient servant,
H. W. HALLECK,
Major-General and Chief of Staff

EXCERPT: CORRESPONDENCE PERTAINING TO THE CAROLINAS CAMPAIGN

Gen. Sherman's concept of "Total War" included acts of violence on not only the property of private citizens but also on their persons. To feed and provide for his vast army marching to the sea and through hated South Carolina, Sherman ordered the use of foragers known as "Sherman's Bummers". Faced with this unprecedented abuse of civilians, some bummers when caught were summarily hung as thieves, murderers and arsonists.

Almost all Federals allegedly lynched by Confederate troops were what were termed "Bummers" or foragers of Sherman's army. It was these bummers who did nearly all of the atrocities that the Federal army was accused of by the Confederates.

The Official Records cites that 46 Federals were reported lynched by Confederate troops. The majority of these incidents occurred above Columbia. Also the lynchings were reportedly done exclusively by Confederate Cavalry. Interestingly enough, the acts occurred almost exclusively when Lt. General Wade Hampton and Major General Matt C.

Butler came into contact with Federal columns in mid-February 1865. These two men, both natives of South Carolina, would be less passive to a Federal army destroying their home state.

Many Confederate Officers, *(particularly those from South Carolina)*, saw the shooting down of foragers caught in the act as a way of deterring their actions in the future.

Heated exchanges occurred between Union and Confederate leaders concerning this situation, for example this sharp debate between Maj. Gen. Sherman and Lt. General Wade Hampton regarding such alleged policies and atrocities.

HDQRS. MILITARY DIVISION OF THE MISSISSIPPI,

In the Field, February 24, 1865.

Lieut. Gen. WADE HAMPTON,

Commanding Cavalry Forces, C. S. Army:

GENERAL: It is officially reported to me that our foraging parties are murdered after capture and labeled "Death to all foragers." One instance of a lieutenant and seven men near Chesterville; and another of twenty "near a ravine eighty rods from the main road" about three miles from Feasterville. I have ordered a similar number of prisoners in our hands to be disposed of in like manner. I hold about 1,000 prisoners captured in various ways, and can stand it as long as you; but I hardly think these murders are committed with your knowledge, and would suggest that you give notice to the people at large that every life taken by them simply results in the death of one of your Confederates. Of course you cannot question my right to "forage on the country." It is a war right as old as history. The manner of exercising it varies with circumstances, and if the civil authorities will supply my requisitions I will forbid all foraging. But I find no civil authorities who can respond to calls for forage or provisions, therefore must collect directly of the people. I have no doubt this is the occasion of much misbehavior on the part of our men, but I cannot permit an enemy to judge or punish with wholesale murder. Personally I regret the bitter feelings engendered by this war, but they were to be expected, and I simply allege that those who struck the first blow and made war inevitable ought not, in fairness, to reproach us for the natural consequences. I merely assert our war right to forage and my resolve to protect my foragers to the extent of life for life.

I am, with respect, your obedient servant,

W. T. SHERMAN,
Major-General, U.S. Army.

To which Hampton replied:

HEADQUARTERS,
In the Field, February 27, 1865.
Maj. Gen. W. T. SHERMAN, U.S. Army:
GENERAL: Your communication of the 24th instant reached me to-day. In it you state that it has been officially reported that your foraging parties are "murdered" after capture. You go on to say that you have "ordered a similar number of prisoners in our hands to be disposed of in like manner; that is to say, you have ordered a number of Confederate soldiers to be "murdered." You characterize your order in proper terms, for the public voice, even in your own country, where it seldom dares to express itself in vindication of truth, honor, or justice, will surely agree with you in pronouncing you guilty of murder if your order is carried out. Before dismissing this portion of your letter, I beg to assure you that for every soldier of mine "murdered" by you, I shall have executed at once two of yours, giving in all cases preference to any Officers who may be in my hands.

In reference to the statement you make regarding the death of your foragers, I have only to say that I know nothing of it; that no orders given by me authorize the killing of prisoners after capture, and that do not believe my men killed any of yours, except under circumstances in which it was perfectly legitimate and proper that they should kill them. It is a part of the system of the thieves whom you designate as your foragers to fire the dwellings of those citizens whom they have robbed. To check this inhuman system, which is justly execrated by every civilized nation, I have directed my men to shoot down all of your men who are caught burning houses. This order shall remain in force so long as you disgrace the profession of arms by allowing your men to destroy private dwellings.

You say that I cannot, of course, question your right to forage on the country--"It is a right as old as history." I do not sir, question this right. But there is a right older, even, than this, and one more inalienable--the right that every man has to defend his home and to protect those who are dependent on him; and from my heart I wish that every old man and boy in my country who can fire a gun would shoot down, as he would a wild beast, the men who are desolating their land, burning their homes, and insulting their women.

You are particular in defining and claiming "war rights." May I ask if you enumerate among these the right to fire upon a defenseless city without notice; to burn that city to the ground after it had been surrendered by the inhabitants who claimed, though in vain, that protection which is always accorded in civilized warfare to non-combatants; to fire the dwelling houses of citizens after robbing them; and to perpetrate even darker crimes than these crimes too black to be mentioned?

You have permitted, if you have not ordered, the commission of these offenses against humanity and the rules of war; you fired into the city of Columbia without a word of warning; after its surrender by the mayor, who demanded protection to private property, you laid the whole city in ashes, leaving amidst its ruins thousands of old men and helpless women and children, who are likely to perish of starvation and exposure. Your line of march can be traced by the lurid light of burning houses, and in more than one household there is now an agony far more bitter than that of death. The Indian scalped his victim regardless of age or sex, but with all his barbarity he always respected the persons of his female captives. Your soldiers, more savage than the Indian, insult those whose natural protectors are absent.

In conclusion, I have only to request that whenever you have any of my men "murdered" or "disposed of," for the terms appear to be synonymous with you, you will let me hear of it, that I may know what action to take in the matter. In the meantime I shall hold fifty-six of your men as hostages for those whom you have ordered to be executed.

I am, yours, &c.,
WADE HAMPTON,
Lieutenant-General.

A very interesting letter from Sherman to one of his Generals illustrates his views on this heated time:

He (General Kilpatrick) reports that two men of his foraging parties were murdered after capture by the enemy and labeled "Death to all foragers." Now, it is clearly our war right to subsist our army on the enemy. Napoleon always did it, but could avail himself of the civil powers he found in existence to collect forage and provisions by regular impressments. We cannot do that here, and I contend if the enemy fails to defend his country we may rightfully appropriate what we want. If our foragers act under mine, yours, or other proper authority, they must be protected. I have ordered Kilpatrick to select of his prisoners man for man, shoot them, and leave them by the roadside labeled, so that our enemy will see that for every man he executes he takes the life of one of his own. I want the foragers, however, to be kept within reasonable bounds for the sake of discipline. I will not protect them when they enter dwellings and commit wanton waste, such as woman's apparel, jewelry, and such things as are not needed by our army. They may destroy cotton and tobacco, because these things are assumed by the rebel Government to belong to it, and are used as a valuable source of revenue. Nor will I consent to the enemy taking the lives of our men on their judgment. They have lost all title to property and can lose nothing not already forfeited, but we should punish for a departure from orders, and if the people resist our foragers I will not deem it wrong, but the Confederate army must not be supposed the champions of any people. I lay down these general rules and wish you to be governed by them. If any of your foragers are murdered, take life for life, leaving a record of each case.

W. T. SHERMAN,
Major-General, U.S. Army.

Footnotes

1.) Tishimingo House- Built in 1857 by Martin Siegrist a Swiss immigrant who designed and Built the Hotel. The hotel was used both as a Union and Confederate Hospital. On January 1865 it was set ablaze by passing Confederate Troop. It stood for just 6 years.

2.) Engaged the Federals South of Iuka

3.) Battle of Iuka Mississippi September 19, 1862- 2 Brigades of Confederate Troops under the Command of General Price. Engaged the Federals South of Iuka. The Confederates captured 9 Union Cannons and the Union Army un General Rosecrans withdrew about 600 yards. The battle was started late in the afternoon. General Henry Little was killed which stalled the Confederate momentum and Price led the Confederate army away from Iuka. With the confederate withdraw the Yankees retained control of the 9 lost cannons. Loss in the battle was U.S. 782 –Confederate 700

4.) Battle of Corinth Mississippi October 4, 1862.

5.) General Newton was Pierre's Brother in Law, He married Anna Starr in 1848. John graduated West Point in 1842. During the war he led regiments and brigades. Newton was at Antietam, Fredericksburg, the Atlanta Campaign and Gettysburg.

6.) General Osterhaus- German born, at age 37 enlisted as a private in the 2nd Missouri. Then appointed Lt. Colonel and ordered to raise a regiment he raised the 12th Missouri Infantry.

7.) Town of Thunderbolt Georgia- The area was settled by general Oglethorpe in 1833. A seaside town.

8.) Gunboat Eollus- Built Newburgh New York as a civilian boat. Purchased by the U.S. Navy in 1864. Transported men, wounded, supplies. Eollus also did coastal watch during the blockade off the coast of North Carolina. 1865   returned to use as a civilian boat. Scraped in 1894.

9.) Jacinto Mississippi -South of Corinth Mississippi. Founded 1836 and named for the Famous Battle of Texas.

10.) George Hovey Cadman Papers, #122, Southern Historical

Collection, The Wilson Library, University of North Carolina at Chapel Hill.

11.) Thomas Hart Seymore- Born September 29, 1807. Democratic and Lawyer from Connecticut. Thomas the 36th Governor of Connecticut for two terms 1850 and 1853. Appointed minister to Russia in 1853 and held the position until 1858. Ran two times unsuccessfully as governor in 1860 and 1863 - lost both times. Attempted to be nominated of the National Democratic party for the presidential election of 1864. Failed to obtain nomination losing to General George B. McClellan.

12.) War of the Rebellion Official Records of the Union and Confederate Armies" Series 1, Volume 17

13) History of Fullers Brigade 1861-1865-Clevleand Ohio 1909

About the Editor

Brad Quinlin noted Historian & Genealogist, he is Author of "Duty Well Performed: The Twenty-first Ohio Infantry in the Civil War" and multiple other books and is currently working on the new United States Colored Troop exhibit for the Atlanta History Center/Cyclorama. He is the official historian for the Marietta National Cemetery in Marietta, Georgia and through in-depth research has identified over 365 US and CSA soldiers buried in Unknown graves. Brad was Historical Advisor and Lead Researcher for the Kennesaw Mountain National Battlefield Park Visitors Center movie: "Kennesaw: One Last Mountain" & the PBS 5-part Mini-Series "Civil War: The Untold Story". Brad is an expert genealogist and movie advisor who is familiar with the National Archives and available for school lectures, private tours and family research.

Website: www.tolearnyourhistory.com

Email: bradquinlin@tolearnyourhistory.com

Book Formatter

Jason Rusk has a Master's Degree in Leadership and 12 years in the financial sector. He is a former U.S. Marine having served in the Gulf War, as an Instructor at the U.S. Marine Corps Officer Candidate School and Colombia, South America hunting Pablo Escobar. He is current Jr. Vice Commandant for the Marietta, Georgia Marine Corps League "L/CPL Squire "Skip" Wells Detachment # 647.